THE PRESIDENT'S CABINET

The President's Cabinet

Gender, Power, and Representation

MaryAnne Borrelli

LYNNE
RIENNER
PUBLISHERS

BOULDER
LONDON

Published in the United States of America in 2002 by
Lynne Rienner Publishers, Inc.
1800 30th Street, Boulder, Colorado 80301
www.rienner.com

and in the United Kingdom by
Lynne Rienner Publishers, Inc.
3 Henrietta Street, Covent Garden, London WC2E 8LU

Library of Congress Cataloging-in-Publication Data
Borrelli, MaryAnne.
   The president's cabinet : gender, power, and representation / MaryAnne Borrelli.
     p. cm.
   Includes bibliographical references and index.
   ISBN 1-58826-094-1 (hc : alk. paper) — ISBN 1-58826-071-2 (pb : alk. paper)
    1. Cabinet officers—United States. 2. Cabinet officers—Selection and
appointment—United States. 3. Women cabinet officers—United States. I. Title.

JK611.B67 2002
352.24'0973—dc21

2002023157

British Cataloguing in Publication Data
A Cataloguing in Publication record for this book
is available from the British Library.

Printed and bound in the United States of America

The paper used in this publication meets the requirements
of the American National Standard for Permanence of
Paper for Printed Library Materials Z39.48-1984.

5 4 3 2 1

*To Katherine Rita Gilboy
and Philomena Borrelli,
two special women in my family*

Contents

Tables

Acknowledgments

Though writing may be done in solitude, writers live in communities and families. I would like to express my thanks to those who have done so much to help with the research, analysis, and production of this book. Though the following list is far from complete, it at least begins to acknowledge those without whom this project could not have been brought to completion.

The folks at Lynne Rienner Publishers have been unfailing in their professionalism and generosity. Dan Eades expressed an early interest in this project, and Leanne Anderson has brought it through to publication. Shena Redmond handled all the production details with unswerving attentiveness, Beth Partin was a wonderful copyeditor, and Liz Miles was outstanding in managing all marketing.

The data presented here were gathered at a series of archives, whose staff cheerfully supplied boxes of documents, photographs, and manuscripts. Thanks go to the archivists at the Dwight D. Eisenhower Library, the Gerald R. Ford Library, the Jimmy Carter Library, the Ronald Reagan Library, and the George H. W. Bush Library. Special thanks go to Barbara Constable at the Eisenhower Library and to Geir Gundersen, William McNitt, and Leesa Tobin at the Ford Library, who guided me through the intricacies of "their" administrations. The archives of the BPW/USA, of Duke University, and of the Schlesinger Library on the History of Women at Radcliffe College of Harvard University also provided crucial materials. The National Women's Political Caucus granted access to their historical records. Meanwhile, at Connecticut College, reference librarian Jim MacDonald painstakingly responded to every request.

Travel and research were supported through several generous grants. The Eisenhower World Affairs Institute and the Gerald R. Ford Foundations each underwrote research at "their" presidential libraries, and the American Political Science Association Research Grants Program funded study at the Jimmy Carter Library. The Center for the Study of the Presidency at the George H. W. Bush School of Government and Public Service of Texas A&M University funded attendance at a presidency research conference and research at the George H. W. Bush Library. The Connecticut College R. F. Johnson Fund for Faculty Development helped to allay costs associated with obtaining documents from the Reagan and Bush Libraries. As the book went through its last revisions, the Women and Public Policy Program at the John F. Kennedy School of Government of Harvard University provided much-needed library and research support.

Colleagues have contributed a great deal to my learning and to this text. Special thanks go to James Q. Wilson and H. W. Perry, who first introduced me to the intricacies of institutional analysis. Georgia Duerst-Lahti's writings and comments have been a constant source of inspiration. As this project took shape, G. Calvin Mackenzie issued an early and continuing challenge with his concern to determine what "difference" women secretaries-designate have made to the presidency. Doris Braendel offered ongoing encouragement. Lisa Wilson and Catherine McNicol Stock read drafts, offering comments that refined the argument. Barbara Burrell and Dorothy McBride Stetson pointed out areas where further explication was required. Ted Jelen graciously shared his knowledge about statistics. Janet M. Martin was a great source of information and ideas, always reminding me to support conceptual arguments with empirical data. Karen Hult provided one of the most thoughtful assessments that my work has ever received.

Research assistants also contributed significantly to the research process. Tracy Barsamian established the database for the secretaries-designate profiles, Cynthia Wilson researched their confirmation hearings and conducted her own analysis of the Perkins and Reno nominations, Cynthia Love studied the dynamics of presidential decisionmaking more generally, and Renée Syzdek demonstrated her accomplishments in cyberspace and in text research. If my colleagues posed questions, my research assistants helped me to find the answers.

As always, my family has been unfailing in its support and understanding. My mother and father, Florence and Joseph Borrelli; my aunt Gertrude Karoghlanian; and my brother and new sister-in-law, Damon and Marianna Borrelli, never doubted that this manuscript would be brought to completion. I relied on their strength, many a time.

This book is dedicated to my aunt Katherine Rita Gilboy, and to my grandmother, Philomena Borrelli. Their boundless compassion and strength, their constant love and support, taught me to recognize heroism and to value courage when I was still very young. I hope they can see the difference that they have made in my life.

1

Introduction: Linking Presidency Research and Gender Studies

Personnel are policy. That familiar adage is especially relevant for the cabinet secretaries, who reveal political priorities even before their first decision. To understand the deeper implications of this truth for the departments, the presidency, and society, cabinet nominations and confirmations must be carefully studied.

In this investigation of cabinet secretaries-designate, I argue that cabinet members make perhaps their most notable contribution to the presidency by serving as representatives. It is therefore essential that we understand the factors and events that shape this service.[1] As a starting point, the constitutive functions of representation can be identified as relationship building and communication. A relationship is essential if the representative is, literally, to re-present a people, an interest, or an ideal. To make present those who are absent, understanding and respect must exist between the representative and the represented. Otherwise, the representative will lack the knowledge and credibility to speak on behalf of the represented. And trust is made possible by communication. Representatives "speak for" people because they have previously "spoken to" those persons.[2]

In selecting the secretaries-designate to serve as representatives, presidents take electoral, policy, and bureaucratic factors into account. A president's past campaign debts and future reelection hopes relate to the individual secretaries-designate, in their own right and as liaisons to particular issue networks. Whether the prospective cabinet members have previously served in the department and their familiarity with the department's policy jurisdiction and with associated Washington networks, as well as their skill in managing large organizations, are all important concerns.[3] As representatives, therefore, cabinet secretaries-designate are expected to perform an array of what might otherwise be viewed as distinctive tasks—building electoral support, making policy, and managing people and programs—while withstanding intense public scrutiny.

Consider, for example, the 1993 nomination and confirmation of Clinton secretary-designate of agriculture Mike Espy. The agriculture secretary has typically represented midwestern states and agribusinesses. Espy, however, was a southerner. An African American and a former member of Congress (D-Miss.), his involvement in agriculture policy had focused on rural poverty and small farmers. The Espy nomination, accordingly, was taken as an indication that there would be a significant shift in the department's priorities. When Espy resigned in 1994, he was replaced by a far more traditional nominee.[4] Like Espy, Agriculture Secretary-Designate Dan Glickman (D-Kans.) was a former member of Congress. Unlike Espy, Glickman was from Kansas; had chaired the Agriculture Subcommittee on Wheat, Soybeans, and Feed Grains; and was considered an expert in agricultural commodities markets. Glickman therefore provided historically dominant agricultural interests with representation. In return, the Clinton administration gained credibility in powerful policy networks.

These nominations begin to suggest the ways in which cabinet secretaries individually and collectively reveal their presidents' perception of key *constituencies*. To be identified as a constituent is to be recognized as "politically relevant."[5] As the Espy and Glickman examples indicate, nominations that alter a constituent's status may or may not effect long-term change. Providing representation for those who have been historically excluded from the political process may be particularly difficult. Though many formerly marginalized peoples are participating more in politics, their networks are sometimes at an earlier stage of development, and their policy perspectives are still emerging. Moreover, it may be difficult for a societal group to be politically unified. Women, for instance, are distinguished from one another by race, ethnicity, socioeconomic status, religion, and many other characteristics. Examining the conflicts generated by the nomination of Clinton attorney general–designate Zoë E. Baird reinforces the impression of diversity rather than unity. It also suggests some of the difficulties associated with providing cabinet representation to women.

As Clinton's attorney general–designate, Baird was the first woman named to the inner cabinet, which is composed of the attorney general and the secretaries of state, treasury, and defense. These departments are identified with issues of national concerns and their executives are often among the president's closest advisers.[6] The nomination of a woman attorney general–designate, therefore, seemed to signal that women had arrived at the apex of the Washington power structure. Already women had been recognized as decisively influencing the outcome of a presidential election: Clinton was significantly indebted to women for his 1992 victory.[7]

Yet it soon became clear that there was no agreement about Baird's role as a representative of women. After her nomination was formally announced and before her confirmation hearing began, a front-page article in the *New York Times* revealed that Baird had broken labor and tax laws in employing undocumented workers in her home. Although these disclosures did not initially compromise her congressional support, polls revealed that the public quickly rejected her nomination. Fifty-six percent of respondents believed that Baird considered herself above the law, and 59 percent felt that her actions had undermined her ability to enforce the law. Seventy-five percent did not believe that she was telling the truth when she claimed to be unable to find qualified "legal" workers for hire.[8] Baird was described as presumptively unwilling to invest in child care, with media commentators (a number of them women) noting that her income as senior vice president and general counsel to Aetna Life and Casualty allowed her to engage highly trained caregivers.[9]

The strongest and angriest statements, therefore, centered on certain aspects of Baird's identity as a *woman* attorney general–designate. As a wife, she was responsible for her home. As a mother, she was responsible for her child. Neither statements that her husband had employed their household workers nor claims of a happy family life could alter the public's judgment. Countervailing political support was limited. Most notable, in light of the debates about Baird's identity, was the silence of the Washington women's and "women's issues" networks. Baird herself had no ties to these organizations, which had unsuccessfully advanced their own candidate for the attorney general's office.[10] Baird's nomination was subsequently withdrawn.

Ultimately, Baird was nobody's representative.[11] Public criticism was vociferous. Washington networks either withdrew their support or failed to provide endorsements. And yet, members of the executive and legislative branches were initially supportive of Baird, accepting her

apologies and viewing her illegal acts as irrelevant to her future contributions as an attorney general.[12] Here is an extraordinary divergence of
opinion about a woman secretary-designate's qualifications and anticipated performance as a representative of women.

For scholars of women in history and politics, the controversy
attending Baird's nomination was entirely predictable. Women had
been excluded from politics, first by legal mandate and later by informal practices, for hundreds of years. Support for that sanction rested on
a series of contentions. Women were identified as inherently unfit for
politics, their instinct to nurture disqualifying them from participating
in a constitutional system premised on self-interest, ambition, and conflict.[13] Other critics contended that women lacked the professional and
political credentials to succeed as policy- and decisionmakers.[14] Of
course, some were advantaged by this exclusion. Withholding influence, authority, and access from everyone except a white male elite
ensured a distribution of goods that was consistently to the benefit of a
few, who were correspondingly well aware of the losses they would
suffer in a more inclusive system.[15] It was only to be expected, therefore, that women would encounter a more stringent review when they
entered high political offices. Women cabinet nominees overturn long-
standing expectations about women's and men's gender roles. What it
means to represent women in the cabinet has consistently been a matter for careful negotiation.

UNDERSTANDING REPRESENTATION

Given that representation encompasses a variety of political actions, it
is understandable that it can also be evaluated along several dimensions. Such assessments have been conducted by a number of scholars,
but those of Hanna Fenichel Pitkin are among the most comprehensive
and detailed. Pitkin focuses on the theory and praxis of representation,
investigating the ways in which ideas and behaviors influence one
another. Identifying relationship building and communication as constitutive of representation, she examines these functions in terms of
four distinct (though related) aspects of representation. These are substantive representation, formal representation, descriptive representation, and symbolic representation.[16]

Substantive representation is concerned with the articulation and
advancement of interests within policymaking arenas. In simple terms,

it is about serving as an advocate for a particular group to secure and increase its resources. In the earlier examples, Agriculture Secretary-Designate Espy's precabinet career led observers to expect that he would be a substantive representative for the rural poor and small farmers, and that Agriculture Secretary-Designate Glickman would be a substantive representative for agribusiness and commodities firms. Yet the most crucial term here is *expected*. A cabinet nominee's loyalties have not yet been fully tested; more than one cabinet member has stressed that cabinet service is like no other. Nominations and confirmations are therefore based on educated guesses about the secretary-designate's future decisions and actions.

In reaching their decisions on these matters, presidents and senators rely on various criteria. There is the nominee's professional and political precabinet career, with all that it suggests about an individual's learning, achievement, and alliances. There are references and recommendations, which indicate both the networks with which a secretary-designate is affiliated and the relationships that will be brought into office. And there are also the connections that the secretary-designate establishes with the chief executive and influential legislators. Time and again, presidents state that they want a certain "chemistry" in their cabinet, and courtesy calls on the members of the Senate confirmation committee are expected of all nominees. Throughout this study of cabinet secretaries-designate, these criteria are carefully pieced together to reveal the expectations of substantive representation that guide nominations and confirmations, singly as well as within and across administrations.

Of the four aspects of representation, substantive representation may be the most familiar to cabinet scholars and political observers. Academic analyses and media commentaries have each considered the secretaries-designate's prior associations with departmental clients and issue networks, as well as their partisan allegiances. Likewise, the "balance" of regions, religions, interests, and party affiliations within the president's cabinet have received a great deal of attention.[17] The addition of gender, race, and ethnicity to this cataloguing of the secretaries-designate is comparatively recent. The significance of these qualities for substantive representation is, as noted in the Baird case study, still a subject for public debate. In this study of women secretaries-designate, I will examine the nominees' credentials and alliances to see whether they might be expected to demonstrate an awareness of women as a distinctive presidential constituency. This assessment parallels the judgments made about other secretaries-designate, with the important proviso that women are a far more diverse societal cohort whose interests are not as easily or as readily advanced. That said, a woman secretary-designate who had been educated at a woman's college, had been active in the Washington women's or "women's issues" network, or had administered government programs for women was viewed as presumably more likely to substantively represent women's interests.

Formal representation refers to the constitutional and statutory provisions that structure governance. The Constitution, in an arrangement that was the result of numerous debates and negotiations, assigned the power to nominate to the president and the power to confirm to the Senate. The relationship between these powers has always been complex, and it has only become more so in recent decades. The factors that distinguish presidential nomination politics have already been mentioned. Meanwhile, ethics legislation, partisan politics, and policy debates have combined to create a confirmation procedure that is an "obstacle course" at best and a "war" at worst.[18] The late Senator Paul Tsongas (D-Mass.) acknowledged as much, concluding that confirmations were the Senate's opportunity to "highlight issues, exact promises, score points, send messages, convey threats and otherwise check and balance the actions of the Administration."[19] These tasks have only been performed with greater thoroughness as the Senate has become increasingly individualized and media-conscious.[20]

Though large Senate majorities typically confirm cabinet nominations, those outcomes cannot be presumed.[21] In 1959, the Senate voted against confirming Commerce Secretary-Designate Lewis Strauss. As chair of the Atomic Energy Commission, Strauss had failed to comply with congressional requests for information. Senators felt that he continued to be evasive during his confirmation hearing. Their negative vote was an expression of Senate views about proper legislative-executive relations in policymaking and oversight.[22] In 1989, the Senate rejected one of its own, Defense Secretary-Designate John Tower. It was the ninth time in history that a cabinet nominee was denied confirmation, but it was only the second that a former senator was denied confirmation and the first that an initial nominee was denied. Though partisanship and policy positions each had their role in this defeat, it was the nominee's character and integrity that received the most attention. These issues had, in their turn, been highlighted by the president-elect's promise to prioritize ethics. The campaign's emphasis on "traditional family values" also worked against Tower, who was portrayed as a hard-drinking womanizer by liberals and conservatives.[23]

In addition to these defeats, there was the previously mentioned 1993 withdrawal of Attorney General–Designate Zoë Baird's nomination and the 2001 withdrawal of Labor Secretary-Designate Linda Chavez's nomination.[24] Like the Strauss and Tower cases, policy and character concerns fueled the debates about Baird and Chavez. Yet gender and race also framed discussions about the two women nominees. Critics challenged Baird as a wife and mother, equating her willingness to hire undocumented caregivers with a lack of dedication to her son. Chavez's opponents described her relationship with a battered and undocumented Latin American woman, who had lived in her home and done some housekeeping, as reinstituting indentured servitude. Their illegal actions opened them to challenge, but Baird and Chavez each confronted questions that were at least as reflective of concerns about their identity as about their credentials for holding cabinet office.[25]

These failed and withdrawn nominations have sensitized both presidents and secretaries-designate to the importance of responding to senators' concerns. Extensive briefings, courtesy calls, and other consultations have become integral to the nominees' preparation for their confirmation hearings. These activities supplement earlier overtures and vetting sessions conducted by the transition team or the White House staff. To understand how the president's representation agenda are formulated and set for the cabinet, therefore, we must critically examine the formal procedures and standards that structure the associated legislative-executive relations. After all, nominations and confirmations set a context for the future relationships between the president, cabinet officers, the Senate, and numerous other interests. At this earliest stage, representatives are valued or dismissed and constituencies are granted or denied representation.

The temptation, however, is to dismiss formal representation as the least significant of the four aspects of representation. Cabinet nomination and confirmation processes are sometimes viewed as "gender neutral," with each secretary-designate presumably encountering similar opportunities and challenges. Such an expectation, however, ignores the implications of men's historic and continuing predominance among cabinet nominees. Political scientists have already considered the ways in which the identities and precabinet careers of the secretaries-designate have affected presidential and Senate evaluations. This study extends that understanding, moving from sex-based comparisons to gender role analysis of the secretaries-designate. Accordingly, successive chapters analyze the presidential nomination decisions; investigate patterns in the precabinet careers of the secretaries-designate; assess media coverage; and, finally, review the Senate confirmation hearings. In every chapter, the focal point is the constitutional and statutory authority of the actors, as its practice reveals the workings of sex and gender in formal representation.

Descriptive representation is about the identity of the representative. If we believe that a representative body should, at least to some extent, reflect its society, then we are concerned about descriptive representation. Historically, descriptive representation has received less attention than substantive representation, though the long-standing interest in the religious and regional affiliations of the secretaries-designate could be construed as a form of descriptive representation. In the modern presidency, however, descriptive representation has become increasingly associated with the nomination of people of color and women to the cabinet. African Americans, Hispanic Americans, Asian Americans, and women have been named as secretaries-designate. These "diversity" nominations have signaled that these demographic groups are recognized—note the visual, descriptive nature of that verb—as the president's supporters.[26] In other words, these peoples are identified as constituents of the president. Not incidentally, such nominations have become more numerous as these voters have become more influential in presidential elections. Though the "diversity" secretaries are rarely present in the cabinet in the same proportions that their demographic cohort is present in society, their provision of descriptive representation is meant to send a message of presidential inclusivity.

At the end of the twentieth century, African American men and white women were among the established presidential constituents. Their absence from the cabinet would cause comment and perhaps cost the president electoral support. African American women, Hispanic women, and Asian Americans have been nominated to the cabinet only recently and much less consistently. Their constituent status, consequently, appears less certain. No Native Americans have yet been named to the cabinet. These people do not yet appear to have been identified as presidential constituents. Further, there has been no widespread protest against or publicity about their absence from the cabinet. In the terminology of feminist scholarship, these people endure an "invisible invisibility."[27]

Even once recognized, previously marginalized constituents still have to continue their efforts to maintain their representation. Otherwise, they are likely to lose their newfound status. At the same time, the provision of descriptive representation may spur debate about the people's substantive interests. For example, thirteen African Americans have held fifteen cabinet nominations in ten departments in seven administrations. Prior to the Clinton and George W. Bush administrations, however, African Americans had been nominated to only three departments—Housing and Urban Development (HUD); Health, Education, and Welfare (HEW)/Health and Human Services (HHS); and Transportation.[28] This practice was protested by some, who argued that these departmental assignments failed to adequately encompass African Americans' diverse political interests.[29] However, leadership of a younger department in the outer cabinet could be an interim stage for previously marginalized peoples, a first step toward more comprehensive cabinet representation.

The cabinet representation provided to women is equally difficult to assess in its intertwining of descriptive and substantive representation. Twenty-one women have received twenty-three cabinet nominations to eleven departments in eight administrations. There are complex patterns in these nominations, which sometimes contradict and sometimes reinforce women's traditional gender role responsibilities. For example, seven women have been secretaries-designate of labor, leading a department whose primary constituency—organized labor—was predominantly male. As secretaries, these women have arguably broadened the department's policy agenda, giving greater attention to the concerns of unorganized workers. Not incidentally, unorganized workers are mostly female. At the same time, the labor post has sometimes been denigrated as the "women's slot." This practice has especially been in evidence during Republican administrations, which had little hope of securing electoral support from organized labor. In these instances, the nomination of a woman secretary-designate seemed designed more to buffer the president against an otherwise formidable interest than to offer women greater representation in executive policy-making circles.

A reader may object, however, that descriptive representation is a very limited form of political access. And to the extent that it is based merely on physical appearance, descriptive representation is a poor and even pathetic undertaking. To expect an African American male nominee (such as Agriculture Secretary-Designate Mike Espy) or a white woman secretary-designate (such as Attorney General–Designate Zoë Baird) to descriptively represent either all African Americans or all women is either incredibly idealistic or hopelessly naive. At the very least, to assign representation of African Americans to a male secretary-designate and representation of women to a white woman secretary-designate is to signal a belief that African Americans are all men and women are all white.[30] This message was one that African American women successfully resisted in 1992 and 1996, acquiring descriptive representatives in Energy Secretary-Designate Hazel R. O'Leary and Labor Secretary-Designate Alexis Herman.[31]

Yet this interpretation of descriptive representation also needs to be resisted in other ways. To the extent that descriptive representation is viewed merely in terms of physical appearance, its deeper implications are neglected. It quickly degenerates into showcasing, essentialism, and stereotyping. Instead, descriptive representation should be understood in the context of a commitment to democratic ideals. The legitimacy of representation in a democratic republic, after all, is partially contingent on its implementation of democratic priorities. Charles Taylor has explained that a people's identity must be accurately and respectfully defined, if their interests are to be properly appreciated and considered.[32] Similarly, Jane Mansbridge has argued that descriptive representatives must be viewed as credible political actors if they are to be effective advocates.[33]

Though credibility is difficult to measure, there are clear indicators of the responses accorded the women secretaries-designate. As already noted, careful consideration of the patterns among their nominations— to departments in the inner or outer cabinet that are relevant to or distant from the president's agenda—suggests the extent to which they will be influential members of a presidential administration. Similarly, the extent to which women have been named to departments in which they possess policy expertise or prior political alliances foreshadows the extent to which their precabinet careers are valued by the administration. Media coverage and Senate confirmation hearing reports put assessments of the nominees on the public record. Their judgments at once capture the essence of descriptive representation and reveal the extent to which it has been provided to women.

Symbolic representation includes the ideals made manifest by the representative. To examine cabinet secretaries-designate as symbolic representatives, it is necessary to ask about the meaning that is implicit in their relationships and communications. The "diversity" secretaries-designate, for example, are often presented as evidence of their administration's democratic inclusivity. Such a portrayal is a statement about the symbolic representation provided by these nominees. "Symbolic," therefore, does not refer to empty gestures, ceremonial acts, or image making. Instead, symbolic representation is about the embodiment and voicing of complex ideologies. It draws connections between the person of the secretary-designate (descriptive representation) and the policy priorities and political alliances of the secretary-designate (substantive representation), in the context of established procedures and relationships (formal representation). In so doing, symbolic representation provides insight about the implications of a nomination for the presidency specifically and the political order generally. The linkages between the different aspects of representation and the consequent implications can be appreciated through a reassessment of the Baird nomination.

Throughout the 1992 campaign, Clinton had repeatedly promised an administration that "looks like America."[34] Indebted to women voters for his victory, Clinton was also reminded of his campaign promise by the Coalition for Women's Appointments (CFWA), a bipartisan alliance of approximately sixty-five women's and "women's issues" organizations. The coalition provided rosters of women candidates for presidential nominations and published almost daily newsletters inventorying nominees by race and by sex.[35] In selecting Zoë Baird, however, the president-elect passed over the CFWA-endorsed candidate for the attorney general's office and selected a woman whose ties were to the white male Washington establishment. Baird's nomination, consequently, did not empower the available institutional leadership (CFWA and its associated networks) of the supporters (women) that the nomination was ostensibly recognizing. As a symbolic representative, therefore, Baird was a complex and even contradictory figure: As a descriptive representative, she was the first woman named to a post in the inner cabinet, apparently demonstrating the president's commitment to democratic inclusivity; as a substantive representative, it seemed probable that she would defer to a male-dominated and male-defined status quo, thereby proving the president's deference to traditionally exclusive networks.

The subsequent media coverage and the confirmation hearing only highlighted these contradictions. Public opinion polling suggested that Baird's failures as a wife and mother were viewed as compromising her ability to stand as a descriptive representative for women. For some senators, Baird's actions and testimony further suggested that she lacked an understanding of "women's issues," which would limit her substantive representation for women. Syndicated columnist Anthony Lewis, however, maintained that the hearing was more indicative of the senators' own gender and class biases than of the nominee's qualifications. Lewis's column provided a commentary on the gendered nature of formal representation as it was manifested in the Baird confirmation hearing.

> Think about the moment in the hearings when Senator Joseph Biden, chairman of the Judiciary Committee, asked Ms. Baird to state how many hours she was away from her child: when she left at [sic] home in the morning and returned at night. Would he have asked that of any male nominee, for any job?
> Or consider Senator Dianne Feinstein's hectoring of Ms. Baird about not resting on her laurels as a magna cum laude graduate but knowing the streets. Would Senator Feinstein have said that to Edward Levi, a reserved intellectual who was the one outstanding Attorney General in the last 20 years?[36]

Though Lewis' argument is appealing from an equal rights–equal treatment perspective, it misses the obvious point: Circumstances are not similar for men and women attorneys general–designate because men and women secretaries-designate are presented and perceived as representing different people. Presidents and media commentators alike describe the woman cabinet nominee as performing a political function—representing women—that a man's sex and gender identities bar him from undertaking.[37] Because they have different political constituencies, women and men cabinet nominees confront different standards for their performance.[38] Thus, sex and gender infuse all facets of representation.

Because the secretaries-designate represent societal and political interests, their nominations and confirmations send important messages about the political priorities of the president and of the Senate. Now that the four aspects of representation—substantive, formal, descriptive, and symbolic—have been differentiated, the character and complexity of this undertaking can be delineated with considerably more precision. Before doing so, however, it is necessary to acknowledge the ways in which gender studies and presidency research can contribute to this analysis.

LINKING GENDER STUDIES AND PRESIDENCY RESEARCH

Gender studies and presidency research have, with some notable exceptions, been pursued as distinct fields.[39] Occasionally, this separation has been defended on the grounds that a woman has never been elected president of the United States. The breadth of the presidency research agenda, however, immediately discounts and dismisses this argument. Presidency scholars have not confined themselves to the Oval Office. Many have investigated advisory and policy networks, which have progressively included women and "women's issues." Similarly, gender studies have never been confined to women. Gender scholars have routinely analyzed masculinity and men.[40] And men have, essentially, created the executive branch and have predominated among its past and present decisionmakers. Examining the presidency and presidency research with the intellectual resources of gender studies, therefore, provides presidency scholars with a better understanding of their own work, helping them to see why some questions are surfacing in their research agendas and others are not.

Though both gender studies and presidency research share a concern for the exercise of power, the subject matter of the latter may seem much more accessible than that of the former. The presidency, after all, is a constitutional entity. In contrast, the effects of gender are often so ordinary and so routine that they are invisible. Accordingly, the foundational concepts of gender studies are set out below, as are their most obvious associations with presidency studies. This information will also set the context for a review of the presidency literature about the cabinet, which follows.

Gender Studies and Cabinet Building

The most basic distinction drawn in gender studies is between sex and gender. *Sex* is a biological characteristic. Election studies, for example, rely on surveys that designate individuals as "male" or "female" based on their physiological appearance. *Gender,* however, refers to the way that society has constructed an identity around sex.[41]

In academic usage, the word gender is neither a euphemism for sex nor a synonym for women. It is a convenient term for describing the varied and continually changing ways people define maleness and femaleness. In sociological terms, gender is a system of ordering

> social relationships based on perceived differences between the
> sexes. Put in more ordinary language, we could say that sex makes
> babies, gender manufactures pink and blue booties. Hence, gender is
> present even when women are not—perhaps especially so.[42]

In traditional terms, females are expected to be feminine, and males are
expected to be masculine. Social mores, often reinforced by law, determine exactly what constitutes "femininity" or "masculinity," as well as
how those traits should be exercised and rewarded.[43]

Quite clearly, sex and gender are related.[44] The identification of a
person's sex often creates presumptions about gender, and gender
refers to behaviors that are typically ascribed to a sex. Still, sex and
gender are distinct elements of an individual's identity, and this is a distinction that political scientists have found useful. If women and men
are only physiologically different—a difference that is immaterial to
political officeholding—their qualifications and credentials can be
compared in simple and exclusive terms.[45] Once that task is completed,
a second step can be taken. The comparisons can be put in a societal
and governmental context so that the meaning of the similarities and
differences among these officeholders can be weighed. In this way,
political scientists have progressed from studying differences between
the sexes to considering the gendered nature of political relationships.

Gender, after all, is about identity and about power.[46] It is about
people learning, and sometimes being coerced into, living within certain normative boundaries. As behaviors are encouraged, rewarded, or
punished, resources are allocated and authority is granted.

> Consider, for example, the opportunity to accrue social resources
> from being a "gender star." . . . The rewards for being quarterback or
> any star player involve some quantity of fame, over several months
> or years, and the direct possibility of further resources such as a col-
> lege scholarship or a professional contract. . . . The homecoming
> queen is famous for a week and finds no systematic way to turn this
> honor into future resources. . . . While both women and men have
> access to gender power, and while . . . sex-role strictures have clearly
> begun to change, that access is highly differential. Masculinism sets
> the contours of that differentiation.[47]

Masculinism, as Georgia Duerst-Lahti explains, is a "meta-ideology," a
set of values so foundational that it is ingrained in our behaviors and
(usually) practiced without question. It is so "ordinary" that there is

resistance even to its being discussed. Masculinism, in particular, is a meta-ideology that values the traits and qualities that have traditionally been associated with men. In a political and governmental system that endorses masculinism, masculinity is advantaged, and femininity is disadvantaged.[48]

Of the three branches, the executive is arguably the most strongly rooted in masculinism. The expectations against which presidents are measured are congruent with Anglo-Saxon traditions of masculinity and "great man" theories of history. Quite simply, the traits attributed to masculinity are more congruent with enduring expectations of the president than are those associated with femininity.[49] In the words of Clinton Rossiter, "The framers of the Constitution took a momentous step when they fused the dignity of a king and the power of a prime minister in one elective office. And, if they did nothing else, they gave us a 'father image' that should satisfy even the most demanding political Freudians."[50] In studying the presidency, then, we are investigating an institution that is infused with gender and that is expressive of masculinism.

Examining cabinet representation with a sensitivity to the historically enduring influence of masculinism raises important questions about the norms that govern secretaries-designate, both women and men, as representatives.[51] The cabinet has always been a gendered institution. It is time to acknowledge as much and to pool the resources of gender studies and presidency research, in order to better understand long-standing political practices.

Presidency Research and Cabinet Politics

The cabinet is an underresearched part of the U.S. presidency, perhaps because it seems to lack continuity in its relationships and practices. Richard F. Fenno, Jr., highlights the ephemeral qualities of the cabinet in his seminal work, *The President's Cabinet: An Analysis in the Period from Wilson to Eisenhower.*[52] In a similar vein, other scholars have noted that cabinet government is a promise made by candidates, an ideal endorsed by presidents-elect, and a practice abandoned by presidents. Such developments are attributed to the numbers and diverse concerns of the cabinet members, which inhibit efficient or effective decisionmaking. Additionally, the loyalties of the secretaries become less certain as they spend time representing their societal and departmental constituencies. Chief executives respond by holding fewer and less substantive cabinet meetings and by centralizing initiatives in the White House.[53]

To view the cabinet as an incidental gathering of departmental chief executives, however, is to miss its contribution to the presidency and to presidential administrations. Studies of cabinet nominations and confirmations have found enduring patterns in secretarial selection. Cabinet nominees selected by presidents-elect, for instance, are consistently different from those selected later in the term. There are also predictable associations between secretaries-designate, departments, and constituencies. These practices, among others, mean that the cabinet is more than a grouping of elites or an organization created anew by each president. It is, instead, a carefully selected collection of representatives.

This claim—that representation is one of the cabinet's most important tasks—draws on a number of approaches that have previously guided cabinet studies.[54] The following is a relatively comprehensive listing of these frameworks:

- *Departmental roles.* The role and influence of the departments can be classified by dividing the cabinet into an inner cabinet and an outer cabinet. The inner cabinet consists of the Departments of State, Treasury, Defense, and Justice, and its agenda centers on matters of nationwide concern. The outer cabinet consists of the remaining departments, and its members mediate among and on behalf of more specialized interests.[55]
- *"Capture" and "issue network" theories.* The chief function of the cabinet secretaries is speaking with and responding to departmental clients and issue networks. Depending on the specific department, the secretary may have little independence from these interests (capture theory) or may act with relative freedom (issue network theory).[56]
- *Presidential expectations of and disappointments with cabinet government.* This approach to cabinet studies assesses whether and how the secretaries, as a collective body, influence presidential decisionmaking.[57]
- *Diversity and "balance" among the secretaries.* Inclusion of individuals from different professions and regions; of different races and ethnicities, sexes, and religions; and with different partisan allegiances is viewed as essential to securing support from the wider polity.[58]

- *Partisan changes in the White House.* Because cabinet nominees are typically members of the president's party, which party
  controls the White House and partisan succession are viewed as
  crucial aspects of cabinet politics.[59]
- *Nomination timing during the presidential term.* As the presidential term progresses, policy and political priorities change,
  and these shifts are reflected in the president's cabinet nominations.[60]
- *Secretaries' ambitions and expectations.* The secretaries' own
  hopes and performance standards influence cabinet politics. The
  secretary-designate, for example, may be associated with a particular policy stance.[61]

To fully appreciate these diverse approaches, we need to look for
connections between them. Their strongest point of agreement is a
question: What defines the cabinet? The first three—departmental
roles, capture and issue network theories, and cabinet government—
answer this question by referring to the departments. These theories
focus on the departments' roles in the executive branch and in the presidential administration. They attribute power to the executive bureaucracy and to the secretarial *office.* They are therefore infused with a
heavy dose of Weberian rationality.

In contrast, the remaining four approaches—diversity and "balance" among the secretaries, partisan change in the White House, nomination timing, and nominee ambitions and expectations—argue that
the secretaries effectively define the cabinet. The personal, professional, and political profile of the cabinet *officer* is viewed as most
influential. These approaches do not abandon the legalistic-rational
model for one that is wholly charismatic, but they do attach considerable importance to the person who is the secretary. Alliances with voters and with parties, nomination timing, political experience, and
expertise are resources possessed (or not possessed) by singular individuals, who consequently use the powers of the secretarial office in
very different ways.

Whether the office or the officer is the determinative force in governmental institutions is one of the oldest debates in politics. In regard
to the cabinet, evidence has favored studying the officer while remembering that the individual acts in the context of a specific office.[62] The
thesis that the cabinet engages in representation supports this conclusion because it seeks to understand how the individual secretaries-des-

ignate build relationships and communicate with political and societal constituencies.

To see the validity of this approach, note first that earlier studies sought to determine which aspect of the secretarial office or office-holder was most influential to the practice of cabinet politics. The representation thesis suggests, instead, that different roles may be of greater or lesser importance at different times. For example, the representation thesis acknowledges that cabinet secretaries are (or should be) loyal advisers to the president. However, it holds that loyal advising is only a part of the cabinet officers' role. They also balance the competing demands and conflicting allegiances that arise from political relationships. Thus representatives mediate, explain, and facilitate but also bungle, confuse, and obstruct.

To begin to understand which relationships are dominant when and why, the representation thesis draws on Nelson Polsby's schema for classifying cabinet secretaries. Polsby argues that presidents' cabinet nominations reveal their perceptions of and calculations about power. A president mindful of the historical relationship between the chief executive and the legislative branch would nominate secretaries-designate who were policy specialists. *Specialists* are reminders of the original legislative-executive programmatic mandate. At the same time, these nominees bring a nonpartisan tone to decisionmaking because they adhere to the canons of their profession.[63] Among the Clinton cabinet nominees, Labor Secretary-Designate Robert Reich was a specialist. A professor of industrial policy prior to his cabinet nomination, Reich had published several books enumerating reforms that could improve workers' lives and was expected to draw on that academic expertise in leading the labor department.

A president who acknowledged the checks placed upon her or his powers by a pluralist system with separated powers would nominate secretaries-designate who could serve as *liaisons* to the departments' clients or issue networks and to the legislative branch. These liaisons would have spent significant portions of their careers in those political environments, so they would be well known and well respected by those whom they represented.[64] For an example of a liaison secretary, there was Clinton secretary-designate of state Madeleine Korbel Albright. Albright had served as a foreign policy adviser in the Senate and as a congressional liaison officer on the National Security Council staff and had been a professor in a foreign service program and the permanent U.S. ambassador to the United Nations. Her precabinet career therefore had brought her into contact with a wide array of foreign policy decisionmakers. She consequently provided the Clinton administration with a greater measure of credibility in this policy arena.

Finally, a president who identifies her or his strength and legitimacy in an electoral mandate would draw on the campaign for the majority of her or his cabinet secretaries-designate. These nominees would be *policy generalists,* with careers centered in law and public relations firms. Their loyalties would be to the president who had nominated them and to their own ambitions.[65] Albright's predecessor, Secretary-Designate of State Warren M. Christopher, was a policy generalist. Though Christopher was an assistant secretary of state in the Carter administration, his contact with foreign policymaking was limited to that experience, and his career otherwise unfolded in a California law firm. He was an adviser during the 1992 Clinton campaign, known for his role in selecting the vice presidential running mate.[66]

Polsby's schema is a good point of departure because it suggests how cabinet nominations link (1) the president's political calculations and (2) the cabinet nominees' career paths to (3) the president's leadership and (4) the representative obligations of the secretaries.[67] In so doing, this classification schema complements the various other approaches to cabinet studies. For example, the conceptualization of liaison secretaries parallels the capture and issue network theories of cabinet nominations. This schema can also be used to reveal the systematic similarities and contrasts in the representation that is expected of the secretaries-designate. The implications of those patterned expectations, for women as officeholders in and constituents of presidential administrations, are the central concern of this book.

STUDYING THE U.S. CABINET

For this study, the *cabinet* was defined as consisting of only the departmental secretaries. Individuals who merely held cabinet rank were removed from consideration.[68] However, every cabinet nomination, including those not confirmed by the Senate, was sampled. The following secretaries-designate were therefore included in the analysis: Roosevelt attorney general–designate Thomas J. Walsh, who died before confirmation procedures began; Eisenhower commerce secretary-designate Lewis Strauss and George H. W. Bush defense secretary-designate John Tower, both of whom were denied confirmation by a negative vote on the floor of the Senate; and Clinton attorney general-designate Zoë Baird, Clinton defense secretary-designate Bobby Ray Inman, and George W. Bush labor secretary-designate Linda Chavez, whose nominations were withdrawn.

Because of the focus on the nominations and confirmations of women secretaries-designate, only those presidential administrations with at least one woman secretary-designate were examined. As a result, the cabinet nominations of eight presidential administrations were examined, namely, those of Franklin D. Roosevelt, Dwight D. Eisenhower, Gerald R. Ford, Jimmy Carter, Ronald Reagan, George H. W. Bush, William J. Clinton, and George W. Bush. Because President George W. Bush had made only initial cabinet nominations as this book went to press, his secretaries-designate were treated as a postscript to the complete rosters of the earlier administrations.

Two ends were served by setting aside the administrations without women secretaries-designate. First, presumptively similar administrations were compared. Though inclusivity is most definitely a relative term, Janet M. Martin has already determined that presidents are markedly different in their receptivity to nominating women.[69] Second, this approach facilitated establishing the dynamics associated with including women on the cabinet. As others have noted, absence is a difficult matter to analyze. First, one needs to have a sense of what "presence" signifies.[70] This study seeks to determine that meaning.

Working within these guidelines yielded a database of 182 nominations. Of these, twenty-three nominations (12.6 percent) were granted women. Two women, Patricia Roberts Harris and Elizabeth Hanford Dole, each had two cabinet nominations. Twenty-one women, therefore, have been secretaries-designate. Two women, Zoë Baird and Linda Chavez, had their nominations withdrawn. Consequently, the Senate confirmed twenty-one cabinet nominations of women.

This population of women secretaries-designate is not large. Yet there are powerful reasons for conducting this study, despite its small sample. Because it is in the early stages of a sex- and gender-based integration, the cabinet reveals how such a development proceeds among elites. Further, an examination of the gendered nature of cabinet politics suggests how constituency status, officeholding, and representation are intertwined. This begins to reveal women cabinet officers' contributions as descriptive, symbolic, and substantive representatives. Such an analysis responds to the question of whether the inclusion of women "makes a difference." At an even more promising and challenging level, this research indicates the role played by the nomination and confirmation powers in governmental-societal and legislative-executive relations.[71]

Like all political developments, the inclusion of women in the cabinet is characterized by advances, reversals, and hesitations. As presidency scholars have already shown, administrations embrace different political ideologies with marked consequences for their policy priorities. This characteristic is especially likely to affect the recognition of women as presidential constituents and the selection of women as cabinet members. Certainly the modern presidents have varied in their responses to women, as evidenced by their electoral appeals to women voters, their positions on "women's issues," and their record of nominating women to high office. Presidents Carter and Reagan, for example, contrasted dramatically on each of these points. Even so, each administration sets a precedent for those that follow. As already noted, the consistency with which successive administrations have nominated white women and African American men to the cabinet suggests that their status as presidential constituents is relatively secure. Their absence from the roster of secretaries-designate is likely to generate criticism. Notably, George W. Bush's initial cabinet nominees included four women, although this president-elect had issued no campaign promises of an inclusive administration and had been similarly circumspect about "women's issues," other than reproductive rights.[72]

Still, tracing political developments among cabinet nominees requires an attentiveness to the Senate and its members, as well as to the presidency and the president. Senators may well be less inclined to alter their perceptions of women as constituents or officeholders. Though the effects of incumbency advantage are less marked in the Senate than in the House, U.S. senators are still reelected to office with great regularity. Unlike presidents, who confront the constraints of a four-year term and a two-term limit, senators have a longer time horizon and a correspondingly more incremental approach to change. Seniority also has its effect in further slowing the pace of developments. Meanwhile, harsh experience has taught presidents that unilateral exercise of the nomination power can result in costly failures. Legislative-executive consultations may, then, further slow the pace of change, limiting the recognition of women as officeholders and constituents.

These eventualities, however, only make it more important to analyze the ramifications of women's presence among the secretaries-designate. This raises the issue of measurement. How is the representation expected of women secretaries-designate to be assessed? How similar or different are the women secretaries-designate who are nominated by different presidents or at different points in the same president's term? Setting out the ways in which these and other questions can be answered is the focus of the following sections.

Regendering Versus Transgendering

To begin, it is important to remember that the political system is not "gender neutral." Instead, as discussed previously, it endorses and practices masculinism. The women's movement in the United States has become increasingly aware of the strength of this gender ideology. In the 1960s and 1970s, the movement and its organizations hoped that the elimination of sex discrimination would secure equality for women. The "male" in "male norm" was viewed as a detachable adjective. More recently, however, as the enduring influence of gender has been recognized, change has been discussed in terms of regendering and transgendering.

Regendering occurs when women and men are accepted into the same profession or nominated to similar offices but are then directed to exhibit gender-distinct behaviors. Women and men may each join the military, for example, and yet their subsequent opportunities may be quite different. Prohibitions against women in combat may be justified by ascribing nurturing instincts to women; requirements of combat for men may be justified by ascribing aggressive instincts to men. *Transgendering,* in contrast, occurs when women and men are viewed as equally capable, though expectations of some gender differences continue. Women and men have often been accepted as competent college and university professors, for example, and yet women continue to be disproportionately present in the less prestigious positions. As these terms indicate, it is not enough to say that "society" is becoming more "open" or "receptive" to women. Instead, it is important to determine how traditional gender roles are being reinforced or weakened.[73]

Regendering and transgendering, therefore, are about the connections between gender and power. Gender roles are performed by individuals and express an identity. These actions, in turn, affect the distribution of power. In a masculinist political order, gender role traditions systematically privilege masculinity and deprecate femininity. Because gender and sex are linked and often conflated, men are more likely and women less likely to have access to power.[74]

Given the strength of history and tradition, a masculinist political system would be more likely to show regendering than transgendering. Regendering allows established gender roles to be preserved, even strengthened. Men continue to prove their worth and gain benefits by practicing traditional masculine traits. Although women may gain entry into new professions or offices, they are subsequently isolated and subordinated. In the cabinet, such practices would be revealed by the departments to which the women secretaries-designate have been named, by the congruence of these departments' policy responsibilities with women's traditional gender roles, and by the importance of these departments to the presidency or the presidential administration.[75] Each of these circumstances would affect the substantive and descriptive representation that could be offered by the women secretaries-designate, by either rejecting or capitalizing on the nominees' credentials, and limiting or extending the definition of "women's issues." A regendered cabinet would merely showcase a few women elites in departments dealing with "women's issues," narrowly defined, and distant from the president's agenda.

Transgendering can be expected in cabinet nominations. Tradition has become less constraining in the wake of Title VII of the 1964 Civil Rights Act; Title IX of the 1972 Education Amendment Act; and innumerable other antidiscriminatory laws, regulations, and judicial rulings. Women have begun to acquire the same credentials as their male colleagues and, in some cases, have been viewed as similarly credible. "Women's issues" have begun to be defined in less stereotypical terms. Accordingly, it is reasonable to expect that women will be nominated to a wider array of departments, including those traditionally associated with masculine gender roles, and of central importance to the presidency and to the policy initiatives of a president. Transgendering would then draw women into politics as constituents and decisionmakers.

Still, speaking in general terms, "seesawing" between regendering and transgendering seems the most likely development. The dynamic will presumably be especially pronounced in higher posts. After all, these offices embody traditional conceptions of men's roles and responsibilities. As such, they exert more influence and more decisionmaking power in the public sphere, and the reallocation of these resources would be likely to generate considerable resistance. These circumstances, though, also mean that women in these offices implicitly and explicitly challenge the presumptions and practices of masculinism.

In the cabinet, swings between regendering and transgendering will be registered in judgments about the representation to be provided by the women secretaries-designate. Regendering and transgendering in cabinet nominations and confirmations will result in qualitative differences in the representation provided by the secretaries-designate. Regendering signals a reinforcement of traditional gender roles. Though women may be nominated and confirmed as secretaries, their presence in the public sphere is merely endured, and their representation is correspondingly limited. Transgendering signals a greater fluidity in gender roles, allowing women and men greater self-expression. The nominees' individual potential becomes the focal point of selection and confirmation politics. Representation becomes substantively richer, encompassing many more issues and viewpoints, and descriptively deeper, as abilities and talents are utilized. It also becomes symbolically powerful, with political deliberations more inclusive of women as constituents and officeholders. Formal representation enforces the prevailing standard, whether it is exclusive (regendering) or inclusive (transgendering). That said, it becomes important to distinguish between the singular and the typical so that these political developments are accurately mapped. This distinction can be made by comparing nominations and confirmations across administrations to determine whether the cabinet is undergoing merely a gendered desegregation or is achieving a gendered integration.

Gender Desegregation Versus Gender Integration

Though women and racial and ethnic minorities each have a history of being excluded from the U.S. political system, there are real differences in both the character of the exclusion and the battles for inclusion. Perhaps no one is more aware of these contrasts than women of color, who have sometimes found themselves unwelcome in movements for gender or racial liberation. Borrowing concepts from ethnic or race analyses to describe gender events, therefore, is a highly problematic undertaking. At the same time, these fields have knowledge to share and learning to gain, and such exchanges are long overdue. The rise of postmodern theory in gender studies has begun to shift the agenda of the women's movement, which has only gradually become more diverse and less centered on the concerns of white women. At the same time, feminists have challenged civil rights movements to think about the ways in which gendered practices magnify oppression. Women of color still encounter requests to dissect their identity, to limit their personhood to their gender, *or* their race, *or* their ethnicity, *or* their sexual orientation.[76] At least sometimes, however, there is also respect for the greater complexities that characterize personalities and lives in experiences and communities.

On these terms, I borrow the concepts of desegregation and integration from studies of racial and ethnic inequality. Particularly in association with legal studies, these terms have been used to describe stages in race relations. In this study, they demarcate stages of gender relations in cabinet representation. *Gender desegregation* in a presidential administration's cabinet nominations and confirmations occurs when there is more regendering than transgendering. The women secretaries-designate are subordinate to the men so that the women's substantive and descriptive representation is closely constrained. Although women are present in the cabinet, their access to its resources is limited and even uncertain. Symbolic representation is qualified, as the desegregated cabinet exhibits little in the way of functional inclusivity. Masculinist values remain dominant because women are showcased but rarely consulted, and men retain their advantaged position.

Gender integration, though, occurs in a presidential administration's cabinet nominations and confirmations when there is more transgendering than regendering. On these occasions, women are expected to act as policy- and decisionmakers, and they are granted the full array of responsibilities and influence. The effects of masculinism may linger in presumptions or opportunities, but women are viewed as thoughtful and accomplished professionals. As gender roles become less dichotomous, representation becomes more complex and more encompassing of socioeconomic concerns. Substantively, policy alternatives proliferate; descriptively, the standards by which the secretaries-designate are assessed become more diversified. Symbolic representation deepens, as the gender-integrated cabinet becomes more inclusive of all its members. Masculinist values become less preeminent, as women are recognized as officeholders and as constituents and as they exercise power and claim authority.

As these definitions should make clear, gender desegregation and gender integration identify stages in the institutional development of the cabinet that have important implications for the polity. A political institution is a routinized set of relationships through which power is exercised, ostensibly on behalf of the public interest. Those relationships and also that exercise of power are predicated on certain ideas. As the discussion of masculinism has made clear, an acceptance of inequality between the genders constitutes one such set of values at work in the political institutions of the United States. As the cabinet nominations and confirmations become more transgendered, as the cabinet shifts from gender desegregation to gender integration, masculinism becomes less normative. In place of a hierarchy of gender roles, relationships begin to reflect individual traits and qualities. Though the changes may be extremely incremental, the dialectic between idea and practice continues and is evident in the discussions about and performance of representation. These discussions are most vibrant—and most public—in connection with the nominations and confirmations because the persons, qualifications, and roles of the secretaries-designate then receive the closest scrutiny.

Given the historic strength of masculinism, the transition from regendering to transgendering in cabinet nominations and confirmations will presumably be extremely difficult. The shift from gender desegregation to gender integration will be even more so because this change requires that the greater proportion of nominations and confirmations evidence transgendering. Masculinism is a powerful and inertial force.

In support of this contention, consider existing analyses of women's incorporation in various other organizations, which have shown that minor changes in the number of "diversity" members generally do not alter enduring practices. Critical mass theory, formulated in bureaucratic analyses and tested in studies of state legislatures, maintains that the representation provided by "diversity" members will be constrained until those individuals hold a significant percentage of the offices in the organization or chamber. This tipping point is estimated to fall somewhere between 40 and 60 percent, when the numbers of "diversity" and majority members are close to even.[77]

As a small organization, the cabinet may evolve in ways that are different from larger bureaucracies. Still, women have rarely been even a significant minority in the cabinet. As Table 1.1 demonstrates, the Clinton administration is the significant outlier in this respect, with women holding a high of 28.6 percent of the secretarial posts. Even so, women secretaries must be viewed as routinized tokens, and women of color secretaries must be considered exceptional cases. Still, there are indications of transgendering in the cabinet, and there may be some foreshadowing of gender integration. Whether and how this change is taking place must be analyzed so that the intertwining of gender and politics in cabinet representation can be understood.

Table 1.1   Maximum Percentage of Women Cabinet Secretaries, by Administration

Administration	Maximum Percentage of Women Secretaries in the Cabinet at One Time
Roosevelt	10.0
Eisenhower	10.0
Ford	9.1
Carter	18.2
Reagan	15.4
G. H. W. Bush	14.3
Clinton	28.6
G. W. Bush (initial nominations only)	21.4

OVERVIEW

The first woman secretary-designate was nominated in the Roosevelt administration, the second in the Eisenhower administration, and the third in the Ford administration. Since that time, women have been almost continuously present in the cabinet. Still, their roles and influence have exhibited considerable variance. Regendering and transgendering have occurred, but gender desegregation has been far more in evidence than gender integration. The cabinet is just beginning to confront and consider its masculinist heritage; its nominations and confirmations indicate that some change has begun, but a more systematic evolution is far from certain. This is a fascinating period of cabinet history, when relationships are shifting, power may be gained or lost, and debates about representation are especially vibrant.

Every one of the assertions in the paragraph above needs to be empirically tested so that its implications for both special and public interests can be carefully considered. Those are the tasks of this book. Drawing on the research of presidency and gender scholars, in this study I determine what significance attaches to the nominations and confirmation of women secretaries-designate. Though these events may have particular meaning for the individual women who enter the cabinet, I firmly believe that their presence as departmental executives is also important for the cabinet and for women in the wider society. As representatives, the cabinet secretaries substantively, descriptively, symbolically, and formally stand for the values and the interests that shape the polity.

In the next chapter, I examine the presidential politics of cabinet nominations. Patterns are identified within and across presidential administrations, and the women's nominations are studied in detail. Though there are some consistencies in the nomination patterns for women and men secretaries-designate, there are also differences. An examination of the nominations, each in the context of its presidential administration, offers further insight into the factors influencing presidential decisionmaking in cabinet nominations. The effects of these decisions on the cabinet's gender desegregation and integration are delineated. Rather than providing answers, a study of the nomination politics associated with the women secretaries-designate generates questions about these representatives and about women's status as presidential constituents.

Chapter 3 then profiles the secretaries-designate by their demographic, educational, professional, and political characteristics. As representatives, the greatest contribution that these individuals make to the cabinet comes through their prioritizing of relationships. The secretaries-designate do not merely acquire their skills and resources when they enter the cabinet; their abilities are developed over the course of a career, with cabinet service a "professional capstone." Overarching patterns among the precabinet careers of the secretaries-designate are identified, with differences between the women and men highlighted. A detailed analysis of the women nominees' careers then allows for a more thorough understanding of the interaction between the president's priorities in selecting cabinet officers and the representation that may be expected of the women secretaries-designate.

Media coverage of the cabinet nominations is the subject of Chapter 4. The *New York Times* is among the most influential of media outlets in the United States. As the nation's newspaper of record, the *Times* enjoys a preeminence that is recognized and thus enhanced by the Washington community. For these reasons, *Times* coverage of cabinet nominations was carefully analyzed. This study is especially important because the primary function of the mass media—communication—is also a constitutive function of representation. As an agent of communication, the mass media may endorse and facilitate, or inhibit and obstruct, the representation provided by the cabinet secretaries. In this chapter, I consider how these possibilities surface in the earliest stages of a cabinet career.

In Chapter 5, I examine the confirmation process. The Senate has routinely confirmed cabinet secretaries-designate by overwhelming majorities after minimal floor debate. All but three cabinet nominations placed on the Senate floor have been confirmed during the twentieth century.[78] This record should not, however, be taken as evidence that confirmation is a purely ceremonial undertaking. Confirmation hearings, summit meetings of legislative and executive representatives, are of particular interest. As such, the hearings have significant implications for the reputation of the secretary-designate and for the institutional development of the cabinet.

What "difference does it make" that women are being nominated and confirmed as cabinet secretaries? Is the cabinet experiencing regendering or transgendering? Is it undergoing a gender desegregation or a gender integration? What is the significance of these changes? To begin to answer these questions, the next chapter turns to the politics of cabinet nominations. As the first expression of formal representation, presidential nomination decisions go a long way toward setting the agenda for descriptive, symbolic, and substantive representation. Notwithstanding their negotiations with organized and unorganized interests, secretaries-designate, and senators, it is presidents who define the basic contours of cabinet representation. A study of cabinet nomination politics, therefore, requires one to confront two of the most basic questions associated with the representation that is provided by the cabinet. First, who are the president's constituents? Second, who represents the president's constituents?

NOTES

1. Representation is also a theme in Jeffrey Cohen's analysis of the cabinet, where it is assessed in terms of responsiveness—policy responsiveness, symbolic responsiveness, service responsiveness, and allocative responsiveness. Also included in his list is communication with constituents. His study places its emphasis upon policy responsiveness and symbolic responsiveness, doing so through a detailed survey of the societal and political backgrounds of the cabinet secretaries. Jeffrey E. Cohen, *The Politics of the U.S. Cabinet: Representation in the Executive Branch, 1789–1984* (Pittsburgh: University of Pittsburgh Press, 1988). See especially pp. 45–48. Joel D. Aberbach and Bert A. Rockman also consider the implications of responsiveness for bureaucratic performance, focusing on the relationships of political appointees and careerists. See *In the Web of Politics: Three Decades of the U.S. Federal Executive* (Washington, D.C.: Brookings Institution, 2000). Gary L. Gregg II suggests that study "through the lens provided by the concept of representation" will unify and advance analyses of the presidency. See "Toward a Representational Framework for Presidency Studies," *Presidential Studies Quarterly* 29, no. 2 (June 1999): 297–305.

2. Legislative scholars have extensively studied the associations among relationship building, communication, and representation. They have demonstrated that a legislative representative's interactions with her or his constituents significantly influence decisionmaking in Washington. The cumulative effect, as each decision registers its impact, is to shape political developments on a grand scale. For example, Morris Fiorina's classic book, *Congress: Keystone of the Washington Establishment,* concluded that members' drive to secure reelection caused them to view casework and pork barrel legislation as dominant concerns in the 1970s. That, in turn, contributed dramatically to the growth of the federal bureaucracy. Fiorina's theory attracted its share of critics, but few disputed the power of the congressional representative's responsibilities and behaviors to shape governmental priorities and processes. See Morris P. Fiorina, *Congress: Keystone of the Washington Establishment* (New Haven: Yale University Press, 1977).

3. On the political calculations and strategizing associated with the appointments and confirmations processes, see G. Calvin Mackenzie, ed., *Innocent Until Nominated: The Breakdown of the Presidential Appointments Process* (Washington, D.C.: Brookings Institution, 2001); *Obstacle Course: The Report of the Twentieth Century Fund Task Force on the Presidential Appointment Process* (New York: Twentieth Century Fund, 1996).

4. Allegations that he had improperly accepted gifts from businesses and lobbyists forced Espy to resign from the cabinet. He was acquitted of thirty of these charges, another eight having been dismissed by the presiding judge, in a jury trial that concluded on 2 December 1998. Bill Miller, "Espy Acquitted in Gifts Case," *Washington Post,* 3 December 1998, p. A1.

5. On the definition of a "constituent" and the importance of representation for citizen interests, see Melissa S. Williams, *Voice, Trust, and Memory: Marginalized Groups and the Failings of Liberal Representation* (Princeton: Princeton University Press, 1998).

6. Thomas E. Cronin, *The State of the Presidency,* 2nd ed. (Boston: Little, Brown, 1980), pp. 276–278.

7. Voter Research and Survey exit polls indicated that 57 percent of the Clinton voters in 1992 were women: 40 percent were white women, 11 percent African American women, and 6 percent Asian American and Hispanic American women. These data were provided through the kindness of Mary Bendyna of Georgetown University. On Clinton's initial statements about nominating a woman as attorney general, see Neil A. Lewis, "Clinton Expected to Name Woman Attorney General," *New York Times,* 9 December 1992, p. 1.

8. These data are taken from a *USA Today* poll conducted on 24 January 1993.

9. ABC and NPR news correspondent Cokie Roberts, a mother of two, remarked, "I'd like to know what she was paying them, frankly, because she made enough money to hire Mary Poppins. . . . [T]he idea that the only people that you could get under these circumstances are people that you have to hire illegally is just not the case with somebody who makes that much money."

Quoted in Benjamin I. Page, *Who Deliberates? Mass Media in Modern Democracy* (Chicago: University of Chicago Press, 1996), p. 87. Also on this issue, see Mary McGrory, "Why Zoe Got Zapped," *Washington Post*, 24 January 1993, p. C1; Judy Mann, "The Raw Nerve of Child Care," *Washington Post*, 27 January 1993, p. D26.

10. Though commonly used, the term *women's issue(s)* is a misnomer insofar as it suggests that only women are interested in policies related to issues such as social welfare and reproductive rights. Throughout this book, therefore, the term is placed in quotation marks. On the silence of the women's and "women's issues" networks, see Erica Jong, "Conspiracy of Silence," *New York Times*, 10 February 1993, p. A23. The favored candidate of these organizations was Brooksley Born, profiled by the Coalition for Women's Appointments as follows: "Brooksley Born, among the first woman partners of Arnold & Porter, is one of Washington's preeminent lawyers. A graduate of Stanford College and Law School, her practice is principally in international business law. She has won numerous awards for her public service work, and she is a longtime leader in the DC Bar and the American Bar Associations, serving on the Board of Governors and chairing such entities as the Standing Committee on the Federal Judiciary [which evaluates candidates for nomination to the federal bench], the Section of Individual Rights and Responsibilities, and the Consortium on Legal Services and the Public. She serves on many boards, including Stanford Law School, National Women's Law Center (chair), National Legal Aid and Defender Association, and Lawyers' Committee for Civil Rights." Coalition for Women's Appointments, "Initial List of Recommendations, November 10, 1992," provided to the author by the National Women's Political Caucus.

11. Terence Moran, "It's Not Just Zoe Baird," *New York Times,* 23 January 1993, p. A21.

12. During the hearing, Senator Howard Metzenbaum (D-Ohio) remarked that his office had received fifty calls opposed to Baird's confirmation and none in support in the evening prior to the hearing (p. 100). Senator Paul Simon (D-Ill.) noted that his Washington office had received eighty-four calls against and three in support (p. 132). U.S. Senate, Committee on the Judiciary, *Nomination of Zoë E. Baird, January 19 and 21, 1993,* 103rd Congress, 1st sess. ABC News reported that calls to Senator Dianne Feinstein's office (D-Calif.) were running 1,500 against to 33 in favor of confirmation. Benjamin I. Page, *Who Deliberates? Mass Media in Modern Democracy* (Chicago: University of Chicago Press, 1996), p. 97. On the matter of nomination withdrawals more generally, see Mark Stence, "Those Who Withdrew," *New York Times*, 23 January 1993, p. A10.

13. Georgia Duerst-Lahti, "Reconceiving Theories of Power: Consequences of Masculinism in the Executive Branch," in *The Other Elites: Women, Politics, and Power in the Executive Branch,* ed. MaryAnne Borrelli and Janet M. Martin (Boulder: Lynne Rienner Publishers, 1997); Georgia Duerst-Lahti and Rita Mae Kelly, eds., *Gender Power, Leadership, and Governance* (Ann Arbor: University of Michigan Press, 1995); Christine Di Ste-

fano, *Configurations of Masculinity: A Feminist Perspective on Modern Political Theory* (Ithaca: Cornell University Press, 1991). See also Kathleen Hall Jamieson, *Beyond the Double Bind: Women and Leadership* (New York: Oxford University Press, 1995).

14. For a critique of the so-called pipeline theory, see Kathryn Dunn Tenpas, "Women on the White House Staff: A Longitudinal Analysis," in *The Other Elites: Women, Politics, and Power in the Executive Branch,* ed. MaryAnne Borrelli and Janet M. Martin (Boulder: Lynne Rienner Publishers, 1997).

15. For the classic theoretical statement of this position, see C. Wright Mills, *The Power Elite* (New York: Oxford University Press, 1957). See also Steven Lukes, *Power: A Radical View* (New York: Macmillan, 1974).

16. Hanna Fenichel Pitkin, *The Concept of Representation* (Berkeley: University of California Press, 1967). See also Jane Mansbridge, "Should Blacks Represent Blacks and Women Represent Women? A Contingent 'Yes.'" *Journal of Politics* 61, no. 3 (August 1999): 628–657.

17. For a comprehensive discussion of alternative approaches to studying the cabinet, see Janet M. Martin, "Frameworks for Cabinet Studies," *Presidential Studies Quarterly* 18 (Fall 1988): 795–798.

18. See *Obstacle Course: The Report of the Twentieth Century Fund Task Force on the Presidential Appointment Process* (New York: Twentieth Century Fund, 1996).

19. Ibid.

20. Of course, the distinction between being "thorough" and being highly partisan is a matter for debate. For example, see Jean Reith Schroedel, Sharon Spray, and Bruce D. Snyder, "Diversity and the Politicization of Presidential Appointments: A Case Study of the Achtenberg Nomination," in *The Other Elites: Women, Politics, and Power in the Executive Branch,* ed. MaryAnne Borrelli and Janet M. Martin (Boulder, Colo.: Lynne Rienner Publishers, 1997). See also Burdett Loomis, "The Senate: An 'Obstacle Course' for Executive Appointments," in *Innocent Until Nominated: The Breakdown of the Presidential Appointments Process,* ed. G. Calvin Mackenzie (Washington, D.C.: Brookings Institution, 2001); Robert Shogan, "The Confirmation Wars: How Politicians, Interest Groups, and the Press Shape the Presidential Appointment Process," in *Obstacle Course: The Report of the Twentieth Century Fund Task Force on the Presidential Appointment Process* (New York: Twentieth Century Fund, 1996).

21. Sharon Lynn Spray, "The Politics of Confirmations: A Study of Senate Roll Call Confirmation Voting, 1787–1994," Ph.D. diss., Claremont Graduate School, 1997, p. 239. Confirmation battles also occurred prior to the modern presidency, which is to say prior to Franklin D. Roosevelt's administration. Coolidge attorney general–designate Charles Warren's nomination, for example, was actually defeated twice on the Senate floor, once by a tie vote (40–40) and once by a negative vote (46–39). On the Warren case, see Richard F.

Fenno, Jr., *The President's Cabinet: An Analysis in the Period from Wilson to Eisenhower* (Cambridge, Mass.: Harvard University Press, 1959), pp. 54–55.

22. U.S. Senate, Committee on Interstate and Foreign Commerce, *Nomination of Lewis L. Strauss*. 86th Cong., 1st sess.; G. Calvin Mackenzie, *The Politics of Presidential Appointments* (New York: The Free Press, 1981), p. 143.

23. U.S. Senate, Committee on Armed Services, *Nomination of John G. Tower to Be Secretary of Defense,* 101st Cong., 1st sess.; Robert Shogan, "The Confirmation Wars: How Politicians, Interest Groups, and the Press Shape the Presidential Appointment Process," in *Obstacle Course: The Report of the Twentieth Century Fund Task Force on the Presidential Appointment Process* (New York: Twentieth Century Fund, 1996), pp. 129–130.

24. Mark Stence, "Those Who Withdrew," *New York Times,* 23 January 1993, p. A10.

25. Notably, public opinion was also highly influential in the Baird and Chavez cases, although Chavez's early withdrawal limited popular protest. Chavez, who had criticized Baird in 1993, stated that her own experience led her to believe that "Baird was treated unfairly," although Chavez did maintain that their actions were quite different. David E. Sanger, "Lessons of a Swift Exit," *New York Times,* 10 January 2001, A1.

26. The members of all marginalized groups, taken together, constitute a majority of the population. "Diversity" is therefore placed in quotation marks. African Americans did achieve proportional representation among the initial Clinton nominees, when four of fifteen initial secretaries-designate (26.7 percent) were African American. The four were Mike Espy (Agriculture), Ron Brown (Commerce), Hazel O'Leary (Energy), and Jesse Brown (Veterans Affairs).

27. Mitsuye Yamada, "Invisibility Is an Unnatural Disaster: Reflections of an Asian American Woman," in *This Bridge Called My Back, Writings by Radical Women of Color,* ed. Cherrie Moraga and Gloria Anzaldua (New York: Kitchen Table, Women of Color Press, 1983).

28. Clinton appointed African American secretaries-designate to the Departments of Agriculture, Commerce, Energy, and Veterans Affairs in 1993 and to Transportation and Labor in 1997. George W. Bush nominated African American secretaries-designate to the Departments of State and Education.

29. Dorothy Gilliam, "Black Women Need a Seat at the Table," *Washington Post,* 19 December 1992, p. B2.

30. For the seminal work challenging this construction, see Gloria T. Hull, Patricia Bell Scott, and Barbara Smith, ed., *All the Women Are White, All the Blacks Are Men, But Some of Us Are Brave: Black Women's Studies* (Old Westbury, NY: Feminist Press, 1982). See also Kimberle Crenshaw, "Demarginalizing the Intersection of Race and Sex: A Black Feminist Critique of Antidiscrimination Doctrine, Feminist Theory and Antiracist Politics," in *Feminist Legal Theory: Foundations,* ed. by D. Kelly Weisberg (Philadelphia: Temple University Press, 1993).

31. Their demand for descriptive representation was based in part on electoral allegiance: 86 percent of African American women had voted for the president-elect. Dorothy Gilliam, "Black Women Need a Seat at the Table," *Washington Post,* 19 December 1992, p. B2.

32. Charles Taylor, *Multiculturalism and "The Politics of Recognition"* (Princeton: Princeton University Press, 1992), passim.

33. Jane Mansbridge, "Should Blacks Represent Blacks and Women Represent Women? A Contingent 'Yes.'" *Journal of Politics* 61, no. 3 (August 1999): 628.

34. Associated Press, "Current Quotes from the 1992 Campaign Trail," 22 May 1992.

35. The president-elect both acknowledged and protested this pressure, describing the women's groups as "bean counters" who were "playing quota games and math games" with the nominations. This outburst came during the press conference that announced the nominations of Energy Secretary-Designate Hazel O'Leary and Education Secretary-Designate Richard Riley. Ruth Marcus, "Clinton Berates Critics in Women's Groups," *Washington Post,* 22 December 1992, p. 1. See also Coalition for Women's Appointments, *The Mirror.* Provided to the author by the National Women's Political Coalition. (*The Mirror* was a newsletter, published throughout the transition, publicizing the sex and race of the Clinton nominees.)

36. Anthony Lewis, "If It Were Mr. Baird," *New York Times,* 25 January 1993, p. A17.

37. In further support of these contentions, it is important to note that media coverage throughout the confirmation process provided evidence that male members of Congress and male secretaries-designate had committed the illegalities for which Baird was pilloried. Yet their actions incited little public attention. It was Baird's descriptive and symbolic representation of women, and its connection with her motherhood, that drew the public's attention. For example, see Karen Tumulty and John M. Broder, "Ron Brown Failed to Pay Employer Tax," *Los Angeles Times,* 8 February 1993, p. A1.

38. It could be argued that this discussion reduces a multifaceted enterprise—symbolic representation—to a one-dimensional, essentialist, time-, and class-bound ideology of woman. Unfortunately, popular political discourse is largely conducted in sound bites. Statements are sweeping, not detailed. Frequently, speakers avoid equivocation and embrace vehemence in order to draw popular attention. This practice is as much in evidence in governing as it is in campaigning. Consequently, coverage and discourse about the Baird nomination constituted a recognizable extreme. Yet Baird's experience is also familiar because it echoes themes seen in each woman secretary-designate's nomination and confirmation. In every instance, the intersection of descriptive and symbolic representation in these cabinet selections has triggered ideological responses that are intellectual and emotional.

39. On this point, see Georgia Duerst-Lahti, "Reconceiving Theories of Power: Consequences of Masculinism in the Executive Branch," in *The Other*

Elites: Women, Politics, and Power in the Executive Branch, ed. MaryAnne Borrelli and Janet M. Martin (Boulder, Colo.: Lynne Rienner Publishers, 1997).

40. The work of Mark E. Kann is particularly outstanding. See, for example, *A Republic of Men: The American Founders, Gendered Language, and Patriarchal Politics* (New York: New York University Press, 1998).

41. Judith Butler, *Gender Trouble: Feminism and the Subversion of Identity* (New York: Routledge, 1990).

42. Laurel Thatcher Ulrich, "Harvard's Womanless History," *Harvard Magazine* 102, no. 2 (November–December 1999): 58.

43. It should be noted that a number of gender scholars argue that there are more than two genders. For a brief discussion of this perspective and also for the oversimplifications that attend categorizing humans physiologically as males or females, see Terrell Carver, *Gender Is Not a Synonym for Women* (Boulder, Colo.: Lynne Rienner Publishers, 1996). See especially the introduction and chap. 1.

44. For a more extended discussion of these identities, see Georgia Duerst-Lahti and Rita Mae Kelly, eds., *Gender Power, Leadership, and Governance* (Ann Arbor: University of Michigan Press, 1995). See also Judith Butler, *Gender Trouble: Feminism and the Subversion of Identity* (New York: Routledge, 1990), especially chaps. 1 and 2.

45. There are, however, rare instances in which the sex of the officeholder is stipulated by law. One example of this is the director of the Women's Bureau, who must be a female. 41 Stat. 987.

46. Terrell Carver succinctly states, "[G]ender is the ways that sex and sexuality become power relations in society." Carver, *Gender Is Not a Synonym for Women* (Boulder, Colo.: Lynne Rienner Publishers, 1996), p. 14.

47. Georgia Duerst-Lahti and Rita Mae Kelly, "On Governance, Leadership, and Gender," in *Gender Power, Leadership, and Governance*, ed. Georgia Duerst-Lahti and Rita Mae Kelly (Ann Arbor: University of Michigan Press, 1995), pp. 20–21.

48. Ibid.

49. Commenting on this point, Georgia Duerst-Lahti notes, "In this gendered construction of a singular leader, cause and effect are blurred and reinforcing; nonetheless, cultural constructions much more readily accord the possibility of individual accomplishment deserving of greatness— accomplishments earned in one's own right, without regards to connections or support—to men. . . . In contrast, women are challenged in at least two ways: in the belief that a woman is or can be singular and in the possibility of be(com)ing 'great.'" Duerst-Lahti, "Reconceiving Theories of Power: Consequences of Masculinism in the Executive Branch," in *The Other Elites, Women, Politics, and Power in the Executive Branch*, ed. MaryAnne Borrelli and Janet M. Martin (Boulder, Colo.: Lynne Rienner Publishers, 1997), p. 22.

50. Clinton Rossiter, *The American Presidency* (New York: Time, 1960), p. 5.

51. A reader may offer two objections to this analysis of masculinism. First, one could argue that women can gain power by adopting masculinist forms of behavior. In the words of a former woman administrator of the Environmental Protection Agency, a woman has to prove that she is "tough enough" in order to succeed in national politics. See Anne M. Burford, *Are You Tough Enough? An Insider's View of Washington Power Politics* (New York: McGraw-Hill, 1986). Second, and alternatively, one could maintain that masculinity and femininity cannot be defined as constant or mutually exclusive categories. What is deemed an appropriate role for a man or a woman varies according to culture. Even within a single country, gender is shaped by race, class, religion, and innumerable other aspects of a people's identity. To this way of thinking, masculinism is merely a rationale for discrimination because it fails to understand the diverse contributions and resources of a society's members.

The first possibility—that women can succeed by practicing masculinism—is an approach that has been endorsed by many women and men leaders. This strategy requires women and men to accept current procedures so that traditionally masculine precepts continue to direct the course of decisionmaking and policy implementation. To the extent that women benefit from existent political and governmental institutions, this arrangement may suffice. Yet women's interests have historically been neglected by masculinist institutions, so endorsing this ideology inevitably means curtailing substantive representation for women. Further, to the extent that women's gender identity is distinct from men's, governing through masculinism means that women are defined as second-class citizens. Insofar as women fail to meet the masculine norm, they fail to achieve the standard set for political participation and governmental representation. This problem obliges one even to ask whether a woman could be credible as a practitioner of masculinism. Could her sex and her gender roles be distinguished sufficiently so that her adoption of masculine behaviors would be accepted?

The second possibility—that masculinism is merely a discriminatory ideology—has merit. As numerous scholars have noted, the false dichotomizing of masculine and feminine attributes and behaviors provides little insight into the richness of personal identities and relationships. See Carol Gilligan, *In a Different Voice, Psychological Theory and Women's Development* (Cambridge, Mass.: Harvard University Press, 1982); Lyn Mikel Brown and Carol Gilligan, *Meeting at the Crossroads* (New York: Ballantine Books, 1992). Yet governmental norms do simplify and generalize in this way. They are, in fact, *essentialist* in their dictates. Numerous kinds of gender diversity are excluded from representation on the cabinet, for example. In the administrations studied, only twelve secretaries-designate had not been married, which suggests that participation in a formally recognized, heterosexual relationship is an informal requirement for cabinet office. More generally, gender scholars have noted that heterosexuality is compulsory for leaders throughout U.S. society. As the operative political ideology directing who should exercise power and to what ends, masculinism does rationalize discrimination and exclusion. If it is to be thoughtfully and successfully challenged, however, it needs to be dissected and understood.

52. Richard F. Fenno, Jr., *The President's Cabinet: An Analysis in the Period from Wilson to Eisenhower* (Cambridge, Mass.: Harvard University Press, 1959). For an early and extensive study of this aspect of the cabinet, see John Fairlie, "The President's Cabinet," *American Political Science Review* (February 1913): 28–44.

53. See Hugh Heclo, *A Government of Strangers* (Washington, D.C.: Brookings Institution, 1977); Stephen Hess, *Organizing the Presidency*, rev. ed. (Washington, D.C.: Brookings Institution, 1988); Terry Moe, "The Politicized Presidency," in *The New Direction in American Politics*, ed. John E. Chubb and Paul E. Peterson (Washington, D.C.: Brookings Institution, 1985); Richard P. Nathan, *The Administrative Presidency* (New York: Macmillan, 1986).

54. This typology is set out in Janet M. Martin's article, "Frameworks for Cabinet Studies," *Presidential Studies Quarterly* 18 (Fall 1988): 793–814.

55. For example, see Thomas Cronin, *The State of the Presidency*, 2nd ed. (Boston: Little, Brown, 1980), pp. 274–286.

56. For example, see Theodore J. Lowi, *The End of Liberalism: Ideology, Policy, and the Crisis of Public Authority* (New York: W. W. Norton, 1969); Hugh Heclo, "Issue Networks and the Executive Establishment," in *The New American Political System*, ed. Anthony King (Washington, D.C.: American Enterprise Institute, 1978). See also Theodore J. Lowi, *The End of Liberalism: The Second Republic*, 2nd ed. (New York: W. W. Norton, 1979).

57. For example, see Stephen Hess, *Organizing the Presidency*, rev. ed. (Washington, D.C.: Brookings Institution, 1988).

58. Janet M. Martin, "Frameworks for Cabinet Studies," *Presidential Studies Quarterly* 18 (Fall 1988): 795–798. For an example of this theme in media coverage of cabinet nominations, see the coverage of the Clinton cabinet nominations during the 1992 transition.

59. For example, see James D. King and James W. Riddlesperger, Jr., "Presidential Cabinet Appointments: The Partisan Factor," *Presidential Studies Quarterly* 14 (Spring 1984): 231–237.

60. For example, see James J. Best, "Presidential Cabinet Appointments: 1953–1976," *Presidential Studies Quarterly* 11, no. 1 (Winter 1981): 62–66; Janet M. Martin, "An Examination of Executive Branch Appointments in the Reagan Administration by Background and Gender," *Western Political Quarterly* 44 (1991): 173–184.

61. For example, see Janet M. Martin, "Cabinet Secretaries from Truman to Johnson: An Examination of Theoretical Frameworks for Cabinet Studies," Ph.D. diss., Ohio State University, 1985.

62. For example, see Herbert F. Weisberg, "Cabinet Transfers and Departmental Prestige: Someone Old, Someone New, Someone Borrowed . . .," *American Politics Quarterly* 15, no. 2 (April 1987): 238–253.

63. Nelson W. Polsby, "Presidential Cabinet Making: Lessons for the Political System," *Political Science Quarterly* 93, no. 1 (Spring 1978): 15–25.

64. Ibid.

65. Ibid.

66. Elizabeth Drew, *On the Edge: The Clinton Presidency* (New York: Simon and Schuster, 1994), pp. 27–28.

67. Nelson W. Polsby, "Presidential Cabinet Making: Lessons for the Political System," *Political Science Quarterly* 93, no. 1 (Spring 1978): 15–25.

68. The distinction is an important one, especially when calculating the number of "diversity" nominees to the cabinet. Ronald Reagan, for example, maintained that his cabinet had a woman from the earliest days of the administration. He argued that the first woman in his cabinet was Jeane Kirkpatrick, who held cabinet rank as the U.S. ambassador to the United Nations. Other presidents have not awarded this position cabinet rank, however. Narrowing cabinet membership to the departmental secretaries is therefore essential to ensuring consistency and comparability across the administrations.

69. Janet M. Martin, *A Place in the Oval Office: Women and the American Presidency* (College Station: Texas A&M Press, forthcoming).

70. For example, see Georgia Duerst-Lahti and Dayna Verstegen, "Making Something of Absence: The 'Year of the Woman' and Women's Representation," in *Gender Power, Leadership, and Governance,* ed. Georgia Duerst-Lahti and Rita Mae Kelly (Ann Arbor: University of Michigan Press, 1995).

71. As is appropriate and possible, this study also draws on research about women officeholders in other settings. These comparisons reveal certain similarities about women's entry into governmental office. Still, the institutional setting exerts a powerful and conditioning effect: Election to a legislature and nomination to the cabinet are not equivalent processes or events. Studying a database of women officeholders, both elected and appointed, would only ignore (and render it impossible to draw) lessons about the cabinet as an institution for representation within the presidency. It would, in other words, be an interesting and valuable study but it would not be *this* study.

72. This research was conducted by Janet M. Martin for a presentation at the American Political Science Association Annual Meeting of 2001.

73. Georgia Duerst-Lahti and Rita Mae Kelly, "On Governance, Leadership, and Gender," in *Gender Power, Leadership, and Governance,* ed. Georgia Duerst-Lahti and Rita Mae Kelly (Ann Arbor: University of Michigan Press, 1995).

74. Ibid.

75. Similar patterns have been observed in state-level bureaucracies, where women and men each predominate in the departments whose jurisdictions most closely conform to their traditional gender roles. See Mary E. Guy, ed., *Women and Men of the States: Public Administrators at the State Level* (Armonk, N.Y.: M. E. Sharpe, 1992); Katherine C. Naff, *To Look Like America: Dismantling Barriers for Women and Minorities in Government* (Boulder, Colo.: Westview Press, 2001).

76. Gloria Anzaldua, *La Frontera: The New Mestiza* (San Francisco: Aunt Lute Books, 1987).

77. Sue Thomas, *How Women Legislate* (New York: Oxford University Press, 1994), pp. 85–87, passim. See also Rosabeth Moss Kanter, *Men and Women of the Corporation* (New York: Basic Books, 1977).

78. The three were Coolidge attorney general–designate Charles Warren, Eisenhower commerce secretary-designate Lewis Strauss, and Bush defense secretary-designate John Tower.

2

Cabinet Nominations: Presidents, Power, Process

The presidents' nomination decisions are among the most intimate and idiosyncratic of their public actions. The selection of the women and men who will advise them, advocate on behalf of their interests, and speak for their concerns involves judgments about politics, professions, and personalities. Still, scholars and political observers often agree that presidents have just two first priorities in selecting their nominees, namely, securing political leadership for and managerial control of the executive branch.

Although political leadership can contribute to good management and vice versa, the two have often been perceived as contradictory. Political demands for change have seemed at odds with a manager's presumed attentiveness to already established programs. Meanwhile, the so-called politicization of the executive branch has sometimes valued ideological conformity more than organizational experience. When judgments about political leadership are premised on public sector standards of effectiveness, while assessments of executive branch management are evaluated by private sector measures of efficiency, the competing priorities can even appear mutually exclusive.[1] And yet the key word is "appear." As practiced by cabinet secretaries, political leadership and executive management share the common purpose of facilitating representation. Ideally, a political leader synthesizes ideas and resolves conflict, establishing programs that are responsive to department clients and more general societal interests. An executive manager ensures that programs fulfill their promises, bringing goods and services to the people on

41

whose behalf the leaders and lobbyists acted. Properly understood, therefore, political leadership and executive management are the skills that enable cabinet members to succeed as representatives.

Because the president has the power to select the secretaries-designate, the president sets the agenda for the cabinet's representation. In doing so, the president-elect or president undertakes four sets of political calculations, the first three relating most to political leadership, whereas the fourth is more about managerial control.

- *Indebtedness* to those who helped the president-elect to win election or the president win reelection to the Oval Office
- *Symbolism* in presenting problem-solving approaches and policy positions
- *Political relationships,* whether sought, sustained, or denied, with the Washington community and the wider polity
- *Managerial needs* to control the bureaucracy for the chief executive[2]

These are the standards by which a president decides who will or will not be represented in the cabinet.[3] Balancing these considerations within and across administrations requires extended and difficult negotiations, as interests and persons are recognized or dismissed as presidential constituents.[4]

When presidents-elect have tried to simplify matters by eliminating or even de-emphasizing one of the four factors, they have encountered extraordinary criticism. During the Carter transition, for example, the president-elect sought to remove indebtedness as a concern and stated as much at a press conference.

> I realize that a lot of different voting entities in our country have helped me become elected. But I completed my own election process, which lasted almost two years, without having made any commitment in private to anyone about an appointment to a Cabinet post or any other post in Government.
>
> And so I'm completely at liberty, absolutely completely at liberty, to make my decisions about the Cabinet membership on the basis of merit and who can do the best job working with me harmoniously to lead our country. There are no other commitments.[5]

The "voting entities," however, strongly objected to the president-elect's self-characterization as "absolutely completely at liberty" in selecting nominees. Their "help" meant that they merited representation in the new administration. In fact, the National Women's Political Caucus believed that Carter *had* made certain commitments at a meeting held during the campaign.[6] Women's nominations and representation for women's interests were discussed in correspondingly pointed terms during this transition.

Although representation remains a constant concern in selecting the secretaries-designate, its functions do change as the presidential term advances. Initial secretaries-designate often focus on advancing new initiatives, seeking to transform the new president's campaign promises into the authorizations and appropriations requisite for departmental action. Midterm secretaries-designate inherit that legislation and work to establish functional programs, seeking to demonstrate the effectiveness of the administration and thus to secure the president's reelection.[7] Thus, communication and relationship building with presidential constituents is ongoing, but the exchanges themselves evolve. In recognition of these eventualities, the skills sought by chief executives in their cabinet representatives also change. *Presidents-elect* emphasize political leadership, paying greatest attention to indebtedness, symbolism, and political relationships. *Presidents* make midterm nominations (sometimes referred to as replacement nominations) with greater concern for managerial needs.

These patterns are, however, seldom clear to the nominating president or the transition team. It is for good reason that the weeks between the election and the inauguration are described as "slightly structured chaos."[8] Time is limited, personnel recruitment is one task among many, and institutional memory and candidates' preparations for office are limited. Presidents-elect juggle staffing for the White House and the cabinet; common wisdom recommends that greatest attention be given to the White House staff, but cabinet posts continue to attract more attention from interest groups, the media, and the general public. Initial secretaries-designate are closely scrutinized as indicators of who will be recognized as presidential constituents and which campaign promises will be fulfilled. Whose interests will the future cabinet members advance? Which individuals are viewed as credible departmental executives? Does the cabinet exhibit inclusivity or exclusivity in its membership? These are questions of substantive, descriptive, symbolic, and formal representation, and they are all first answered in the selection of the initial secretaries-designate. Those questions are revisited when midterm secretaries-designate are nominated, oftentimes with an added awareness of the president's impending reelection campaign.

To delineate and assess the ways in which cabinet representation changes across a presidential term, James King and James Riddlesperger compared initial and midterm cabinet nominations from the Truman administration through the first two and a half years of the Reagan administration. Their analysis found consistent differences along partisan lines between initial secretaries-designate in Democratic and Republican administrations. In Democratic administrations, initial secretaries-designate had more extensive experience in the national government. These nominees were more highly educated than their Republican counterparts and were more likely to be members of Congress, attorneys, and academics. They also included relatively more southerners. Republican initial secretaries-designate were more consistently recruited from the private sector. Their governmental experience was more often at the state or local level. Republican initial nominees also included higher proportions of political party officeholders and midwesterners. These differences were absent among the midterm secretaries-designate, however, who were comparatively similar in terms of their governmental experience, political party service, professional profile, educational attainment, and regional distribution.[9] Rather than partisan contrasts, common concerns for executive branch politics seemed to be the dominant influence in the later cabinet nominations. What does this mean for the representation that is expected of the cabinet nominees?

To answer this question, it is necessary to conduct an even more detailed comparison of the initial and midterm secretaries-designate. Studying their precabinet contacts with the Washington community, policy networks, and the president and assessing their expertise in the issue jurisdiction of their future department indicates the representation that they can be expected to provide as cabinet members. In so doing, the connections between presidential nominations and cabinet representation are revealed because who is selected as a cabinet secretary-designate is indicative of who is recognized as a presidential constituent.

PRESIDENTIAL PRIORITIES AND
THE SECRETARIES-DESIGNATE

If political leadership and executive management are crucial to the performance of representation by cabinet secretaries, then the anticipated performance of the secretary-designate can best be gauged by reference to two sets of relationships. The first set includes those that the secretary-designate has already established with members of the Washington community. Leadership and management require a knowledge of people and process, and the difficulties associated with running a department are somewhat eased by past governmental experience. At the same time, campaign promises of new perspectives and "fresh faces" dictate the nomination of Washington outsiders to the cabinet. So, the balance of insiders and outsiders is suggestive of the weight given to established routines and to alternative approaches, as well as of the priority given to proven expertise. If a president values Washington insiders, especially among initial secretaries-designate, the Washington community gains influence, and cabinet representation is unlikely to undergo many changes. In contrast, the nomination of Washington outsiders may allow for changes in representation, though their lack of familiarity with D.C. folkways may cause these secretaries-designate to be somewhat less successful in advocating on behalf of their constituents.[10] Such a conclusion mirrors the analysis of Joel D. Aberbach and Bert A. Rockman, who observe that prior experience in government service does contribute to the effectiveness of presidential and political appointees.[11]

The second set of relationships indicative of the secretary-designate's leadership and management includes those classified by Nelson W. Polsby's schema. Specialists are experts in their prospective department's issue jurisdiction; liaisons have long-standing relationships with their prospective department's clients or issue networks and with the legislative branch; policy generalists are chosen from the campaign leadership and from among the president's closest friends. Each of these associations will affect cabinet representation, influencing the conversations and the relationships that are valued by the secretaries. Though any secretary-designate may more readily embrace the status quo than work for change, representation is especially likely to remain constant when liaisons are nominated. With strong ties already forged to powerful department clients and networks, these cabinet members may not even see the need for innovation. Whether specialists will reach out to new constituents depends on their assessments of the programs already being administered. The representation provided by generalists is also somewhat uncertain. By definition, secretaries-designate whose prior relationships are with historically underrepresented interests will be classified as generalists. Their dependence on the chief executive may delimit their ability to advocate on behalf of those interests.

In this chapter, nomination patterns throughout the presidential term are delineated. The presence of Washington insiders and outsiders and of specialists, liaisons, and generalists among initial and midterm secretaries-designate is established across the presidential administrations. This analysis at once supplements and augments the previously cited work of King and Riddlesperger, as it relies on new categories for profiling the secretaries-designate and includes the initial cabinet nominations of George W. Bush.

Acknowledging the Washington Community: Insiders and Outsiders

In each administration, as the presidential term advanced, the percentage of Washington insiders increased among the secretaries-designate, while the percentage of outsiders decreased. This conclusion rested on a rigorous definition of a Washington insider: To qualify as an insider, a secretary-designate had had a primary career in the national government, *or* had entered the cabinet directly from the subcabinet, *or* had transferred directly from another cabinet post. Any nominee that did not meet at least one of these criteria was designated an outsider. As Table 2.1 demonstrates, the percentages and magnitude of this change varied, but the shift toward insiders was consistent for every administration except that of George H. W. Bush. In this administration, the trend was reversed: The percentage of insiders decreased, and the percentage of outsiders increased across the presidential term.[12] Typically, then, the opportunities for outsiders—and presumably for innovations in cabinet representation—were greater at the beginning of the presidential term.

The initial favoring of outsiders can be attributed to campaign promises and to partisan turnover in the Oval Office. Presidential candidates routinely promise to draw new leadership into their administration. Even George H. W. Bush, an insider with at least twenty-four years experience in government and politics, promised to nominate "new faces."[13] The one president who had not been elected to office—Gerald R. Ford—confronted similar popular expectations of change, as his nomination decisions were influenced by a concern to mitigate the lingering effects of the Watergate scandal.[14]

Partisan turnover also virtually dictates the selection of outsiders, because presidents seldom nominate either members of the opposing party or supporters of their primary opponents to the cabinet. Indeed,

Table 2.1   Cabinet Secretaries-Designate as Insiders or Outsiders, by the Timing of the Nomination and by Administration (percentages, with frequency counts in parentheses)

	Initial	Midterm	Total
Roosevelt			
Insider	27.3 (3)	60.0 (9)	46.2 (12)
Outsider	72.7 (8)	40.0 (6)	53.8 (14)
Eisenhower			
Insider	0 (0)	72.7 (8)	38.1 (8)
Outsider	100.0 (10)	27.3 (3)	61.9 (13)
Ford			
Insider	40.0 (2)	62.5 (5)	53.8 (7)
Outsider	60.0 (3)	37.5 (3)	46.2 (6)
Carter			
Insider	36.4 (4)	50.0 (5)	42.9 (9)
Outsider	63.6 (7)	50.0 (5)	57.1 (12)
Reagan			
Insider	30.8 (4)	55.0 (11)	45.5 (15)
Outsider	69.2 (9)	45.0 (9)	54.5 (18)
G. H. W. Bush			
Insider	71.4 (10)	62.5 (5)	68.2 (15)
Outsider	28.6 (4)	37.5 (3)	31.8 (7)
Clinton			
Insider	20.0 (3)	62.5 (10)	41.9 (13)
Outsider	80.0 (12)	37.5 (6)	58.1 (18)
Totals			
Insider	32.9 (26)	60.2 (53)	47.3 (79)
Outsider	67.1 (53)	39.8 (35)	52.7 (88)
Postscript: G. W. Bush			
Insider	33.3 (5)		
Outsider	66.7 (10)		

Note: Percentages may not add up to 100 because of rounding.

when presidents do step across these boundaries, they are likely to be criticized for doing so.[15] Of the eight administrations studied here, there were only two instances of partisan continuity, namely, the Ford and George H. W. Bush administrations.[16] Electoral forces, therefore, create pressures to recruit cabinet members from outside the Washington community and thus to initiate a wider array of political relationships.

Insiders, however, predominate among midterm nominees. As such, they are indicative of the changing role of departmental secretaries during the presidential term, their greater familiarity with Washington networks facilitating the implementation of new programs. The increased proportion of insiders may also reflect the practice of recruiting midterm secretaries-designate from within the administration, as when subcabinet members are promoted or secretaries are transferred from one department to another. These nominations allow presidents to reward—and further benefit from—the loyalty and skillfulness of initial nominees.[17] When the midterm nominee is selected from the Washington community, its influence increases and its standards for representation are endorsed. When the midterm nominee is recruited from within the administration, representation may be sustained, but it will seldom be enhanced.

In the George W. Bush administration, the percentage of insiders (33.3 percent) among the initial secretaries-designate was comparable to other administrations. Like many of his predecessors, George W. Bush's election resulted in partisan change in the White House. Additionally, George W. Bush's political career was not centered in Washington to the same extent as his father's. It therefore seems likely that the cabinet nominations in the George W. Bush administration will conform to the patterns seen in virtually every other administration.

Why were George H. W. Bush's nominations so unusual? During this Bush administration, the percentage of insider cabinet nominees decreased, and the percentage of outsider nominees increased across the presidential term.[18] A sitting vice president who was elected president, George H. W. Bush followed the lead of other presidents and recruited his cabinet officers from his career networks. An insider himself, he nominated insiders. After eight years of Republican control of the White House, it was also true that the presidential nominee candidate pool had been somewhat depleted of outsiders. George H. W. Bush's exceptional cabinet nominations, therefore, were likely to be a product of his exceptional circumstances. At the same time, this exception did prove the more general rule that in exercising the power to nominate, a chief executive expresses his priorities for executive leadership and management.

Capitalizing on Past Relationships: Specialists, Liaisons, and Generalists

In each administration, the percentage of policy generalists increases and the percentage of liaisons decreases across the presidential term.[19] As shown in Table 2.2, the changes are most dramatic in the Roosevelt and Eisenhower administrations. Policy specialists are consistently rare. The exceptions, in this instance, are the Gerald Ford and Bill Clinton administrations.

Table 2.2   Cabinet Secretaries-Designate as Specialists, Liaisons, or
            Generalists, by the Timing of the Nomination and by
            Administration (percentages, with frequency counts in
            parentheses)

	Initial	Midterm	Total
Roosevelt			
Specialist	9.1 (1)	6.7 (1)	7.7 (2)
Liaison	63.6 (7)	33.3 (5)	46.2 (12)
Generalist	27.3 (3)	60.0 (9)	46.2 (12)
Eisenhower			
Specialist	10.0 (1)	0 (0)	4.8 (1)
Liaison	70.0 (7)	45.5 (5)	57.1 (12)
Generalist	20.0 (2)	54.5 (6)	38.1 (8)
Ford			
Specialist	40.0 (2)	0 (0)	15.4 (2)
Liaison	20.0 (1)	62.5 (5)	46.2 (6)
Generalist	40.0 (2)	37.5 (3)	38.5 (5)
Carter			
Specialist	9.1 (1)	0 (0)	4.8 (1)
Liaison	54.5 (6)	40.0 (4)	47.6 (10)
Generalist	36.4 (4)	60.0 (6)	47.6 (10)
Reagan			
Specialist	0 (0)	0 (0)	0 (0)
Liaison	61.5 (8)	40.0 (8)	48.5 (16)
Generalist	38.5 (5)	60.0 (12)	51.5 (17)
G. H. W. Bush			
Specialist	0 (0)	0 (0)	0 (0)
Liaison	50.0 (7)	37.5 (3)	45.5 (10)
Generalist	50.0 (7)	62.5 (5)	54.5 (12)
Clinton			
Specialist	6.7 (1)	6.3 (1)	6.5 (2)
Liaison	40.0 (6)	43.8 (7)	41.9 (13)
Generalist	53.3 (8)	50.0 (8)	51.6 (16)
Totals			
Specialist	7.6 (6)	2.3 (2)	4.8 (8)
Liaison	53.2 (42)	42.0 (37)	47.3 (79)
Generalist	39.2 (31)	55.7 (49)	47.9 (80)
Postscript: G. W. Bush			
Specialist	0 (0)		
Liaison	46.7 (7)		
Generalist	53.3 (8)		

Note: Percentages may not add to 100 because of rounding.

Liaison secretaries have strong relationships with their departments' traditionally dominant clients or issue networks. They are often
nominated as part of a presidential effort to recruit or reward those
interests or to court the legislative branch.[20] These political relationships may empower liaisons to act as comparatively independent power

brokers. Campaign indebtedness also spurs the selection of liaisons in the initial nominations: The nomination of a liaison secretary-designate provides a department client or issue network with representation. By extension, it demonstrates the president-elect's own responsiveness to those interests.

As reelection approaches, however, presidents favor secretaries-designate whose loyalties and dependence are less equivocal, and thus they nominate proportionately more generalists. The careers and relationships of these secretaries-designate are more closely tied to the president. Though they may have previously served in the national government, they have few alliances with their department's clients and issue networks. Although liaisons are likely to experience cross-cutting loyalties and may even function as an internalized loyal opposition, policy generalists are presidency-centered actors.[21]

These nomination patterns are also reflective of developments in legislative-executive relations that have occurred over the past decades. In the mid–twentieth century—represented in this study by the Franklin Roosevelt and Eisenhower administrations—cabinet secretaries had considerable discretion. Departments essentially operated as independent fiefdoms. In return for this freedom, secretaries met expectations that they would deliver votes on Capitol Hill and support from constituency groups to the president. Secretarial autonomy in this period, therefore, yielded more benefits than it incurred costs.[22]

By the 1970s, however, policymaking and decisionmaking processes had become more pluralistic. The number of interest groups had proliferated and lobbying had intensified. Departments were expected to report to more committees and subcommittees. The change shocked Health, Education, and Welfare (HEW) Secretary Joseph A. Califano, Jr., who compared his experiences in the Johnson White House with those he had as a member of the Carter cabinet.

> Power has been fragmented in Washington, not just within the executive branch, but by legislative mandate within individual departments, and not just between the executive and Congress, but within Congress itself. We have been and always will be a nation of special interest politics. But to a degree few Americans appreciate, these interests have been institutionalized in law and regulation, in both the congressional and executive bureaucracies. More than forty committees and subcommittees claimed jurisdiction over one or another part of HEW and each month demanded hundreds of hours of testimony and thousands of documents from top department appointees.[23]

Congressional and electoral votes became harder for the secretaries to deliver. Meanwhile, greater media coverage meant that disagreements between the president and the cabinet secretaries became more costly for the president. The secretaries, however, could potentially increase their political capital by publicizing confrontations with the chief executive. The benefits of independent cabinet secretaries having diminished and the costs having significantly risen, presidents moved toward centralizing their administrations and securing the loyalty of their nominees.[24] The executive branch became more politicized, and representation was correspondingly narrowed to reflect the political priorities of the president.

As an exception to the practice of appointing proportionately more liaisons initially and more generalists at midterm, the Ford administration was also unusual for its historical context. During this administration, the percentage of policy generalists decreased, and the percentage of liaisons increased across the presidential term. Centralization was not an acceptable organizational practice for the successor to the "Palace Guard" regime.[25] Also, as an unelected president who had to campaign for office soon after he entered the Oval Office, Ford needed to recruit voter support. These events, which were unique to this administration, explain the exceptional profile of this president's cabinet nominations. Even so, the Ford secretaries-designate resembled those of all the other administrations in that they provided contacts with the president's constituents and thus signaled the administration's policy priorities as cabinet representatives.

Similar considerations may explain why the initial and midterm cabinet nominations in the Clinton administration were roughly equal in their respective proportions of specialists, liaisons, and generalists. Throughout his two terms, Clinton encountered a variety of challenges—legislative confrontations, investigations, and impeachment hearings—that motivated him to select liaison secretaries-designate who could serve as his emissaries to established interests. Political representatives, after all, mediate between government officers and sociopolitical interests.

Thus, representation is a constant concern in the selection of cabinet secretaries-designate. And with few exceptions, that representation evolves in a predictable fashion across the presidential term, with more insiders and more generalists nominated as programmatic implementation and loyalty to the president become more pressing concerns. From the perspective of the White House, this change facilitates ideological congruence within the presidential administration (a crucial element of political leadership) and greater control of the departmental bureaucracies (a primary managerial concern). Departments, however, may find this practice very disruptive. Generalists lack both the professionalism of policy specialists and the political expertise of the liaisons. They may fail to meet the departments' needs. When successive generalists are nominated to one department, long-standing programmatic and political alliances may be compromised. Career civil servants may feel obliged to end-run their secretary more frequently. Alternatively, the nomination of generalists may generate contacts with new interests and actors, leading to new constellations of department clients and issue networks. Which of these possibilities is realized and why is assessed in regard to the women secretaries-designate in the following section.

Gender and Power in Cabinet Nominations

In the seven administrations with initial and midterm nominations, 47.4 percent of the women and 47.3 percent of the men are insiders, leaving 52.6 percent of the women and 52.7 percent of the men outsiders. Three of the ten initial women nominees are insiders (30.0 percent), and seven are outsiders (70.0 percent). Among the midterm women nominees, six of the nine are insiders (66.7 percent), and three are outsiders (33.3 percent). Women and men, therefore, are similar in this regard. The George W. Bush cabinet is likely to conform to these practices. Among the initial cabinet nominees, none of the women and 54.5 percent of the men are insiders, leaving room for a rise in the proportion of insiders as the presidential term progresses.[26]

Women and men secretaries-designate contrast, however, in their profiles as specialists, liaisons, and generalists. Although the men are liaisons and generalists in almost similar proportions (51.7 and 43.5 percent, respectively; see Table 2.3), the overwhelming majority of the women are policy generalists (84.2 percent). This pattern holds even though 52.6 percent of the women are initial nominees. Thus, the patterns observed among the men secretaries-designate are not observed among the women secretaries-designate. In fact, the two women liaison secretaries-designate nominated before the George W. Bush administration were nominated at midterm, contrary to the pattern prevailing among the men secretaries-designate.[27] Specialists are rare among both the women and the men, with only 5.3 percent (one nominee, Perkins) of the women and 4.8 percent (seven) of the men having these creden-

Table 2.3 Summary Profile of the Secretaries-Designate Through the Clinton Administration (percentages, with frequency counts in parentheses)

	Women	Men	Total
Nomination timing			
Initial	52.6 (10)	46.9 (69)	47.3 (79)
Midterm	47.4 (9)	53.1 (79)	52.7 (88)
Nomination status			
Inner cabinet	15.8 (3)	40.5 (60)	37.7 (63)
Outer cabinet	84.2 (16)	59.5 (88)	62.3 (104)
Nominee status			
Insider	47.4 (9)	47.3 (70)	47.3 (79)
Outsider	52.6 (10)	52.7 (78)	52.7 (88)
Nominee relation to the department policy area			
Specialist	5.3 (1)	4.8 (7)	4.8 (8)
Liaison	10.5 (2)	51.7 (77)	47.3 (79)
Generalist	84.2 (16)	43.5 (64)	47.9 (80)

Note: Percentages may not add up to 100 because of rounding.

tials. There were no specialists among the initial nominees to the George W. Bush cabinet (see Table 2.4).

The nominations of the women secretaries-designate therefore show *both* regendering and transgendering. Transgendering is evident, at least potentially, in the pattern common to both the women and the

Table 2.4 Summary Profile of the Secretaries-Designate; Postscript: George W. Bush Initial Cabinet Nominees (percentages, with frequency counts in parentheses)

	Women	Men	Total
Nomination timing			
Initial	26.7 (4)	73.3 (11)	100.0 (15)
Nomination status			
Inner cabinet	0.0 (0)	36.4 (4)	26.7 (4)
Outer cabinet	100.0 (4)	63.6 (7)	73.3 (11)
Nominee status			
Insider	0.0 (0)	45.5 (5)	33.3 (5)
Outsider	100.0 (4)	54.5 (6)	66.7 (10)
Nominee relation to the department policy area			
Specialist	0 (0)	0 (0)	0 (0)
Liaison	25.0 (1)	54.5 (5)	46.7 (7)
Generalist	75.0 (3)	45.5 (5)	53.3 (8)

Note: Percentages may not add up to 100 because of rounding.

men, namely, that of selecting greater proportions of outsiders as initial nominees and of insiders as midterm nominees. It seems that women's and men's credentials are being similarly acknowledged, with women officeholders being recognized as talented decisionmakers. To the extent that this is true, women secretaries-designate are providing women with a rich descriptive representation. Depending upon the credentials of the insider secretaries-designate, which will be examined in the next chapter, it may be an especially powerful message.

Yet regendering appears dominant. Women are being nominated to the cabinet, but they are disproportionately generalists and are correspondingly more dependent on the president for political advancement. Though women are present in the cabinet, this practice suggests that they hold consistently subordinate positions. Only one specialist and three liaisons are numbered among all the women secretaries-designate, which is to say that very few women have had the political resources to act as independent power brokers. Here is strong evidence that the women secretaries-designate can offer only weak descriptive representation and that they are in fact more showcased for their sex than respected for their abilities.

This preliminary finding is in keeping with the masculinist precepts of the presidency. This ideology holds that men provide and protect and that leaders distinguish themselves by their selfless concern for the polity. Dependence in any form is therefore problematic because the president is expected to act as a powerful and autonomous leader. Dependence on a woman is even more threatening to masculinist standards of strength and individuality. Reinforcing masculinism is the norm of *homosociability*. In U.S. society, people tend to be most comfortable with those who most closely resemble themselves. The effects of this psychological trait have been repeatedly demonstrated in private and public bureaucracies, and they are no less evident in the presidency. As G. Calvin Mackenzie, a scholar of presidential appointments, has concluded, "White male Presidents have created personnel staffs composed primarily of other white males who have done the bulk of their recruiting through predominantly white male contacts in the government and in the private sector. That they should come up with a majority of candidates in their own image is probably only natural."[28] To grant women officeholders influence in keeping with their credentials, thereby providing all women with a meaningful form of descriptive representation, overturns accepted political and social practices to such a degree that it might be considered revolutionary. The nominations of women generalists minimize these sorts of challenges. These women are relatively dependent on the president for their success and advancement. Lacking both alliances with established department clients interests and substantive policy expertise, these women secretaries-designate cannot challenge or modify presidential initiatives. Their likely influence within the administration and their strength as representatives are correspondingly minimized.

And yet, there is some evidence of transgendering in the midst of regendering. There are the women Washington insiders who have been midterm secretaries-designate. There are also the three women liaison secretaries-designate, one in the George H. W. Bush administration, a second in the Clinton administration, and a third in the George W. Bush administration. Bush commerce secretary-designate Barbara Franklin was nominated so late in the term that she had already distinguished herself as a fundraiser in the president's reelection campaign. Her contributions as a representative were correspondingly limited. Clinton secretary-designate of state Madeleine Albright, however, was nominated at the beginning of the president's second term in office. At the time, the administration had lost its standing with the various foreign policy communities, and Albright was nominated to correct this situation. Bush interior secretary-designate Gale Norton was an initial nominee, named to a department that was associated with several well-remembered campaign promises. Thus, in recent administrations, women liaisons have been nominated progressively earlier in the term and have been granted correspondingly greater opportunities to participate as leaders in their departments and administrations. Accordingly, they have offered women more meaningful descriptive representation and have seemed to stand for greater inclusivity as symbolic representatives.

Three interrelated questions emerge from this preliminary survey of the presidents' nomination patterns and the nominees' political profiles. First, given that the vast majority of women secretaries-designate have been generalists, there is a need to delineate the circumstances of women's nominations. The selection of a generalist rather than a liaison signifies that the president is—to some extent—dismissing a historically influential constituency of the executive branch. To do so while nominating a woman may send a particularly strong message of rejection. Not only are established interests being set aside, but "their" department will now be led by an individual who—given both her generalist status and the workings of masculinism—is likely to be marginalized within the cabinet. That much has been publicly acknowledged and strongly protested by clients of the labor, housing and urban development, and energy departments in several different administrations. Why would a president so dramatically alter the representation being provided by a cabinet office?

Second, the representation expected from each of the women secretaries-designate needs to be more carefully delineated. To the extent that the women have been showcased for their sex rather than recruited for their political skills and resources, they have not offered descriptive representation to women. To the extent that they have been marginalized as generalists, their substantive and symbolic representations have been similarly compromised. Presidential decisionmaking, an important mechanism in formal representation, would then be upholding masculinism. What caliber of representation has been promised by the women secretaries-designate? What has it meant for the regendering and transgendering of the cabinet?

Third, it is important to look for trends across the nominations and administrations. Always remembering that political developments are rarely linear or progressive, there is a need to assess how the cabinet is being changed by the nomination of women as secretaries-designate. To what extent is the cabinet undergoing gender desegregation or gender integration? Is there evidence of movement from one to the other? To the extent that the cabinet is undergoing gender desegregation, it exposes the endurance of masculinism. To the extent that the cabinet is undergoing gender integration, it indicates when and why a formerly excluded people may be viewed as capable of exercising power and authority. From patterns in representation, then, one discerns patterns in power and in political development, with implications for individuals and for the wider society.

NOMINATING THE WOMEN SECRETARIES-DESIGNATE

To better understand the representation provided by the women secretaries-designate and its implications for regendering or transgendering and for gender desegregation or integration within the cabinet, the nominations are first studied as a group. The political resources of the nominees, the politics and networks of the departments, and the relevance of the departments to the presidents' agendas are each examined. Because summary measures can oversimplify and even neglect developments, however, the factors influencing presidential decisionmaking in each nomination are considered. Together, these discussions reveal the changes effected by the selection of women secretaries-designate.

Gender and Representation

Although the preceding analysis considered the relevance of the nominees' precabinet political alliances to their anticipated representation, it did not put those data in the context of the departments and administrations in which the nominees were nominated. The policy jurisdiction and networks of each department and its history and status within the cabinet powerfully condition the secretary's role. The distinctive concerns and priorities of each president also have an effect. These pressures for stability and for change, as manifested in the nominations of the women secretaries-designate, are recorded in Table 2.5.

Looking across the table, what may be most striking are the commonalities among the women secretaries-designate. Across administrations, partisanship and political changes in the presidency notwithstanding, the women secretaries-designate are far more similar than different in their profiles. As much has already been suggested in the preceding analysis, which noted that although women are Washington insiders and outsiders in almost equal proportions—57.9 and 42.1 percent, respectively—there is an extraordinary preponderance of generalists (84.2 percent; see Table 2.3), and an associated scarcity of liaisons (10.5 percent) and specialists (5.3 percent). Here was a preliminary indication of the strength of masculinism, in that women secretaries-designate were nominated to departments in which they had little policy expertise and few prior political relationships. They were thus more dependent on the president. The descriptive representation and symbolic representation that they promised to women was correspondingly circumscribed, as their opportunities for full participation as decisionmakers and presidential constituents were likely to remain elusive.

The departmental context of the women's nominations did little to alter this assessment. Women have routinely been named to young departments in the outer cabinet. Women were the first secretaries of the Health, Education, and Welfare and the Education Departments. Arguably, nomination to younger (or new) departments may provide the women secretaries-designate with more opportunities to respond to women as presidential constituents because the departmental structures and processes are still mutable. However, these circumstances also

Table 2.5 The Women Secretaries-Designate and Their Departments and Nominations

Name	Secretarial Profile	Department	Year Dept. Founded	Inner or Outer Cabinet Department	Link to President's Agenda	Department's Traditional Gender Profile
Frances Perkins	Specialist Outsider	Labor	1913	Outer	Distant	Constituency male; Policy jurisdiction masculine
Oveta Culp Hobby	Generalist Outsider	HEW	1952	Outer	Distant	Constituency male and female; Policy jurisdiction feminine
Carla Anderson Hills	Generalist Insider	HUD	1965	Outer	Distant	Constituency male; Policy jurisdiction masculine
Juanita Kreps	Generalist Outsider	Commerce	1913	Outer	Distant	Constituency male; Policy jurisdiction masculine
Patricia Roberts Harris	Generalist Outsider	HUD	1965	Outer	Distant	Constituency male; Policy jurisdiction masculine Second woman HUD secretary
	Generalist Insider	HEW/HHS	1952/1979	Outer	Somewhat related	Constituency male and female; Policy jurisdiction feminine Second woman HEW/HHS secretary
Shirley M. Hufstedler	Generalist Outsider	Education	1979	Outer	Somewhat related	Constituency male and female; Policy jurisdiction feminine
Elizabeth Hanford Dole	Generalist Insider	Transportation	1966	Outer	Distant	Constituency male; Policy jurisdiction masculine
	Generalist Insider	Labor	1913	Outer	Distant	Constituency male; Policy jurisdiction masculine Second woman labor secretary

continues

Table 2.5 Continued

Name	Secretarial Profile	Department	Year Dept. Founded	Inner or Outer Cabinet Department	Link to President's Agenda	Department's Traditional Gender Profile
Margaret M. Heckler	Generalist Insider	HHS	1952/1979	Outer	Distant	Constituency male and female; Policy jurisdiction feminine Third woman HEW/HHS secretary
Ann Dore McLaughlin	Generalist Insider	Labor	1913	Outer	Distant	Constituency male; Policy jurisdiction masculine Third woman labor secretary
Lynn Martin	Generalist Insider	Labor	1913	Outer	Distant	Constituency male; Policy jurisdiction masculine Fourth woman labor secretary
Barbara Hackman Franklin	Liaison Outsider	Commerce	1913	Outer	Somewhat related	Constituency male; Policy jurisdiction masculine Second woman commerce secretary
Donna E. Shalala	Generalist Outsider	HHS	1952/1979	Outer	Related	Constituency male and female; Policy jurisdiction feminine Fourth woman HEW/HHS secretary
Hazel Rollins O'Leary	Generalist Outsider	Energy	1977	Outer	Distant	Constituency male; Policy jurisdiction masculine
Zoë E. Baird	Generalist Outsider	Justice	1789/1870	Inner	Related	Constituency male; Policy jurisdiction masculine
Janet Reno	Generalist Outsider	Justice	1789/1870	Inner	Related	Constituency male; Policy jurisdiction masculine

continues

Table 2.5 Continued

Name	Secretarial Profile	Department	Year Dept. Founded	Inner or Outer Cabinet Department	Link to President's Agenda	Department's Traditional Gender Profile
Madeleine Korbel Albright	Liaison Insider	State	1789	Inner	Related	Constituency male; Policy jurisdiction masculine
Alexis Herman	Generalist Insider	Labor	1913	Outer	Somewhat related	Constituency male; Policy jurisdiction masculine Fifth woman labor secretary
Ann M. Veneman	Generalist Outsider	Agriculture	1862	Outer	Distant	Constituency male; Policy jurisdiction masculine
Gale A. Norton	Liaison Outsider	Interior	1849	Outer	Related	Constituency male; Policy jurisdiction masculine
Linda Chavez	Generalist Outsider	Labor	1913	Outer	Distant	Constituency male; Policy jurisdiction masculine Sixth woman labor secretary-designate
Elaine Lan Chao	Generalist Outsider	Labor	1913	Outer	Distant	Constituency male; Policy jurisdiction masculine Sixth woman labor secretary

lower the departments' status within the cabinet, especially since their political contributions have yet to be proven. The dominant effect of nominating women to younger departments in the outer cabinet, then, is to constrain the women's prospective participation in decisionmaking, thereby also limiting their descriptive representation.

At the same time, the women confronted significant gender challenges from their departments' constituents and policy jurisdictions. Tradition having reserved the public sphere to men, one could argue that political actors and actions are masculine by definition. Such a perspective, however, neglects the ways in which women have historically been present in the public sphere and also the ways in which the public and private spheres have overlapped. The Departments of Health, Education and Welfare/Health and Human Services (HHS) and Education have always been identified with feminine gender roles. Women have been named as secretaries-designate to both of these departments, serving in HEW and HHS on a relatively frequent basis. (There have been four women secretaries in this department.) In other departments, however, women have been "gender outsiders" in relation to both the policy jurisdictions and constituencies. Organized labor, the traditional client of the Labor Department, has only gradually included a significant number of women among its members. The same could be said of professions related to engineering and national infrastructure, which were the constituents of the Transportation, Housing and Urban Development, Energy, Agriculture, and Interior Departments. The nomination of women secretaries-designate to these departments could have the effect of shifting established agendas and relationships, if the women secretaries-designate entered office with the requisite political resources and the president's endorsement. Instead, women generalists were named to these departments, their lack of expertise and prior relationships limiting their opportunities to effect change.

In the majority of nominations (14; 60.9 percent), women were also named to departments distant from the president's policy agenda. Four women (17.4 percent) were nominated to departments "somewhat related" to the president's agenda and five others (21.7 percent) to departments that were "related." Those that were only "somewhat related" provide little indication of greater opportunities for women as officeholders or constituents. Two women were named to departments that the sitting president had promised to reorganize or create; these were President Carter's nominations of Patricia Roberts Harris as secretary-designate of health, education, and welfare, and of Shirley M.

Hufstedler as secretary-designate of education. These women found themselves focusing more on managerial issues than on policies and programs. The two other women were nominated to departments whose clients had traditionally supported the party of the sitting president, so the secretaries-designate were expected to perform as caretakers rather than innovators. These nominees were George H. W. Bush commerce secretary-designate Barbara H. Franklin and Clinton labor secretary-designate Alexis M. Herman. Though their departments played a role in administration initiatives, these four secretaries-designate entered office with little expectation of exercising significant influence.

The five instances in which women were nominated to departments "related" to the president's agenda are far more encouraging in terms of women's participation in policymaking. Clinton secretaries-designate Donna E. Shalala (HHS), Zoë E. Baird (Justice), Janet Reno (Justice), and Madeleine Korbel Albright (State), as well as George W. Bush secretary-designate Gale A. Norton (Interior), were each nominated to lead departments essential to the presidency or to their administrations.[29] Still, these nominations are limited to the most recent administrations, so it is not yet certain that these opportunities will continue to be provided to women cabinet nominees. If not, the enhanced descriptive and symbolic representation offered by these women will be delimited to their tenure in office.

Across the nominations and administrations, then, there is far more evidence of regendering than transgendering. Descriptive representation is limited in the vast majority of instances, as women secretaries-designate are routinely generalists in young departments in the outer cabinet, with policy jurisdictions distant from the president's agenda. This fact suggests that women are valued more for their ability to showcase the presence of women in an otherwise predominantly male administration than for their contributions as leaders or executive managers. As symbolic representatives, the women secretaries-designate therefore convey a message of exclusivity, not inclusivity. In sum, the mechanisms of formal representation reinforce the precepts of masculinism. The extent and strength of this regendering suggests that the cabinet is undergoing gender desegregation.

Still, women secretaries-designate have been liaisons, they have been nominated to the inner cabinet, and they have led departments important to the president's policy agenda. These nominations suggest that the representation promised by the women secretaries-designate may be changing. Their descriptive representation may begin to have content, as women are recognized as capable decisionmakers; their symbolic representation may denote a correspondingly greater measure of inclusivity; and their formal representation may begin to mitigate and even erode masculinism. And yet these nominations and nominees are present only in recent administrations. Transgendering, therefore, appears to be a comparatively new phenomenon, and the push toward gender integration is still in its earliest stages.

If presidential nominations of women to the cabinet have been more about regendering than transgendering, why have presidents included women among their secretaries-designate? This question leads to others about the ways in which appearance and substance intersect in cabinet nominations and how cabinet representation has been interpreted by the media and endorsed by the Senate. Before those concerns can be addressed, however, the first query must be answered: Why have presidents nominated their women secretaries-designate?

Gender Politics and Presidential Selection of Women Secretaries-Designate

Though political developments are neither progressive nor linear, studying the women's cabinet nominations in chronological order provides insight into the factors that have influenced the presidents' selection of women secretaries-designate. Such an approach further aids in discerning regendering and transgendering in the cabinet.

Franklin D. Roosevelt and Frances Perkins. The nomination of Frances Perkins as labor secretary-designate reflected the president-elect's willingness to acknowledge his campaign debts and his desire to avoid political entanglements with organized labor. Electorally, the Women's Division of the Roosevelt campaign had been extremely active, and their speakers and publications had been perceived as contributing to FDR's victory. Its leader, Mary "Molly" Dewson, was well-known to Roosevelt and was absolutely committed to securing presidential appointments for those women who would advocate on behalf of progressive initiatives. In addition to speaking with Roosevelt personally, Dewson generated "an endless chain of letters" from renowned social reformers in support of a cabinet nomination for Perkins.[30]

Even as Dewson was lobbying for Perkins, the president-elect was making his other initial cabinet nominations. These suggested that he had three priorities. First, he selected initial secretaries-designate whom he knew well. Many were close friends who had participated in the campaign, so their loyalty had been tested and proven.[31] Second, he balanced the cabinet in regional and partisan terms. Roosevelt's ties to the Northeast were evident, but secretaries-designate were also drawn from the South and from the West. Moderate and progressive Republicans, as well as the full ideological spectrum of the Democratic Party, were all represented.[32] Third, although Roosevelt acknowledged the influence of special interests, none of his secretaries-designate had been closely affiliated with a departmental client or issue network organization.[33] Prospective Labor Secretary-Designate Frances Perkins satisfied each of these criteria, providing a form of representation that was congruent with the president-elect's standards for his initial cabinet.

Perkins had been well acquainted with Roosevelt since his 1928 campaign for the governor's office.[34] At that time, she had campaigned with Roosevelt, introducing him to labor leaders throughout upstate New York. Subsequently, as a member of Roosevelt's gubernatorial cabinet, Perkins was generally recognized as his primary resource on social welfare issues. Her politics were liberal. Until 1912, Perkins was a member of the Socialist Party. Later, she described herself as an independent. Her policy ties were to social workers and reformers, including the future first lady. Perkins had won the support of New York's unions while leading the state's labor department. However, she was not associated with any one of them.[35] Roosevelt therefore first disappointed all the unions by nominating Perkins and then appeased them with subcabinet posts.[36] In so doing, he maintained his independence from individual labor leaders while sustaining contact with the wider issue network.

With decades of experience in labor policy, Frances Perkins is the sole specialist among the women secretaries-designate. Given her strong ties to Progressive Era reform networks populated largely by women, she could be expected to advance women's interests. Her record as a lobbyist and state administrator indicated that she would not hesitate to wield her expertise, and her prior relationship with the president-elect suggested that she would be able to effect significant policy innovations. Though the enmity of organized labor meant that she would encounter formidable opposition in office, she had previously worked constructively with unions and union leaders. In this instance, a woman secretary-designate was selected to protect a president-elect from established clients of the executive branch but also to provide a president with good contacts to a prospective presidential constituency.

Women, meanwhile, were to be represented by a cabinet member who could provide substantive representation for their concerns, descriptive representation for their abilities, and symbolic representation of their attentiveness to politics. Frances Perkins's selection as labor secretary-designate, therefore, satisfied the needs of the nominating president and began to transgender the cabinet office.

Dwight D. Eisenhower and Oveta Culp Hobby. There are significant similarities between Roosevelt's nomination of Frances Perkins and Eisenhower's nomination of Oveta Culp Hobby. In both instances, the presidents-elect knew the women secretaries-designate, though Hobby's contacts were less extensive. Also in both instances, the women met the president-elect's informal requirements for cabinet service even more fully than several of their male colleagues. Hobby's involvement in the 1952 campaign, for example, surpassed that of almost all the other initial secretaries-designate, with the exceptions of Attorney General-Designate Herbert Brownell (campaign manager), Commerce Secretary-Designate Sinclair Weeks (an early Eisenhower supporter and chair of the National Republican Finance Committee), and Postmaster General-Designate Arthur E. Summerfield (Republican National Committee chair).[37] As the editor of the *Houston Post,* Hobby could claim managerial experience in the private sector. She also had prior government experience, having led the Women's Auxiliary Army Corps during World War II. Finally, her nomination offered representation to three constituencies—the South, conservative Democrats, and women.[38] In the Roosevelt and in the Eisenhower administrations, then, the woman secretary-designate had the credentials to prove her loyalty to the president, her political skills, and her managerial competence. Here was the promise of descriptive representation, not mere showcasing.

Like Roosevelt, however, Eisenhower seems to have been cautious in his cabinet selection. In both administrations, the women were nominated to lead the youngest department in the outer cabinet.[39] Also in both instances, there were indications that the nominating president did not expect the department that was led by a woman to be central to his policy agenda. Perkins pushed her way onto a series of task forces, wielding her credentials as a social reformer and as a labor representative. As a generalist, Hobby was dependent on the president for her career opportunities and advancement.

When we turn from the similarities between Perkins and Hobby to their differences, therefore, it seems that women lost some ground with this second cabinet posting. With decades of experience in labor policy, Perkins was a specialist who could draw on policy networks for support. As a generalist, Hobby was more dependent on the president. The representation—substantive, descriptive, and symbolic—provided to women was correspondingly constrained in the Eisenhower administration. Unquestionably, Hobby provided women with some descriptive representation, which they had lacked throughout the Truman administration. As a symbolic representative, however, she testified more to the marginalization of women in governmental decisionmaking. Thus, while the Perkins nomination had a transgendering effect, the Hobby nomination tipped toward regendering. A woman was nominated to the cabinet, but her participation and her influence were delimited, and the cabinet underwent only a mild gender desegregation.

Gerald R. Ford and Carla Anderson Hills. Carla Anderson Hills, named housing and urban development secretary-designate on 13 February 1975, was Ford's second cabinet nomination. She was the first woman cabinet member in three administrations. Then an assistant attorney general in the Civil Division of the Justice Department, Hills had no experience with housing or urban policy. She was most definitely a policy generalist, and she knew that it left her politically vulnerable.

> I told the President, "I believe you will have some political flack in not nominating someone with a background in the area concerned." He said he didn't believe so. Anyway, he said that if he appointed a Governor the Mayors would object; if he appointed a Mayor then the Loan Companies would object; if he appointed a consumer group person, then business would object; if he appointed a builder then the budgeteers would object. What he needed was an administrator and I had a reputation as such.[40]

Once again, a woman secretary-designate was selected to serve as a buffer against influential departmental constituencies, though Hills lacked Perkins's precabinet record of constructive relationships with those interests at the state level. Hills was primarily expected to be the president's representative.

Hills had already been under consideration for a cabinet post, appearing on a list titled, "Other Special Women to Be Considered." She was then described in the following terms: "First-rate lawyer, attractive, relatively young, gets high marks on performance at Justice so far. Represents moderate to liberal (Finch wing) of Republican Party in California. She could fill an even higher post at Justice."[41] Hills's sex would—and clearly already had—drawn attention. However, the memo indicates that she was also valued for her Republican Party connections in a state with a large number of electoral votes.[42]

The political circumstances and characteristics of Hills's nomination are therefore remarkably similar to those of her predecessors. The women's movement had gained considerable momentum, and women had become more politically involved since the Perkins and Hobby nominations. However, women secretaries-designate continued to protect the president from powerful departmental clients while remaining dependent on the chief executive. They also continued to serve in young departments in the outer cabinet, with jurisdictions distant from their administration's principal policy concerns. The transgendering suggested by Perkins's nomination was clearly muted in the Hobby and Hills nominations. Though both provided a measure of descriptive representation to women, doing far more than merely showcasing the president's ostensible receptivity to women, their symbolic representation was suggestive of limited presidential inclusivity. Evidence from the presidential selection processes suggests that women were nominated to the cabinet because (1) there were women available who were exceptionally qualified to be named as secretaries-designate, and (2) there were open cabinet posts that would curb their influence. Masculinism endured. The cabinet resumed the gender desegregation that had been suspended when Hobby left the cabinet in 1955.

Jimmy Carter and Juanita Kreps, Patricia Roberts Harris, and Shirley M. Hufstedler. The Carter administration effected a number of advances in women's nominations to the cabinet. First, with one brief lapse, there were always two women in the cabinet. The increase was small but significant, as was the fact that women had now served in the cabinet throughout two successive presidential administrations. Republican and Democratic administrations were both granting women some recognition as presidential constituents. Second, the Carter administration named the first woman of color to the cabinet: Patricia Roberts Harris was nominated to lead the Department of Housing and Urban Development (1977) and the Department of Health, Education, and Welfare/Health and Human Services (1979). Given that Harris was transferred to HEW at a time when political leadership and managerial acumen were being critically assessed and highly valued by the presidential administration, she provided women of color with rich descriptive representation.[43] Third, Juanita Kreps was named the first woman commerce secretary-designate, nominated to work in a policy area—finance and business—traditionally associated with men. She therefore pushed the gender boundaries of departmental leadership in the cabinet. Fourth, this administration named women as midterm secretaries-designate. Midterm nominees have typically attracted less attention than do the initial secretaries-designate, so there was less political capital to be gained from showcasing a "diversity" secretary-designate. Descriptive representation, accordingly, could be stronger and symbolic representation more oriented toward women's full participation in the cabinet.

Other developments in the selection of the women secretaries-designate were somewhat qualified. All the Carter women nominees served in the outer cabinet. Patricia Roberts Harris and Shirley M. Hufstedler were nominated to lead departments that had previously had a woman secretary (Housing and Urban Development and HEW) or had jurisdictions associated with women's private sphere responsibilities (HEW/HHS and Education). Further, all the Carter women secretaries-designate were generalists. Still, there were mitigating standards associated with this practice. Harris provided descriptive representation to African Americans, which made her somewhat less dependent on the president. Hufstedler's generalist standing actually enhanced her political credibility, since she was nominated to lead a department (Education) criticized for close ties with special interest lobbies.[44] Of the three, only Kreps (later) stated that her generalist standing limited her effectiveness as a cabinet officer.[45]

Presidential selection politics during the Carter administration suggest that the symbolic representation promised by the women secretaries-designate was a little stronger—the inclusivity was a little less cautious, a little less restricted. Women nominees were still generalists in the outer cabinet, in departments distanced from the president's agenda. Regendering was therefore still predominant. But there were also hints of change. As women were being recognized as officeholders and constituents, cabinet nominations were (again) being transgendered. The possibility of gender integration in the cabinet was, however, rejected by the Reagan administration.

Ronald Reagan and Elizabeth H. Dole, Margaret M. Heckler, and Ann Dore McLaughlin. There were no women among Reagan's initial secretaries-designate.[46] For the most part, however, the president-elect was able to avoid comment or criticism because he had never made a campaign promise to nominate women.[47] Women, at least at the outset of this administration, were no longer recognized as a distinctive constituency of the president and lost their representation in the cabinet. When women were nominated as secretaries-designate at midterm, it was because the widening gender gap suggested that women voters could deny the president reelection.[48] Though previous nominations had been awarded in acknowledgment of women's past electoral support of the president, these selections marked the first time that a woman's cabinet nomination was made in acknowledgement of an electoral threat. The effect of this change on cabinet representation, though, was not entirely positive.

Reagan's cabinet nominees were renowned for their long-standing loyalty to the president and their conformity with his conservative ideology, with the notable exception of the women secretaries-designate.[49] During the transition, Elizabeth Hanford Dole was rejected as a prospective commerce secretary-designate because she received a negative recommendation from former President Richard M. Nixon.[50] The fact that she had been a Democrat before her marriage to Senator Robert Dole (R-Kans.) was doubtless also a factor. As a member of the House of Representatives, Margaret Heckler opposed 56 percent of the administration's proposals. She attracted considerable attention by wearing an Equal Rights Amendment (ERA) button even after President Reagan refused to support the amendment. Heckler said that the initials stood for "Endorsing Reagan Anyway."[51] Nominated, respectively, as transportation secretary-designate and HHS secretary-designate, Dole and Heckler were generalists whose precabinet political records left them exceptionally vulnerable.[52] Their descriptive representation was correspondingly minimal, and their nominations showcased women rather than proved their credibility as political executives. Similarly, their symbolic representation was about the appearance, not the practice, of participation. The strength of this regendering and the extent to which the women secretaries-designate were marginalized meant that formal representation strengthened masculinism during this administration.

The nomination of Ann Dore McLaughlin as labor secretary-designate did not alter this outcome. Nominated late in the second term, she was primarily expected to campaign for the Republican Party.[53] In the words of one White House aide, "[White House Chief of Staff Howard Baker] wants a woman in the Cabinet to assist in the campaign next year. . . . Ann's paid her dues and the consensus is that she's competent. Her husband is well-connected with right-wing political groups. . . . The job of labor secretary isn't as important as it used to be."[54] Like the earlier Reagan women secretaries-designate, then, McLaughlin was an image maker rather than a representative.

To the extent that there was any gender change in the cabinet during the Reagan administration, it was most definitely regendering. No women were among the initial nominees. Though women were selected as midterm secretaries-designate, they provided little descriptive or symbolic representation. Showcasing and image making, not responsiveness to women as officeholders or as constituents, distinguished this administration's cabinet nominations.[55] The gender integration of the cabinet halted, and even its gender desegregation was qualified.

George H. W. Bush and Elizabeth H. Dole, Lynn Martin, and Barbara H. Franklin. As in previous administrations (with the exception of the Reagan administration), the women and men secretaries-designate nominated by George H. W. Bush were more similar than different. The Bush cabinet nominees were drawn from the same candidate pools, namely, the White House staffs of previous Republican administrations, the Congress, and the campaign organization. They had proven their collegiality and had significant political accomplishments. They had also demonstrated their loyalty to the chief executive. Women secretaries-designate were still distant from the inner circle, but they seemed to take a small step away from the margins.[56]

One advance was evident in the political affiliations of the women secretaries-designate. Although Labor Secretaries-Designate Elizabeth Hanford Dole and Lynn Martin were generalists,[57] Commerce Secretary-Designate Barbara H. Franklin was a liaison nominee. The first liaison among the women secretaries-designate, she had long-standing associations with the business issue networks and clients of the Commerce Department.[58] Appointed at the close of the Bush administration, Franklin could provide only limited representation to women. Still, her nomination suggested the possibility that the generalist standard for women secretaries-designate might be weakened. With that change came the possibility of stronger descriptive representation, as women officeholders gained more opportunity to capitalize on their precabinet political affiliations. There might also be further opportunities for substantive representation if the women secretaries-designate used their political resources to respond to women as presidential constituents. The greater autonomy and influence of the liaison secretaries, meanwhile, would move the women's symbolic representation from image making toward full participation.

There was more regendering than transgendering in George H. W. Bush's cabinet nominations of women, but there was some transgendering. As evidence of regendering, the women secretaries-designate were tightly grouped in the Labor and Commerce Departments, two departments that were originally founded as one. Both departments had previously had women secretaries, so no new precedents were set or challenges issued with these nominations. This administration also set aside a department as the "woman's seat" on the cabinet. Not incidentally, that department—the Labor Department—was in the outer cabinet, and its constituents were unlikely to provide the president with electoral support. Thus, the women secretaries-designate found themselves routinely serving as buffers against critical or even hostile interests. And yet, Franklin's liaison profile suggested transgendering to the extent that it indicated a modicum of presidential dependence on a prospective woman secretary's expertise. The Bush administration provided somewhat more representation for women in the cabinet than had the Reagan administration. However, the achievements of the Carter administration—particularly the nomination of a women secretary-designate of color—had yet to be equaled.

Bill Clinton and Donna E. Shalala, Hazel R. O'Leary, Zoë E. Baird, Janet Reno, Madeleine Korbel Albright, and Alexis M. Herman. The 1992 Clinton campaign repeatedly promised "an administration that looks like America," a pledge that was sometimes softened to "an administration that looks more like America."[59] Media scrutiny of the nominees was correspondingly great, as was the activism of the Coalition for Women's Appointments, both of which pushed Clinton to build on the advances of the Carter and the Bush administrations, at least in his cabinet nominations. Like Carter, Clinton recognized the electoral power of women and people of color and nominated members of those cohorts—including two women of color—to the cabinet. Also like Carter, Clinton nominated women to a wide range of departments, including those associated with traditionally masculine areas of expertise. The most notable of these transgendering nominations were to secretarial offices in the Departments of Energy (with disarmament and scientific responsibilities), Justice (the nation's lawyer, with the responsibility to review the actions of the president), and State (an important figure in foreign policy decisions). None of these positions had ever before been held by a woman. Further, the nominations to Justice and State put women in the inner cabinet, closer to the inner circle of presidential decisionmaking.

Like George H. W. Bush, Clinton nominated a liaison woman secretary-designate. Clinton, however, went further than Bush. Whereas Barbara Franklin was nominated in the last year of the Bush administration, Secretary-Designate of State Madeleine Albright was named at the outset of Clinton's second term. The administration's foreign policy was then in disarray, desperately in need of a charismatic, credible, and effective advocate. Albright was therefore mandated to make significant contributions to the president's policy agenda. The norms of homosociability and masculine autonomy were broken, as the president's dependence on a woman cabinet officer was widely recognized. Attorney General Janet Reno exerted influence throughout the eight years of Clinton's presidency, but it was Albright who combined the power of an inner cabinet secretary with the authority of a well-respected liaison. Her descriptive and symbolic representation affirmed that women were the president's constituents.

Even as transgendering predominated in the Clinton cabinet nominations, regendering continued. Women were again named to lead the Labor and the HHS Departments, which became the departments with the greatest number of women secretaries-designate. Still, the limitations imposed through regendering were less stringent. Since this Democratic administration was dependent on constructive relations with labor unions and committed to health and welfare reform, these posts did provide women with an opportunity to contribute to presidential decisionmaking. Here again was descriptive and symbolic representation that valued women's public sphere contributions. The strength of masculinism in formal representation was weakened. And, as the nominations gave more evidence of transgendering than regendering, the cabinet began to undergo a gendered integration.

Postscript: George W. Bush and Ann M. Veneman, Gale A. Norton, Linda Chavez, and Elaine Lan Chao. George W. Bush's initial secretaries-designate were remarkably similar, suggesting that the president-elect applied consistent criteria in making these nominations. Five secretaries-designate (33.3 percent) had played significant roles in the presidential campaign. Nine secretaries-designate (60.0 percent) had previous executive branch experience, four of them in cabinet or cabinet-rank positions. Such experience tends to predominate among midterm rather than initial appointees; these proportions suggested that this administration had an early appreciation for the cabinet's role in managing and directing the executive bureaucracy. Four secretaries-designate (26.7 percent) were current or former members of Congress. Seven secretaries-designate (46.7 percent) had held positions in state or local government. Overall, four secretaries-designate (26.7 percent) had held positions in more than one level of government, suggesting that the future cabinet would be able to draw on significant political resources.[60]

Further evidence in support of this conclusion is seen in the profile of the generalist secretaries-designate. Eight nominees (53.3 percent) were classified as such, but few were unacquainted with the policies or the networks of their department.[61] Agriculture Secretary-Designate Ann Veneman, for example, lacked connections with midwestern grain and commodities interests. However, she had served previously in her department as a deputy secretary and had been California's food and agriculture secretary. In this and other instances, the nomination of a generalist signaled a shift in emphasis, but not one so dramatic as to make the nominee heavily dependent on the president.

Campaign debts and reelection hopes were intertwined in a number of Bush's initial nominations. Republican conservatives gained representation in the Justice, Interior, and Labor posts. Some voting groups were rewarded, and others were courted. Two African Americans, two Hispanic Americans (one withdrawn), and two Asian Americans were named as secretaries-designate. Four women were nominated, two of them women of color—though one was a replacement for the other, whose nomination was withdrawn. Ultimately, Bush initially named seven white males and eight "diversity" secretaries-designate, a ratio comparable to Clinton's record of six white males and nine "diversity" initial secretaries-designate.

The nominations of the women secretaries-designate, specifically, evidenced both regendering and transgendering. Once again, a Republican administration nominated women generalists as labor secretaries-designate, this time selecting women of color to resume the pattern of marginalization seen throughout the Reagan and George H. W. Bush administrations. And yet, women were also nominated to lead two other departments—Agriculture and Interior—that had previously had only male secretaries-designate. Both of these women had ties to the president-elect or to his political networks. Agriculture Secretary-Designate Veneman was a generalist, but, as noted above, she had considerable expertise in her department's issue area. Interior Secretary-Designate Gale A. Norton was a liaison and would be responsible for fulfilling a number of the president-elect's campaign promises. Here was a more affirmative promise of recognition for women as presidential constituents. Consequently, although initial cabinet nominations in the Bush administration slowed gender integration in the cabinet, they did not necessarily signal a return to gender desegregation.

*   *   *

Why, then, did presidents nominate women to the cabinet? Presidents included women among their cabinet nominees largely in response to electoral pressures. In the Roosevelt, Eisenhower, Carter, and Clinton administrations, women voters contributed significantly to the president's margin of victory. In the Republican administrations, there was a concern to court women voters to secure reelection. This motivation was particularly pronounced in the Reagan administration, in which women were nominated to the cabinet only after the president's reelection was threatened by a widening gender gap. Quite simply, then, presidents acknowledged women as their constituents and provided them with a measure of representation because doing so served their needs as elected officeholders.

As for selecting the actual women secretaries-designate, presidents chose women who met (and often exceeded) the standards guiding their cabinet nominations. The women nominees possessed credentials and could lay claim to political resources that equaled and often exceeded those of the men with whom they were nominated. In the vast majority of women's nominations, however, chief executives capitalized on just one set of qualifications, namely, the women's proven loyalty to their president. The typical woman secretary-designate was a generalist, "nominated away" from the departments in which she would have been a specialist or liaison. In the process, women cabinet members also found that their descriptive representation was compromised and that their symbolic representation was about exclusivity. Formal representation continued to support the precepts of masculinism. Regendering was predominant, and the cabinet experienced only a gradual gender desegregation.

Still, the decisionmaking associated with the nomination of women to the cabinet did evidence transgendering. Across the administrations, women were nominated to a more diverse set of departments, including those whose constituents were predominantly male.[62] Though descriptive representation was not consistently strengthened—nominations of women as secretaries-designate in the Reagan administration, for example, merely showcased elite individuals—some improvements were made in the Clinton and George W. Bush administrations. In more recent administrations, presidents nominated women as liaison secretaries-designate; they also nominated women to lead departments that would play influential roles in their administrations. In signaling their willingness to rely on a woman's political expertise and judgment, these presidents provided women with the opportunity to act as more autonomous and creative decisionmakers, enhancing their provision of descriptive and symbolic representation. A measure of gender integration was initiated.

The character of regendering and transgendering, as well as the balance between them, has remained uncertain and even volatile. Rather than being mutually exclusive, therefore, gender desegregation and gender integration have been shown to mark different points on a spectrum of gender inclusivity. Presidential administrations have positioned themselves at various places on this spectrum, as the seesawing between regendering and transgendering, desegregation and integration, has continued. Clearly, change is not yet predictable in cabinet nominations. And yet the change is likely to continue, as women are valued for their electoral support, and presidential self-interest dictates that they be given some cabinet representation.

GENDER DESEGREGATION, GENDER INTEGRATION, AND THE PRESIDENTS' CABINET NOMINATIONS

Political scientists have described presidential nominations as efforts to recruit political leaders and executive branch managers based on calculations about campaign indebtedness, policy symbolism, political relationships, and executive branch experience. Those generalities are demonstrably true for women and for men secretaries-designate, but the listing is far from complete. The selection of the cabinet secretaries-designate also testifies to the enduring influence of masculinism in the executive branch, which disadvantages women as officeholders and constituents. From this conclusion come three corollaries about the gendered evolution of cabinet nomination politics.

First, the power of masculinism notwithstanding, women have been offered representation in the cabinet with increasing frequency over the course of the modern presidency. In the Roosevelt, Eisenhower, and Ford administrations, nominating a woman secretary-designate was unusual. These were exceptional decisions, with approximately twenty years stretching between each nomination. Only with hindsight is the Ford nomination recognized as setting a precedent. In the later administrations, a woman in the cabinet—and gradually more than one—has become the norm. Thus, women have gained recognition as officeholders and as presidential constituents. At the same time, as has been shown, the more frequent nomination of women to the cabinet has not always provided women constituents with more meaningful representation.

Second, women secretaries-designate have been nominated to posts that constrained their opportunities to provide women with descriptive and symbolic representation. In the vast majority of instances, presidents have nominated women to the cabinet because doing so was in the president's electoral interest, because there were exceptionally qualified women available, *and* because women could be nominated to posts that would curb their influence. Presidents, therefore, have decided not to take full advantage of the expertise and political resources of women officeholders, just as they have also chosen to limit their recognition of women constituents.

Third, the nominations have generally regendered cabinet office, contributing to the gender desegregation of the cabinet. Transgendering and gender integration are less frequent phenomena. And yet, for all that masculinism has been sustained, every administration that included women in its cabinet ultimately enhanced women's representation. Even the Reagan administration made its contribution; its nominations explicitly acknowledged the connection between women in the electorate and women in the cabinet. This third corollary is the logical counterweight to the first two. Having recognized the normative strength of masculinism and its consequent power to limit change, it is important also to recognize that change has occurred.

This assessment of presidential nomination decisions has focused on descriptive and symbolic representation that are most directly related to the secretary-designate's anticipated performance as a political leader and executive manager. In the following chapter, attention shifts to the secretaries-designate themselves. In what ways are the women and the men secretaries-designate similar and different? What do those similarities and differences mean for cabinet representation? During briefings and consultations, White House and departmental advisers, as well as senators and their staff, study the nominees' pre-cabinet careers for indications of the substantive representation that they might be expected to offer. Have the women secretaries-designate, in particular, possessed the expertise and the experience to challenge established issue agendas, to resist dichotomizing the political interests of women and of men, and to offer new perspectives on behalf of women as presidential constituents? Also to be considered are the likely connections these secretaries-designate will forge among substantive, descriptive, and symbolic representation, with their implications for regendering or transgendering cabinet service. In the calculus of expectations that distinguish nomination politics, these judgments are the basis for the media portrayals and the Senate confirmation hearings that introduce the secretary-designate to the general public.

NOTES

1. For an assessment of these competing priorities in presidential nominations, see Joel D. Aberbach and Bert A. Rockman, *In the Web of Politics, Three Decades of the U.S. Federal Executive* (Washington, D.C.: Brookings Institution, 2000), pp. 26–27; Carl M. Brauer, *Presidential Transitions: Eisenhower Through Reagan* (New York: Oxford University Press, 1986); James P. Pfiffner, "Presidential Appointments: Recruiting Executive Branch Leaders," in *Innocent Until Nominated: The Breakdown of the Presidential Appointments Process,* ed. G. Calvin Mackenzie (Washington, D.C.: Brookings Institution, 2001); George C. Edwards, III, "Why Not the Best? The Loyalty-Competence Trade-Off in Presidential Appointments," in *Innocent Until Nominated: The Breakdown of the Presidential Appointments Process,* ed. G. Calvin Mackenzie (Washington, D.C.: Brookings Institution, 2001); *Obstacle Course: The Report of the Twentieth Century Fund Task Force on the Presidential Appointment Process* (New York: Twentieth Century Fund, 1996); G. Calvin Mackenzie, *The Politics of Presidential Appointments* (New York: Free Press, 1981); Terry Moe, "The Politicized Presidency," in *The New Direction in American Politics,* ed. John E. Chubb and Paul E. Peterson (Washington, D.C.: Brookings Institution, 1985); Thomas J. Weko, *The Politicizing Presidency: The White House Personnel Office, 1948–1994* (Lawrence: University Press of Kansas, 1995). For a discussion of private-public distinctions, see James Q. Wilson, *Bureaucracy: What Government Agencies Do and Why They Do It* (New York: Basic Books, 1989). To identify just one private-public conflict, note that management in the private sector assesses performance in terms of profit. It therefore prizes an optimal relationship between measurable inputs

and outputs, that is, efficiency. Public sector leadership, however, evaluates management in terms of providing services. It therefore values the intangibles of responsiveness, accountability, and equity, that is, effectiveness. Private sector and public sector leaders, therefore, are seeking different goals. When a cabinet officer defines her or his managerial responsibilities by private sector standards, a conflict with the public nature of political leadership is inevitable. In this instance, management and leadership priorities will only be reconciled if the goals themselves are critically reviewed. That is one of the tasks of the cabinet nomination process.

2. G. Calvin Mackenzie, *The Politics of Presidential Appointments* (New York: Free Press, 1981), pp. 4–9.

3. Mackenzie and others were commenting on nominations and appointments made across an entire administration; the rank and responsibilities of the departmental secretaries mean that cabinet nominations are somewhat distinctive. Still, the same four factors have been identified in association with the selection of the secretaries-designate. James P. Pfiffner, "Presidential Appointments: Recruiting Executive Branch Leaders," in *Innocent Until Nominated: The Breakdown of the Presidential Appointments Process,* ed. G. Calvin Mackenzie (Washington, D.C.: Brookings Institution, 2001); George C. Edwards, III, "Why Not the Best? The Loyalty-Competence Trade-Off in Presidential Appointments," in *Innocent Until Nominated: The Breakdown of the Presidential Appointments Process,* ed. G. Calvin Mackenzie (Washington, D.C.: Brookings Institution, 2001); *Obstacle Course: The Report of the Twentieth Century Fund Task Force on the Presidential Appointment Process* (New York: Twentieth Century Fund, 1996); G. Calvin Mackenzie, *The Politics of Presidential Appointments* (New York: Free Press, 1981).

4. As an illustration of these difficulties, there is also the Clinton selection of an interior secretary-designate in 1992. At various points, the president-elect appeared to have selected Tim Wirth (a former senator and strong campaign supporter), Bill Richardson (a former Congress member and a Hispanic American), and Bruce Babbitt (a former governor favored by environmentalists). Each of these men was a westerner and would have satisfied, in some measure, the principal regional constituency of the department; each would additionally have satisfied a different element of Clinton's election coalition.

5. Press Conference, 14 December 1976, as quoted in G. Calvin Mackenzie, *The Politics of Presidential Appointments* (New York: Free Press, 1981), p. 63.

6. "Candidate Jimmy Carter, in his meeting with the Women's Caucus at the 1976 Democratic Convention, promised that if elected he would nominate a significant number of women to decision-making positions in his administration. No sooner were the election returns in, than the National Women's Political Caucus began lobbying the President-Elect to nominate nationally known women to his cabinet." "Proposal: The Women's Appointment Network," ca. 1977. "Appointments Project" Folder, 92-M162, Box 17, National Women's Political Caucus Files, Arthur and Elizabeth Schlesinger Library on

the History of Women in America, Radcliffe College, Harvard University. See also Ad Hoc Coalition for Women, "Summary of Priority Requests Made by Coalition in Meeting with President Carter and Vice President Mondale at White House Meeting, March 10, 1977." BPW/USA Archives.

7. See, for example, the comments of midterm nominee, Reagan transportation secretary Elizabeth Hanford Dole, in Robert D. Hershey, Jr., "Working Profile: Elizabeth H. Dole, Transportation Secretary," *New York Times,* 22 August 1983, sec. 2, p. 8.

8. G. Calvin Mackenzie, "The Presidential Appointment Process: Historical Development, Contemporary Operations, Current Issues," in *Obstacle Course: The Report of the Twentieth Century Fund Task Force on the Presidential Appointment Process* (New York: Twentieth Century Fund, 1996), p. 51.

9. James D. King and James W. Riddlesperger, Jr., "Presidential Cabinet Appointments: The Partisan Factor," *Presidential Studies Quarterly* 14 (Spring 1984): 231–237. See also James D. King and James W. Riddlesperger, Jr., "Unscheduled Presidential Transitions: Lessons from the Truman, Johnson, and Ford Administrations," *Congress and the Presidency* 22, no. 1 (Spring 1995): 1–17.

10. For a discussion of these calculations in regard to the initial Carter cabinet secretaries-designate, see "The View from the Top of the Carter Campaign," *National Journal,* 17 July 1976, p. 997; Hedrick Smith, "Carter Urges Aides to Find a Broad 'Mix' for Posts in Cabinet," *New York Times,* 19 November 1976, p. 1; Hedrick Smith, "A Neatly Balanced Cabinet," *New York Times,* 24 December 1976, p. A10.

11. Joel D. Aberbach and Bert A. Rockman, *In the Web of Politics: Three Decades of the U.S. Federal Executive* (Washington, D.C.: Brookings Institution, 2000), pp. 72–78.

12. King and Riddlesperger found this pattern also prevailed in the administrations that are not included in this study, namely, those of Truman, Kennedy, Johnson, and Nixon. See "Presidential Cabinet Appointments: The Partisan Factor," *Presidential Studies Quarterly* 14 (Spring 1984): 231–237. See also James J. Best, "Presidential Cabinet Appointments, 1953–1976," *Presidential Studies Quarterly* 11, no. 1 (Winter 1981): 62–66.

13. For a listing of these campaign promises, see Janet M. Martin, "Women Who Govern: The President's Appointments," in *The Other Elites: Women, Politics, and Power in the Executive Branch,* ed. MaryAnne Borrelli and Janet M. Martin (Boulder, Colo.: Lynne Rienner Publishers, 1997), p. 52.

14. Ford's early appointments were focused on the White House staff, in response to ongoing concerns about Watergate. However, he was quickly encouraged to give equal consideration to the cabinet. For example, see Letter, Representative Clarence J. Brown to President Ford, 12 August 1974, "FG 10 The Cabinet, 8/9/74-12/31/74" Folder, Box 72, White House Central Files, Subject File, Gerald R. Ford Library, Ann Arbor, Mich.; Letter, Senator James B. Pearson to President Ford, 8 November 1974, "FG 10 The Cabinet, 8/9/74-12/31/74"

Folder, Box 72, White House Central Files, Subject File, Gerald R. Ford Library, Ann Arbor, Mich. Throughout Ford's term, there are also memoranda evaluating cabinet meetings and giving suggestions for enhancing their contribution to the policymaking process. For example, see Memorandum, James E. Connor to Donald Rumsfeld, "Attendance at Cabinet Meetings," 2 January 1975, "Cabinet Meetings—Attendance and Seating Policy" Folder, Box 1, James E. Connor, Cabinet Secretary Subject File, Gerald R. Ford Library, Ann Arbor, Mich.; Memorandum, Jim Connor to Dick Cheney, "Cabinet Meetings," 14 June 1976, "Cabinet—General (3)" Folder, Box 1, James E. Connor, Cabinet Secretary Subject File, Gerald R. Ford Library, Ann Arbor, Mich.

15. The criticisms may be voiced even when the president nominates from an opposing wing of his own party, as Eisenhower learned. Agriculture Secretary-Designate Ezra Taft Benson had been a supporter of Senator Robert A. Taft (R-Ohio), Eisenhower's Republican opponent in the presidential primaries. Among the responses to this nomination was a letter from a citizen who wrote, "How, now, can I, or any other American citizen who voted for you, have confidence in you when you have elevated an opposition leader to a position of influence in your cabinet?" In reply, Sherman Adams wrote:

> Throughout the campaign, the President frequently stated his intention to establish an administration which would be representative of all Americans and which would draw upon the most able and talented of Americans for leadership. He would, he said, consider the solution of every problem on the basis of the single question, "Is this good for America?" There were, of course, certain fundamental principles correlative to this proposition, such as integrity, opposition to waste, and devotion to the American tenets of freedom, which would motivate every policy of the new administration. / In making his selections for Cabinet posts as well as for all other positions in his administration, President Eisenhower has been guided by these principles. I believe you will agree that all of the men and women appointed by the President share these convictions and that none of them can properly be termed "opposition leaders." The policy adopted by the President in this respect will insure that the new administration, and the Republican Party, will be truly representative of the American people; and it will encourage the formation of a real and effective two-party system.

Letter, William Michael Anderson to President Dwight D. Eisenhower, 27 February 1953, "8 Cabinet (collectively), 1952–1953" Folder, Box 174, White House Central Files, General File, Dwight D. Eisenhower Library, Abilene, Kans.; Letter, Sherman Williams to William Michael Anderson, 18 March 1953, "8 Cabinet (collectively), 1952–1953" Folder, Box 174, White House Central Files, General File, Dwight D. Eisenhower Library, Abilene, Kans. Benson's was not the only "opposition" nomination, though he was the most recent Taft supporter in the cabinet. Treasury Secretary-Designate G. M.

Humphrey had supported Taft in 1948. Leo Egan, "G. M. Humphrey to Get Treasury Post and Brownell Attorney Generalship; Stassen Will Direct Mutual Security," *New York Times,* 22 November 1952, p. 1.

16. Partisan turnover has actually been the historic norm. As James Pfiffner observed, "President [George H. W.] Bush was the first president elected to succeed a predecessor of his own party since 1928 and the first sitting Vice-President to be elected in his own right since 1836." "Establishing the Bush Presidency," *Public Administration Review* (January–February 1990): 64.

17. James Best referred to secretaries who are moved from one cabinet post to another as "managerial 'technocrats.'" These secretaries are typically expected to control departments whose programs are too diversified for easy coherence (HEW/HHS), whose internal divisions threaten presidential agendas (Defense, Commerce), or whose jurisdictions directly affect presidential fortunes (Justice). The ultimate managerial technocrat could be Elliot Richardson, who served as the as secretary of health, education and welfare, secretary of defense, and attorney general in the Nixon administration and was secretary of commerce in the Ford administration. James J. Best, "Presidential Cabinet Appointments, 1953–1976," *Presidential Studies Quarterly* (Winter 1981): 64. See also Herbert F. Weisberg, "Cabinet Transfers and Departmental Prestige: Someone Old, Someone New, Someone Borrowed . . .," *American Politics Quarterly* 15, no. 2 (April 1987): 238–253.

18. George H. W. Bush is widely viewed as making his first three cabinet nominations while still a vice president, having considerable influence in Reagan's nomination of Treasury Secretary-Designate Nicholas Brady, Attorney General-Designate Richard Thornburgh, and Education Secretary-Designate Lauro Cavazos. Each of these three secretaries-designate qualified as an outsider when they were Reagan midterm nominees. When renominated to the Bush cabinet in 1989, however, each qualified as an insider. When these exceptional cases are removed from the count of George H. W. Bush initial nominees, the insider-outsider trend in Bush cabinet nominations is slightly modified. Without these three insiders, initial nominees are 63.4 percent insiders (7) and 36.4 percent outsiders (4). Midterm nominees, as demonstrated in Table 2.1, are 62.5 percent insiders (5) and 37.5 percent outsiders (3). Thus, when the exceptional cases are set aside, George H. W. Bush nominated similar proportions of insiders and outsiders in both his initial and his midterm cabinet nominations. This pattern still contrasts with those of the other administrations.

19. Though he does not use the specialist-liaison-generalist classification schema, James J. Best reports similar cabinet nomination patterns in administrations not included in this study, namely, those of Kennedy, Johnson, and Nixon. See James J. Best, "Presidential Cabinet Appointments, 1953–1976," *Presidential Studies Quarterly* 11, no. 1 (Winter 1981): 62–66.

20. For example, in 1992, in an effort to improve his standing with veterans, Clinton named Jesse Brown, then executive director of Disabled American Veterans, as veterans affairs secretary-designate. Also among Clinton's ini-

tial nominees were Senator Lloyd Bentsen (D-Tex.), then chair of the Senate Finance Committee, who was named treasury secretary-designate; and Representative Les Aspin (D-Wis.), then chair of the House Armed Services Committee, who was named defense secretary-designate. Clinton's replacement nominees also included former members of Congress, often selected to repair strained relationships. Among these were Representative Dan Glickman (D-Kans.), from the House Agriculture Committee (General Farm Commodities Subcommittee), and former Senator William Cohen (R-Maine), from the Senate Armed Services Committee.

21. Clinton health and human services (HHS) secretary-designate Donna E. Shalala, an initial nominee, was a generalist. Shalala had federal government experience, having served as a housing and urban development assistant secretary in the Carter administration. However, her policy expertise in HHS was limited to grant-related negotiations with the National Institutes of Health, which she conducted as a university president. Yet she was a loyal Democrat and Clinton supporter who could be depended on to advance the president's agenda. In fact, Shalala was cautioned in her confirmation hearing not to be too deferential to Oval Office priorities. U.S. Senate, Committee on Labor and Human Resources, *Nomination* [Donna E. Shalala, of Wisconsin, to be Secretary of Health and Human Services], 103rd Con., 1st sess., 1993.

22. Thomas J. Weko, *The Politicizing Presidency: The White House Personnel Office, 1948–1994* (Lawrence: University Press of Kansas, 1995), pp. 46–50.

23. Joseph A. Califano, Jr., *Governing America: An Insider's Report from the White House and the Cabinet* (New York: Simon and Schuster, 1981), p. 23. Quoted, in part, in Thomas J. Weko, *The Politicizing Presidency: The White House Personnel Office, 1948–1994* (Lawrence: University Press of Kansas, 1995), p. 73.

24. Thomas J. Weko, *The Politicizing Presidency: The White House Personnel Office, 1948–1994* (Lawrence: University Press of Kansas, 1995). pp. 72–76.

25. Samuel Kernell and Samuel L. Popkin, eds., *Chief of Staff: Twenty-five Years of Managing the Presidency* (Berkeley: University of California Press, 1986).

26. The women secretaries-designate nominated by George W. Bush had held positions in state government and in various nonprofit organizations during the eight years of the Clinton administration. All of them had, however, served in national government during previous Republican administrations.

27. The two midterm women liaisons were Commerce Secretary-Designate Barbara Franklin in the George H. W. Bush administration and Secretary-Designate of State Madeleine Albright in the Clinton administration. The third woman liaison was Interior Secretary-Designate Gale A. Norton, an initial cabinet nominee in the George W. Bush administration.

28. G. Calvin Mackenzie, *The Politics of Presidential Appointments* (New York: Free Press, 1981), p. 256.

29. Shalala was the most liberal of Clinton's cabinet nominees and was nominated to the department that was expected to be the site of the most liberalizing reforms. Susan Chira, "Emphasis on Action: Donna Edna Shalala," *New York Times*, 12 December 1992, p. 11; "Bill Clinton's Pragmatists," *New York Times*, 12 December 1992, p. 22; Elizabeth Drew, *On the Edge: The Clinton Presidency* (New York: Simon and Schuster, 1994), p. 22. On the Albright nomination, see Craig R. Whitney, "Nominees Raise Both Hope and Worry Abroad," *New York Times*, 7 December 1996, p. 7.

30. Mary W. Dewson, *An Aid to the End*, pp. 33, 40–49, 110–111, 124–125. M-133, Reel A3 of the Molly Dewson Collection of the Arthur and Elizabeth Schlesinger Library on the History of Women, Radcliffe College, Harvard University; Susan Ware, *Partner and I: Molly Dewson, Feminism, and New Deal Politics* (New Haven: Yale University Press, 1987); Susan Ware, *Beyond Suffrage: Women in the New Deal* (Cambridge, Mass.: Harvard University Press, 1981); Eleanor Roosevelt and Lorena A. Hickok, *Ladies of Courage* (New York: G. P. Putnam's Sons, 1954), p. 277. For published endorsements of Perkins as labor secretary, see "Our Next Cabinet," *The Forum* (January 1933): 11–12; "Letter to the Editor, by Jane Addams," *The Forum* (February 1933): ix–x; "The Department of Labor: A Challenge," *The Nation* (22 February 1933): 192; "The Common Welfare: Madam Secretary Perkins," *Survey* (March 1933): 110.

31. Treasury Secretary-Designate William H. Woodin, Interior Secretary-Designate Harold L. Ickes, and Postmaster General-Designate James A. Farley all fit into this category.

32. The southerners were Secretary-Designate of State Cordell Hull (Tenn.) and Navy Secretary-Designate Claude A. Swanson (Va.), while the westerners were War Secretary-Designate George H. Dern (Utah) and Attorney General-Designate Thomas J. Walsh (Mont.). Moderate and progressive wings of the Republican Party were represented, respectively, by Treasury Secretary-Designate William H. Woodin and Interior Secretary-Designate Harold L. Ickes.

33. "Hull and Woodin Named for Cabinet to Speed Action on World Economics: Roosevelt Confers with French Envoy," *New York Times*, 22 February 1933, p. 1; "Woodin Advocate of Sound Money," *New York Times*, 22 February 1933, p. 1; "Public Services of the Ten Prospective Members of Roosevelt's Cabinet," *New York Times*, 23 February 1933, p. 3; James A. Hagerty, "Roosevelt Names Farley, Wallace as Cabinet Aides," *New York Times*, 27 February 1933, p. 1; James A. Hagerty, "Roosevelt Names Swanson and Ickes," *New York Times*, 28 February 1933, p. 5; James A. Hagerty, "Roosevelt Names Last of Cabinet," *New York Times*, 1 March 1933, p. 1. For a secondary source discussing Roosevelt's cabinet nominations, see Rexford G. Tugwell, *The Democratic Roosevelt* (Garden City, N.Y.: Doubleday, 1957), pp. 267–269.

34. The two had actually met at a tea dance in 1910. Perkins subsequently observed Roosevelt in the New York Senate, while she was lobbying for various social reforms, and her impressions were not especially positive. "I have a

vivid picture of him operating on the floor of the Senate: tall and slender, very active and alert, moving around the floor, going in and out of committee rooms, rarely talking with the members, who more or less avoided him, not particularly charming (that came later), artificially serious of face, rarely smiling, with an unfortunate habit—so natural that he was unaware of it—of throwing his head up. This, combined with his pince-nez and great height, gave him the appearance of looking down his nose at most people. . . . I think he started that way not because he was born with a silver spoon in his mouth and had a good education at Harvard (which in itself constitutes a political handicap), but because he really didn't like people very much and because he had a youthful lack of humility, a streak of self-righteousness, and a deafness to the hopes, fears, and aspirations which are the common lot. The marvel is that these handicaps were washed out of him by life, experience, punishment, and his capacity to grow. He never wholly ignored these youthful traits himself. He once said to me when he was President, 'You know, I was an awfully mean cuss when I first went into politics.'" Frances Perkins, *The Roosevelt I Knew* (New York: Viking Press, 1946), pp. 11–12.

35. Perkins felt that the unions should have one of their own leaders in the secretarial office, and she initially lobbied against her own nomination. Frances Perkins Oral History, the Oral History Research Project, Butler Library, Columbia University. See also Lillian Holmen Mohr, *Frances Perkins, "That Woman in FDR's Cabinet!"* (Great Barrington, Mass.: North River Press, 1979); George Martin, *Madam Secretary, Frances Perkins* (Boston: Houghton Mifflin, 1976).

36. Rexford Tugwell wrote, "Presidents had until then allowed themselves to be guided by organized labor in making this appointment and had usually discovered that they lost by it both the regard of labor and the respect of ordinary citizens. . . . Frances had demonstrated her competence; as much as anyone, she was responsible for the advancement of New York's labor law and the excellence of their administration. But she was not identified with any of labor's warring factions." Rexford G. Tugwell, *The Democratic Roosevelt* (Garden City, N.Y.: Doubleday, 1957), p. 268. See also Mary W. Dewson, *An Aid to the End*, pp. 40–49, 110–111, 124–125, M-133, Reel A3 of the Molly Dewson Collection, Arthur and Elizabeth Schlesinger Library on the History of Women, Radcliffe College, Harvard University.

37. Hobby had been a campaign donor, a member of Eisenhower's campaign committee, and the leader of the "Democrats for Eisenhower" organization. Letter, Keith McCanse to Oveta Culp Hobby, 9 May 1952, "1952 Eisenhower—Citizens for, Advisory Counsel" Folder, Box 1, Oveta Culp Hobby Papers, Dwight D. Eisenhower Library, Abilene, Kans.; Press Release, Citizens for Eisenhower-Nixon, 20 October 1952, "1952 Eisenhower—Material Brought in by Mrs. Hobby" Folder, Box 1, Oveta Culp Hobby Papers, Dwight D. Eisenhower Library, Abilene, Kans.; Telegram, Howard Peterson and Paul Hoffman to Oveta Culp Hobby, 6 July 1952, "1952 Eisenhower—Citizens for, Advisory Counsel" Folder, Box 1, Oveta Culp Hobby Papers, Dwight D.

Eisenhower Library, Abilene, Kans.; Letter, Tex McCrary to Oveta Culp Hobby, 15 July 1952, "1952 Eisenhower—Citizens for, Advisory Counsel" Folder, Box 1, Oveta Culp Hobby Papers, Dwight D. Eisenhower Library, Abilene, Kans.; Letter, Herbert Brownell to Sherman Adams, 9 December 1958, "A (1)" Folder, Box 66, Herbert Brownell Papers, Dwight D. Eisenhower Library; Lucius D. Clay, Sr. Oral History, Conducted 20 February 1967, p. 46, Dwight D. Eisenhower Library, Abilene, Kans..

38. As a representative of women, Hobby was endorsed for the cabinet office by the American Association of University Women, which submitted a roster of eighteen women for "administrative and policy-making positions in the Government" on 24 November 1952. "A.A.U.W. Recommends 18 Women to Eisenhower for High Posts," St. Louis [Missouri] Post-Dispatch, 25 November 1952, "1952 (2)" Folder, Box 67, Oveta Culp Hobby Papers, Dwight D. Eisenhower Library, Abilene, Kans. Hobby also used her Texas connections to influence Democratic opposition leaders in the House (then Minority Leader Sam Rayburn) and in the Senate (then Democratic Whip Lyndon Johnson). James C. Haggerty's diary records the following exchange among these actors: "While I was with [the President] I told him that the reaction I had already received on his remarks about the Health Reinsurance Bill were very favorable. He was delighted and asked me to get in touch with Mrs. Hobby and work out measures to keep the pot boiling on this one and to keep the pressure on the boys up on the Hill. I called Mrs. Hobby and the first thing we decided to do was to put pressure through Texas on Sam Rayburn who had called the bill 'stupid and a blundering way to start.' Mrs. Hobby sent word through Lyndon Johnson that her many years of friendship with Rayburn had been ended in three minutes by the speech that Rayburn made. Johnson, of course, relayed this remark to Rayburn and within an hour Johnson was calling Mrs. Hobby back to tell her that 'Rayburn was amazed and hurt' at Mrs. Hobby's attitude. 'Do you know what I told Lyndon?' Mrs. Hobby asked me. 'I told him to tell Rayburn just one word "nuts."'" Mrs. Hobby is getting her people in Texas to really put the heat on Rayburn and to let him know that this time we will not forget what he did. Whether it will have any effect or not is another matter, but all in all, I think it is a good procedure." 14 July 1954, "Haggerty Diary; July 1954" Folder, Box 1, James C. Haggerty Papers, Diary Entries, Dwight D. Eisenhower Library, Abilene, Kans.

39. Hobby was instrumental in securing congressional passage of Eisenhower's Reorganization Plan No. 1, which united previously disparate bureaus and agencies into the single Department of Health, Education, and Welfare. This was accomplished in the first months of the Eisenhower administration, though the plan owed much to work done in the Truman administration.

40. Anthony J. Bennett, The American President's Cabinet: From Kennedy to Bush (New York: St. Martin's Press, 1996), pp. 63–64.

41. "The Cabinet," "Transition (1974) White House and Cabinet Personnel Report, ca. 9/74" Folder, Box 12, Richard Cheney Files, Gerald R. Ford Library, Ann Arbor, Mich.

42. These partisan and campaign considerations notwithstanding, the First Lady subsequently claimed some credit for Hills's nomination. Betty Ford had been publicly campaigning for the nomination of a woman to the cabinet for several months. Following her lead, media coverage—apart from the trade journals of Housing and Urban Development's traditional clients—presented the secretary-designate as a role model for women throughout the society, highlighting Hills's professional accomplishments. The drawbacks associated with her generalist status were often dismissed. See "Women's Unit Hails Betty Ford," *New York Times*, 7 May 1975, p. 33; "Excellent Choices," *Washington Star News*, 17 February 1975, in U.S. Senate, Committee on Banking, Housing, and Urban Affairs, *Hearings on the Nomination of Carla A. Hills to Be Secretary of the Department of Housing and Urban Development*, 94th Cong., 1st sess., p. 15.

43. "Two for One Deal," *Time*, 3 January 1977, p. 44; Dennis Williams, "A Question of Loyalty," *Newsweek*, 30 July 1979, p. 30; Robert Reinhold, "Mrs. Harris Is Expected to Alter H.E.W. Subtly," *New York Times*, 21 July 1979, p. 17; Jimmy Carter, *Keeping Faith: Memoirs of a President* (New York: Bantam Books, 1982), pp. 76, 117; "Carter and Secretary Harris," *Christian Science Monitor*, 3 August 1979, p. 24. But see also Alvin F. Poussaint, "To Get and to Get Not," *New York Times*, 13 March 1977, p. 23.

44. Memo, Robert Barnett to Dick Moe, 2 December 1976, "[Minority Appt—Recommendations] [O/A 1165]" Folder, Box 9, Hamilton Jordan Papers, Jimmy Carter Library, Atlanta, Georgia. Marjorie Hunter, "Congress Approves Dept. of Education; Victory for Carter," *New York Times*, p. 1; Terrence Smith, "Home State Labor Backs Kennedy; Education Group Supports Carter," *New York Times*, 29 September 1979, p. 1; U.S. Senate, Committee on Labor and Human Relations, 1979. Nomination [Shirley M. Hufstedler, of California, to be Secretary of Education]. 96th Cong., 1st sess. p. 20.

45. "Gentlewoman," *Washington Post*, 5 November 1979, A22; Hobart Rowen, "Kreps: Introspective Farewell," *Washington Post*, 3 November 1979, p. A1.

46. Jeane Kirkpatrick, the U.S. representative to the United Nations, was granted cabinet rank and was advertised as Reagan's woman in the cabinet. The *New York Times* coverage of the Kirkpatrick nomination had the following as its page 1 lead: "President-elect Ronald Reagan today announced the selection of five more Cabinet members, including the first woman, who is also the first Democrat, and the first black that he has nominated." The "first woman" held cabinet rank as the U.S. ambassador to the United Nations; the "first black" was Housing and Urban Development Secretary-Designate Samuel R. Pierce. The two did not have equal status as cabinet members; Steven R. Weisman, "Black and a Woman Are Among 5 Named to Reagan Cabinet," *New York Times*, 23 December 1980, p. 1. To illustrate the recognized distinction between cabinet "rank" and actual cabinet membership, consider the following commentary on Bill Richardson. Richardson was first nominated as U.S. ambassador to the United Nations and then was later nominated

energy secretary-designate. "Richardson will become the highest ranking Hispanic in the Clinton administration. And he won't just have a Cabinet-level post as he did at the United Nations but an actual Cabinet secretary's job." David Ivanovich, "Richardson Perplexes the Pundits," *Houston Chronicle,* 19 June 1998, p. 1.

47. Maureen Reagan, the president-elect's daughter, voiced one of the few critical statements about this panel's personnel decisions; it was dismissed by the president. "On the way to his doctor's appointment, Mr. Reagan was asked about a comment by his daughter, Maureen, that he had not chosen enough women for his Cabinet. 'She'd like fifteen,' he said with a laugh." Steven R. Weisman, "Black and a Woman Are Among 5 Named to Reagan Cabinet," *New York Times,* 23 December 1980, p. 1.

48. See Tanya Melich, *The Republican War Against Women: An Insider's Report from Behind the Lines* (New York: Bantam Books, 1996).

49. Dom Bonafede, "Reagan and His Kitchen Cabinet Are Bound by Friendship and Ideology," *National Journal,* 11 April 1981, pp. 605–608; Thomas J. Weko, *The Politicizing Presidency: The White House Personnel Office, 1948–1994* (Lawrence: University Press of Kansas, 1995), pp. 96, 187 n. 114; Shirley Anne Warshaw, *Powersharing: White House–Cabinet Relations in the Modern Presidency* (Albany: State University of New York Press, 1996), pp. 135–136.

50. Helene Von Damm, *At Reagan's Side* (New York: Doubleday, 1989), pp. 129–133.

51. "Mrs. Heckler's Record," *New York Times,* 21 January 1983, p. 16; Juan Williams, "President Names Ex-Rep. Heckler as Head of HHS," *Washington Post,* 13 January 1983, pp. 1, A6; Robert Pear, "Mrs. Heckler Disputes 'Token' Woman Label," *New York Times,* 15 January 1983, p. 24; Susan Trausch, "Heckler's ZigZag Line in Congress," *Globe,* "Margaret Heckler/Dole app'ts," Folder, Box 4, National Women's Political Caucus Records 91-M118, Arthur and Elizabeth Schlesinger Library on the History of Women, Radcliffe College, Harvard University.

52. Though Dole had acquired some capital as the director of White House public liaison, Heckler entered office with little credibility in the administration. Further, the Reagan administration had promised significant cuts in social services, and the White House had selected an HHS deputy secretary, John Svahn, with a proven record of success in doing so. In her confirmation hearing, as during her tenure at the department, Heckler faced criticism that Svahn was the true leader of the department. See U.S. Senate, Committee on Finance, *Nominations of Margaret Heckler, to be Secretary of HHS and John A. Svahn, to be Under Secretary of HHS.* 98th Cong., 1st sess.; U.S. Senate, Committee on Labor and Human Resources, *Additional Consideration of Margaret M. Heckler, of Massachusetts, to be Secretary, Department of Health and Human Services,* 98th Cong., 1st sess. See also Robert Pear, "New Chief's Deputy Is Used to Running the Show," *New York Times,* 11 March 1983, p. 20.

53. Dole and Heckler had each campaigned extensively in the 1984 presidential campaign. James Lake, communications director for Reagan/Bush '84, found Heckler particularly valuable as an advocate for the president, remarking, "Because the HHS secretary 'isn't a typical Reaganite . . . she frankly is more credible. . . .'" Burt Schorr, "HHS's Mrs. Heckler: A Leader for the Poor or Just a Poor Leader?" *Wall Street Journal,* 29 February 1984, p. 1. See also Robert Pear, "Softening Some Images, If Not Policies," *New York Times,* 26 June 1983, p. E4.

54. William Neikirk, "Reagan Picks Woman as New Labor Secretary," *Chicago Tribune,* 4 November 1987, I5.

55. Similar practices may have prevailed in Reagan's appointments of people of color to the cabinet. At the very least, the president's contacts with all these cabinet members were limited. Reagan could not even identity Samuel Pierce, an African American, as his secretary of housing and urban development, when the two met at a White House conference.

56. Gerald M. Boyd, "Bush Names James Baker as Secretary of State; Hails 40-State Support for 'My Principles,'" *New York Times,* 10 November 1988, p. 1; Gerald M. Boyd, "Bush Is Reported to Have Chosen Gov. Sununu as His Chief of Staff," *New York Times,* 16 November 1988, p. 1; Bernard Weinraub, "Bush Will Retain Webster at C.I.A.; Fills 4 More Posts," *New York Times,* 7 December 1988, p. 1; Gerald M. Boyd, "Bush Names Tower to Pentagon Post, Ending Long Delay," *New York Times,* 17 December 1988, p. 1; Gerald M. Boyd, "Kemp, Picked as Chief of H.U.D., Pledges to Combat Homelessness," *New York Times,* 20 December 1988, p. 1; Gerald M. Boyd, "Bush Picks Doctor Who Was Chided on Abortion Views," *New York Times,* 23 December 1988, p. 1; Burt Solomon, "Bush Promised Fresh Faces But He's Hiring Old Friends," *National Journal,* 21 January 1989, pp. 142–143.

57. The president-elect stressed that Dole was nominated to the cabinet on her own merits, not for her sex or her marital relationship with his former presidential opponent Robert Dole. The president-elect added, though, that any "dividend" in the nomination would be cheerfully accepted. "Excerpts from Bush's News Conference with Elizabeth Dole," *New York Times,* 25 December 1988, p. 22. In introducing Martin, George H. W. Bush described her as "a cherished friend." A former member of the House of Representatives, she helped Bush to prepare for the vice presidential debates against Geraldine Ferraro in the 1984 election. In the 1988 election, she was an early co-chair of Bush's campaign. While in Congress, however, her AFL-CIO rating was 29 percent, which organized labor concluded "did not reflect a sensitivity to the needs of workers" on the part of the labor secretary-designate. Frank Swoboda, "Bush Picks Rep. Lynn Martin to Head Labor Department," *Washington Post,* 15 December 1990, p. A2; Andrew Rosenthal, "Lawmaker Selected as Labor Secretary," *New York Times,* 15 December 1990, p. 11; Albert R. Klarr, "Bush's Choice of Lynn Martin Brings Tough Fiscal Conservative to Labor Post," *Wall Street Journal,* 17 December 1990, p. B6. Martin's relationship with organized labor did not improve over the course of her cabinet service. See Frank Swo-

boda, "Labor Secretary Martin Finds Criticism Is Par for the Political Course," *Washington Post*, 9 March 1992, p. A15.

58. Franklin was serving on seven corporate boards at the time of her nomination. She received considerable praise for her board leadership during the confirmation hearing. U.S. Senate, Committee on Commerce, Science, and Transportation, *Nomination of Barbara Hackman Franklin to Be Secretary of Commerce*, 102nd Cong., 2nd sess., 1987, pp. 1–5.

59. Associated Press, "Current Quotes from the 1992 Campaign Trail," 22 May 1992. For a discussion of this promise and its consequences during the transition, see Janet M. Martin, "Women Who Govern: The President's Appointments," in *The Other Elites, Women, Politics, and Power in the Executive Branch*, ed. MaryAnne Borrelli and Janet M. Martin (Boulder: Lynne Rienner Publishers, 1997), pp. 51–52.

60. Evans, Chao, Martinez, Thompson, and Veneman had played roles in the presidential campaign. Norton, Veneman, Chavez, Chao, and O'Neill had previously held posts in the executive branch; Powell, Rumsfeld, Mineta, and Principi had held cabinet or cabinet-rank posts. The former or current members of Congress were Rumsfeld, Ashcroft, Mineta, and Abraham. The seven secretaries-designate who had held state or local office were Ashcroft, Norton, Veneman, Martinez, Mineta, Thompson, and Paige. Ashcroft, Norton, Veneman, and Mineta had served in more than one level of government. The secretaries-designate did have different records of achievement as political and governmental actors. Attorney General-Designate John Ashcroft, for example, had been defeated after just one term in the Senate. Energy Secretary-Designate Spencer Abraham, similarly, was in his first Senate term when he accepted the cabinet nomination.

61. The following George W. Bush initial secretaries-designate were classified as generalists: Secretary-Designate of State Colin Powell, Attorney General–Designate John Ashcroft, Agriculture Secretary-Designate Ann Veneman, Commerce Secretary-Designate Donald Evans, Labor Secretary-Designate Linda Chavez, Labor Secretary-Designate Chao, Health and Human Services Secretary-Designate Tommy Thompson, and Energy Secretary-Designate Spencer Abraham. All of them had some policy experience in their future department's issue jurisdiction. Those arguably the least acquainted with the policies were Evans, Chavez, Chao, and Abraham.

62. The State Department has been found guilty of sex discrimination in several legal cases. See Nancy E. McGlen and Meredith Reid Sarkees, *Women in Foreign Policy: The Insiders* (New York: Routledge, 1993).

3

The Secretaries-Designate

Presidential nominees are often treated as interchangeable, their distinctive traits lost in studies of their shared circumstances as members of an administration. Their offices, the decisionmaking routines in which they participate, and the policies that they recommend are the focus of attention. And yet, political analysts repeatedly acknowledge that individuals "matter," that the personal and professional and political experiences that officeholders bring into government influence every undertaking. Those experiences and their implications for cabinet representation are the subject of this chapter.

Some assessments of the nominees' precabinet careers were offered in the previous chapter. As Washington insiders or outsiders, as specialists or liaisons or generalists, secretaries-designate already have relationships with networks and decisionmakers. And yet, these classifications provide little insight on the career choices of the secretaries-designate. In particular, the shape and content of their political ambition remain unknown, even though this may reveal a great deal about their interests and priorities as prospective cabinet officers and representatives.

Accordingly, this chapter focuses on the cabinet nominees, systematically examining their career paths. This undertaking details the positions that the secretaries-designate have held throughout their professional lives, allowing assessments to be made about the nominees' political and entrepreneurial skills. Their prior political alliances indicate the relationships that they will presumptively bring into the cabinet and the interests that will thereby gain access to policymaking. In a very real sense, then, this chapter identifies the nominees' constituents—the actors that the secretaries-designate have, in their precabinet careers, recognized as politically relevant. It also involves considering whether the women secretaries-designate have indicated an awareness of women as their constituents.

SURVEYING THE SECRETARIES-DESIGNATE

Scholars of presidential nominations have examined the careers of the secretaries-designate in terms of three sets of variables. *Demographic variables* constitute the first set. Age, sex, race and ethnicity, marriage, and children preliminarily define a secretary-designate's life. Interpreting these variables, however, is difficult. Age is especially slippery. It can be indicative of generational experiences, which are often relevant to political decisionmaking.[1] Yet this conclusion must be carefully formulated and tested to ensure that the identified historical events actually had a formative effect.

Sex, race and ethnicity, marital status, and children are revelatory of societal strictures and expectations. Until recently, it has been the rare presidential appointee or nominee who was not male, white, married, and a father.[2] The classic Brookings Institution study, *Men Who Govern: A Biographical Profile of Federal Political Executives* (1967), was well named for its time.[3] Whites have similarly dominated in U.S. politics and in every profession from which cabinet officers have been recruited. Moreover, both men and whites have held on to their advantages with discriminatory practices that have denied women and people of color innumerable opportunities. Marriage and family also cut in two directions. First, a supportive spouse is an important emotional and professional resource. Second, a heterosexual marriage and children put the secretary-designate in obvious conformity with society's traditional normative standards.

Because demographic variables are the nominees' most easily identified characteristics, they are popular indicators of cabinet representation. Recognizing the significance of appearance, President Clinton carefully introduced his white male and "diversity" secretaries-designate in pairs in 1992 and 1996. The attendant press conferences and photo opportunities included extensive commentary on Clinton's commitment to an inclusive cabinet and administration. Though George W. Bush did not echo Clinton's campaign promises to diversify presidential nominations, he nonetheless continued the practice of pairing white male and "diversity" nominees in his initial introductions. Of course, as noted in the previous chapter, descriptive and symbolic representation turn on far more than the appearance of the cabinet nominees. Position, credibility, and prospective influence must be considered, none of which can be measured by demographic variables.[4]

Educational variables are the second set of descriptors for the secretaries-designate. The degrees they have earned, as well as the institutions attended as undergraduates and postgraduates, provide insight on the nominees' socioeconomic status and professional training. Matriculation from an elite college or university often confers access to powerful networks because these institutions participate in an elite credentialing process.[5] As much social as intellectual, an individual's educational experience fundamentally shapes his or her understanding. Education may also be suggestive of individual ambitions. With due consideration given patterns of economic and social segregation in the United States, the nominees' educational decisions may be indicative of their early career goals. The association between opportunity and ability is likely to be especially complex for the women secretaries-designate because many universities and professional schools were predominantly male until comparatively recently. Education thus affects a secretary-designate's performance as a representative along several dimensions, even years after the degrees have been received.

The third set of variables centers on the nominees' *occupation(s) or profession(s)*, both in their own right and as the basis for political alliances. The skills and abilities that secured the secretary-designate's success in other venues will transfer only approximately to the cabinet. The CEO of a Fortune 500 firm, for example, will not necessarily be an effective cabinet secretary.[6] Still, a nominee's precabinet employment is likely to be suggestive of her or his generalized approach to political leadership and departmental management.[7] Precisely because so many secretaries-designate have similar career paths, those experiences constitute a shared wisdom that may condition cabinet officers' responses to the presidency, their departments, and their constituents. Profession and politics become interactive, both ideologically and pragmatically, as values and proposals are conditioned by the nominees' working careers.[8] In brief, political and governmental variables forecast the nominees' practice of representation.

Profiling the secretaries-designate in terms of demographic, educational, and professional variables, then, provides insight into the representation that can be expected from these individuals. Similarities and differences, especially those systematically identified across generations, administrations, and sexes, suggest how representation has evolved throughout the modern presidency. As always, the concern is to identify the ways in which the individual and the office interact, either to regender or transgender the cabinet office, to contribute to the gender desegregation or integration of the cabinet.

Demographic Profiles

Societal developments occurring throughout the years spanned by this study have been extraordinary. The United States emerged from the Great Depression and began to participate in global markets. Technological innovations changed every aspect of life. The country engaged in wars, police actions, and innumerable smaller conflicts, and the provision of education through the G.I. Bill dramatically altered individual lives and national resources. There were civil rights movements for several races and ethnicities, women, and gays and lesbians. There were also backlashes that sometimes reversed and sometimes consolidated the accomplishments of these movements. This listing could continue indefinitely, and yet, in the midst of so much dynamism, the demographic profile of the cabinet secretaries-designate remained remarkably consistent.[9]

In the seven administrations with both initial and midterm nominees, secretaries-designate averaged 54.1 years of age at the time of their nomination (see Table 3.1). The youngest cabinet was Gerald Ford's, with an average age of 51.5 years at nomination. The oldest cabinets were those of Franklin Roosevelt and Dwight Eisenhower, whose secretaries-designate averaged 56.2 and 56.3 years, respectively. George W. Bush's initial cabinet was also considerably older, with his secretaries-designate averaging 57.5 years, but this may drop with his midterm nominations.

Categorizing the secretaries-designate by party era, Jeffrey Cohen found that the mean age of the nominees was as follows: 1789–1824, 43.6 years; 1825–1860, 50.6 years; 1861–1896, 52.9 years; 1897–1932, 54.0; and 1933–1984, 52.5 years. The cabinet nominees of both parties have therefore been "consistently and historically middle-aged."[10] (Increases in the average lifespan are taken by some to suggest that today's secretaries-designate are relatively younger than those in earlier generations.) Similarly, the Brookings study noted that cabinet nominations typically come at an individual's "vocational peak."[11] In this sense,

Table 3.1   Average Age of the Secretaries-Designate at the Time of Their
Nominations, by Administration (years, with frequency counts
in parentheses)

	Average Age	Women's Average Age	Men's Average Age
Roosevelt	56.2 (26)	51.0 (1)	56.4 (25)
Eisenhower	56.3 (21)	48.0 (1)	56.8 (20)
Ford	51.5 (13)	41.0 (1)	52.4 (12)
Carter	52.5 (21)	54.5 (4)	52.1 (17)
Reagan	54.8 (33)	48.3 (3)	55.5 (30)
G. H. W. Bush	55.7 (22)	52.3 (3)	56.5 (19)
Clinton	52.8 (31)	52.3 (6)	52.9 (25)
Average (overall)	54.1 (167)	51.0 (19)	54.5 (148)
Postscript: G. W. Bush's initial secretary-designates	57.5 (15)	49.8 (4)	60.3 (11)

the precabinet career justifies the nomination and conditions expectations about the secretary-designate's performance as a representative.

Comparing the women and men secretaries-designate, however, reveals that the women are typically younger. In fact, women have averaged 0.6 years (Clinton) to 11.4 years (Ford) younger than their male colleagues; only in the Carter administration was the average age of the women secretaries-designate (54.5 years) higher than that of the men (52.1 years).[12] In the George W. Bush initial cabinet, women secretaries-designate were, on average, 10.5 years younger than the men with whom they were nominated. These age differences provide the first indication of underlying differences in the women's and men's career paths. For successful professionals such as the cabinet nominees, the forties and fifties are years when a career begins to flourish. Younger secretaries may or may not have had the associated opportunities and experiences. Thus, their career development—and the breadth or extent of their representation—may be correspondingly more limited.

The vast majority of the secretaries-designate are white and male (see Table 3.2). There were 149 nominations (89.2 percent) of whites, 11 (6.6 percent) of African Americans, six (3.6 percent) of Hispanics, and one (0.6 percent) of Asian Americans.[13] The proportions of cabinet nominations of people of color ranged from zero (Roosevelt and Eisenhower) to 32.3 percent (Clinton). Among George W. Bush's initial cabinet nominees, 39.9 percent were people of color. Although the record is far from complete, this administration may provide people of color with more representation than any previous cabinet. Similarly, the proportion

Table 3.2   **Race and Ethnicity of the Secretaries-Designate, by Administration (percentages, with frequency counts in parentheses)**

	African American	Asian American	Hispanic	White
Roosevelt	0 (0)	0 (0)	0 (0)	100.0 (26)
Eisenhower	0 (0)	0 (0)	0 (0)	100.0 (21)
Ford	7.7 (1)	0 (0)	0 (0)	92.3 (12)
Carter	9.5 (2)[a]	0 (0)	0 (0)	90.5 (19)
Reagan	3.0 (1)	0 (0)	3.0 (1)	93.9 (31)
G. H. W. Bush	4.5 (1)	0 (0)	9.1 (2)	86.4 (19)
Clinton	19.4 (6)	3.2 (1)	9.7 (3)	67.7 (21)
Totals	6.6 (11)	0.6 (1)	3.6 (6)	89.2 (149)
Postscript: G. W. Bush's initial secretaries-designate	13.3 (2)	13.3 (2)	13.3 (2)	60.0 (9)

Notes: Percentages may not add to 100 because of rounding.

a. Patricia Roberts Harris received two cabinet nominations in the Carter administration and so is counted twice. A similar practice was followed for the "repeat players" in other administrations.

of cabinet nominations awarded to women ranged from 3.8 percent (in the Franklin Roosevelt administration) to 19.4 percent (in the Clinton administration). Here again George W. Bush set a high with his initial nominations, of whom 26.7 percent were women (see Table 3.3).[14]

Two conclusions are immediately clear from these tables. First, people of color and women have remained statistical tokens in the cabinet.[15] If, as the critical mass theorists predict, organizational change is effected only when 40 percent of the members share the formerly marginalized identity, then the cabinet is still in the early stages of its racial or gendered evolution. Second, the numbers—and the proportions—of people of color and of women nominees have increased most markedly in the later administrations, when the number of cabinet departments has also increased. Since "diversity" secretaries-designate are typically named to the younger departments in the outer cabinet, it is worth noting that their presence coincides with the "thickening" of government described by Paul Light.[16] For the women secretaries-designate, the effect has been to constrain their contributions as representatives and to slow the cabinet's gendered development, even as their relatively greater numbers seem to suggest that the administrative elite is becoming more "diversified."[17]

Table 3.3 Sex of the Secretaries-Designate, by Administration
(percentages, with frequency counts in parentheses)

	Female	Male
Roosevelt	3.8 (1)	96.2 (25)
Eisenhower	4.8 (1)	95.2 (20)
Ford	7.7 (1)	92.3 (12)
Carter	19.0 (4)	81.0 (17)
Reagan	9.1 (3)	90.9 (30)
G. H. W. Bush	13.6 (3)	86.4 (19)
Clinton	19.4 (6)	80.6 (25)
Totals	11.4 (19)	88.6 (148)
Postscript: G. W. Bush's initial secretaries-designate	26.7 (4)	73.3 (11)

Note: Percentages may not add to 100 because of rounding.

Marital status must be considered in simple terms (see Table 3.4). Secretaries-designate are incredibly reserved in regard to this aspect of their personal lives. Even the biographical profiles provided to the Senate confirmation committees seldom disclose divorces or annulments. It can be said with confidence, however, that the vast majority of secretaries-designate (93.4 percent) are married at the time of their nominations. As is true for people of color and women, higher proportions of unmarried people were nominated by Clinton (19.4 percent) and George W. Bush (13.3 percent).

Table 3.4 Marital Status of the Secretaries-Designate at the Time of
Their Nominations, by Administration (percentages, with
frequency counts in parentheses)

	Unmarried	Married	Unknown
Roosevelt	3.8 (1)	96.2 (25)	0 (0)
Eisenhower	4.8 (1)	95.2 (20)	0 (0)
Ford	0 (0)	100.0 (13)	0 (0)
Carter	4.8 (1)	95.2 (20)	0 (0)
Reagan	0 (0)	100.0 (33)	0 (0)
G. H. W. Bush	4.5 (1)	90.1 (20)	4.5 (1)
Clinton	19.4 (6)	80.6 (25)	0 (0)
Total	6.0 (10)	93.4 (156)	0.6 (1)
Postscript: G. W. Bush's initial secretaries-designate	13.3 (2)	86.7 (13)	0 (0)

Note: Percentages may not add to 100 because of rounding.

Table 3.5   Children of the Married Secretaries-Designate at the Time of
Their Nominations, by Administration (frequency counts in
parentheses)

	No Children (percent)	Have Children (percent)	Unknown (percent)	Among Nominees with Children (range)	Among Nominees with Children (average no.)
Roosevelt	11.5 (3)	69.2 (18)	19.2 (5)	1–7	2.67
Eisenhower	0 (0)	100.0 (21)	0 (0)	1–6	3.14
Ford	0 (0)	100.0 (13)	0 (0)	1–4	2.69
Carter	9.5 (2)	90.5 (19)	0 (0)	1–9	3.60
Reagan	3.0 (1)	97.0 (32)	0 (0)	1–10	3.24
G. H. W. Bush	0 (0)	90.9 (20)	9.1 (2)	1–10	3.50
Clinton	3.7 (1)	83.9 (26)	3.2 (1)	1–5	2.0
Overall Values	4.2 (7)	89.2 (149)	4.8 (8)	1–10	3.1
Postscript: G. W. Bush initial secretaries-designate	20.0 (3)	80.0 (12)	0 (0)	0–4	2.6

Notes: "Children" included stepchildren and adopted children. In instances in which the secretaries-designate were divorced, it was not possible to accurately determine which parent had custody; for the sake of consistency, it was therefore presumed that custody was always with the secretary-designate.

Percentages may not add up to 100 because of rounding.

Most married secretaries-designate have children (see Table 3.5). The number of children ranges from one to ten, with the average at just slightly over three. As with age, however, there are differences between the women and the men. Among the secretaries-designate with children the women have a narrower range of children than the men, with one-to-seven children for the women and one-to-ten children for the men. Moreover, when the women have more children, it is often as the result of marrying into a large family. George H. W. Bush labor secretary-designate Lynn Martin, for example, has two biological children and five stepchildren. Ford housing and urban development (HUD) secretary-designate Carla Anderson Hills has the greatest number of biological children (four).

Smaller families may be part of the women nominees' career planning. Appointments scholar Janet M. Martin hypothesizes as much, drawing on the example of Jane Cahill Pfeiffer. An IBM vice president, Pfeiffer declined a cabinet nomination in the Carter administration because she had recently married into a family of ten children. Pfeiffer felt that her responsibility to the children precluded her accepting the nomination. Juanita Kreps, the mother of three adult children, was nominated in her place.[18]

Family planning to accommodate professional ambitions, however, does run contrary to traditional conceptions of women's gender role. Particularly among the older generations of nominees, this decision would place the women secretaries-designate at odds with the societal norm. In more recent decades, it has become more accepted for women not to marry, to have childless marriages, or to delay having children. It does not seem coincidental that the proportions of unmarried women nominees rose dramatically in the Clinton and George W. Bush cabinets. Likewise, the number of children born to married women secretaries-designate dropped in these administrations. A woman secretary-designate contradicts one societal norm; an unmarried or childless woman secretary-designate contradicts several more, and thus these women entered the cabinet only after the strength of those norms had been weakened. To the extent that descriptive representation is about the appearance of the secretary-designate, then, the women secretaries-designate have shown some parallels with women in society in their marital and child-bearing profiles.

Demographically, there are important similarities and differences among the women and men secretaries-designate. Both women and men nominees are typically white and married, but the women are usually younger and have fewer children than the men. Thus, the women and men nominees are typically in conformity with and advantaged by certain societal expectations. Women, however, may enter the cabinet with less professional experience than men (a function of their age at nomination) and with greater awareness of the tensions between private lives and professional careers (given their family planning). If the women secretaries-designate perceive these patterns as inequitable and implicitly discriminatory, it may contribute to their substantive representation of women's interests in the cabinet. Such a calculus, however, would require the women nominees to generalize from their identities and ambitions *to* their policy agendas and recommendations. Such connections are not encouraged in all administrations. Still, the demographic variables suggest a difference in life experiences that could leave the women nominees at least more aware of women's distinctive social and economic circumstances.

Educational Profiles

Turning to the second set of variables, education, we see that the secretaries-designate were more extensively educated as the century progressed (see Table 3.6). As elites, the cabinet secretaries have been highly educated since the founding of the United States. By the Roosevelt administration, some college attendance had become the norm,

Table 3.6 Highest Educational Attainment of the Secretaries-Designate, by Administration (percentages, with frequency counts in parentheses)

	Roosevelt	Eisenhower	Ford	Carter	Reagan	G.H.W. Bush	Clinton	Average Percentage (across admin.)
All appointees								
Less than h.s.	—	4.8 (1)	—	—	—	—	—	0.6 (1)
High school	3.8 (1)	9.5 (2)	—	—	—	—	—	1.8 (3)
Attended college	19.2 (5)	14.3 (3)	15.4 (2)	9.5 (2)	—	—	3.2 (1)	8.4 (14)
College graduate	23.1 (6)	38.1 (8)	15.4 (2)	4.8 (1)	30.3 (10)	4.5 (1)	6.5 (2)	21.0 (35)
Master's degree	3.8 (1)	4.8 (1)	—	—	9.1 (3)	27.3 (6)	6.5 (2)	7.8 (13)
Law degree	42.3 (11)	28.6 (6)	38.5 (5)	61.9 (13)	45.5 (15)	27.3 (6)	64.5 (20)	44.9 (75)
Doctorate	—	—	30.8 (4)	23.8 (5)	15.2 (5)	27.3 (6)	19.4 (6)	13.8 (23)
Unknowns	7.7 (2)	—	—	—	—	13.6 (3)	—	1.8 (3)
Total	100.0 (26)	100.0 (21)	100.1 (13)	100.0 (21)	100.0 (33)	100.0 (22)	100.0 (31)	100.1 (167)
Women								
Less than h.s.	—	—	—	—	—	—	—	—
High school	—	—	—	—	—	—	—	—
Attended college	—	100.0 (1)	—	—	—	—	—	5.3 (1)
College graduate	—	—	—	—	33.3 (1)	33.3 (1)	16.7 (1)	15.8 (3)
Master's degree	100.0 (1)	—	—	—	—	33.3 (1)	—	10.5 (2)
Law degree	—	—	100.0 (1)	75.0 (3)	66.7 (2)	33.3 (1)	50.0 (3)	52.6 (10)
Doctorate	—	—	—	25.0 (1)	—	—	33.3 (2)	15.8 (3)
Unknowns	—	—	—	—	—	—	—	—
Total	100.0 (1)	100.0 (1)	100.0 (1)	100.0 (4)	100.0 (3)	99.9 (3)	100.0 (6)	100.0 (19)

continues

Table 3.6 Continued

Men	Roosevelt	Eisenhower	Ford	Carter	Reagan	G.H.W. Bush	Clinton	Average Percentage (across admin.)
Less than h.s.	—	5.0 (1)	—	—	—	—	—	0.7 (1)
High school	4.0 (1)	10.0 (2)	—	—	—	—	4.0 (1)	2.0 (3)
Attended college	20.0 (5)	10.0 (2)	16.7 (2)	11.8 (2)	—	5.3 (1)	4.0 (1)	8.8 (13)
College graduate	24.0 (6)	40.0 (8)	16.7 (2)	5.9 (1)	30.0 (9)	26.3 (5)	8.0 (2)	21.6 (32)
Master's degree	—	5.0 (1)	—	—	10.0 (3)	26.3 (5)	—	7.4 (11)
Law degree	44.0 (11)	30.0 (6)	33.3 (4)	58.8 (10)	43.3 (13)	26.3 (5)	68.0 (17)	43.9 (65)
Doctorate	—	—	33.3 (4)	23.5 (4)	16.7 (5)	15.8 (3)	16.0 (4)	13.5 (20)
Unknowns	8.0 (2)	—	—	5.9 (1)	—	—	—	2.0 (3)
Total	100.0 (25)	100.0 (20)	100.0 (12)	100.0 (18)	100.0 (30)	100.0 (19)	100.0 (25)	99.9 (148)

Postscript: G. W. Bush's initial secretaries-designate

	Women	Men	Total
Less than h.s.	—	—	—
High school	—	—	—
Attended college	—	—	—
College graduate	25.0 (1)	18.2 (2)	20.0 (3)
Master's degree	25.0 (1)	27.3 (3)	26.7 (4)
Law degree	50.0 (2)	45.5 (5)	46.7 (7)
Doctorate	—	9.1 (1)	6.7 (1)
Total	100.0 (4)	100.1 (11)	100.1 (15)

Notes: So that trends are more obvious, "0" has been replaced with a "—". Percentages may not add to 100 because of rounding.

and this trend was reinforced in later administrations.[19] More specifically, 69.2 percent of the Roosevelt secretaries-designate had graduated from college; in the Clinton cabinet, it was 96.8 percent. Every Reagan secretary-designate and every George W. Bush initial secretary-designate achieved this level of education. In regard to graduate degrees, the Democratic cabinets showed a steady increase, from 46.2 percent (Roosevelt) to 85.7 percent (Carter) to 90.3 percent (Clinton). After a leap upward, the Republican cabinets seem to have leveled off at a lower proportion, with 33.3 percent (Eisenhower) rising to 69.2 percent (Ford), then 69.7 percent (Reagan) and 68.2 percent (George H. W. Bush). The George W. Bush administration may bring another boost upward, with 80.0 percent of the initial nominees having graduate degrees. These statistics and trends set a high standard for the secretaries-designate, as only the most privileged of women would have the educational credentials to enter the cabinet as strong descriptive representatives for women.

Still, the women secretaries-designate have had educational credentials that typically equaled or exceeded those of their male colleagues.[20] With the exception of Eisenhower health, education, and welfare secretary-designate Oveta Culp Hobby, every woman secretary-designate has had a college degree. With the further exception of four labor secretaries-designate—Ann Dore McLaughlin, Lynn Martin, Alexis Herman, and Linda Chavez—the women nominees have also held professional or graduate degrees. Moreover, nine of the women (56.3 percent of those with advanced degrees) graduated from the same prestigious institutions (e.g., Harvard, Yale, Columbia, Duke, and Stanford Universities) attended by significant numbers of their male colleagues.[21] It is important to note that the women with less education, in relative terms, are clustered in the Labor Department. An outer cabinet post that is often distant from the president's agenda, this nomination granted women little influence in the cabinet and thereby constrained the possibility of meaningful symbolic representation. The relative lack of educational credentials on the part of some of the women labor secretaries-designate reinforces that pattern by diminishing the possibility of descriptive representation for women.

In general, however, the women secretaries-designate are among the most extensively educated women of their generations. They are even more singular because they have attended the same institutions of the elite men of their generations. Yet, once again, there are important contrasts in the life experiences of the women and men secretaries-designate. Carter education secretary-designate Shirley M. Hufstedler was one of two women in her Stanford Law School class. She graduated tenth in the class of 1949, having served as a law review editor, and was inducted into the Order of the Coif.[22] Reagan health and human services (HHS) secretary-designate Margaret Heckler was the only woman in the Boston College Law School class of 1956. She won the moot court competition every year, was an editor of the law review, and graduated sixth in her class.[23] Hufstedler and Heckler therefore earned high honors. Yet each was a token in her law school, subjected to heightened scrutiny and lacking a same-sex support network. Under these circumstances, mere endurance would be an achievement. These tokens, however, thrived. They successfully negotiated both the formal and the informal power structures of their predominantly male institutions. These skills and the associated trait of self-reliance are evident in every woman secretary-designate's educational history. Here are the character traits that suggest the women nominees will be able to capitalize on opportunities to provide meaningful representation for women. That not all women would be able to do so suggests the importance of the wider political context.

Professional, Partisan, and Political Profiles

The professions that feed into the cabinet have been consistent throughout its history, though they have been represented by varying proportions of secretaries-designate over the decades. Government service, business, education, and the legal profession have contributed the majority of cabinet nominees. (The political parties are another source, although fewer secretaries-designate have been drawn from their leadership across the modern presidency.[24]) The constancy with which secretaries-designate have been recruited from particular professions suggests that those professions are providing (and even controlling) the credentials deemed essential for cabinet officers. In doing so, these professions gain an opportunity to shape the character and extent of the representation offered by the cabinet nominees. For women, the extent of regendering or transgendering within the professions influences how (and even whether) these processes occur within the cabinet. This close relationship between the so-called feeder professions and cabinet representation dictates that the primary careers of the secretaries-designate be given careful consideration (see Table 3.7).[25]

Table 3.7 Primary Careers of the Secretaries-Designate, by Administration (percentages, with frequency counts in parentheses)

	Roosevelt	Eisenhower	Ford	Carter	Reagan	G.H.W. Bush	Clinton	Total
All secretaries-designate								
Governmental sector								
State, local	15.4 (4)	9.5 (2)	7.7 (1)	14.3 (3)	15.2 (5)	9.1 (2)	23.6 (7)	14.4 (24)
Members of Congress	11.5 (3)	0 (0)	7.7 (1)	14.3 (3)	9.1 (3)	27.3 (6)	23.6 (7)	13.8 (23)
Noncareer federal	11.5 (3)	0 (0)	7.7 (1)	9.5 (2)	9.1 (3)	9.1 (2)	0 (0)	6.6 (11)
Career federal	0 (0)	0 (0)	0 (0)	9.5 (2)	3.0 (1)	4.5 (1)	3.2 (1)	3.0 (5)
Public service (gen.)	11.5 (3)	14.3 (3)	15.4 (2)	9.5 (2)	9.1 (3)	18.2 (4)	0 (0)	10.2 (17)
Other	3.8 (1)	14.3 (3)	0 (0)	0 (0)	0 (0)	0 (0)	6.5 (2)	3.6 (6)
Subtotal	53.8 (14)	38.1 (8)	38.5 (5)	57.1 (12)	45.5 (15)	68.2 (15)	54.8 (17)	51.5 (86)
Private sector								
Business, banking	26.9 (7)	42.9 (9)	7.7 (1)	19.0 (4)	30.3 (10)	13.6 (3)	9.7 (3)	23.2 (37)
Law	3.8 (1)	4.8 (1)	15.4 (2)	9.5 (2)	13.1 (4)	9.1 (2)	16.1 (5)	10.2 (17)
Education, research	0 (0)	4.8 (1)	38.5 (5)	14.3 (3)	9.1 (3)	9.1 (2)	13.9 (4)	10.8 (18)
Political party	3.8 (1)	0 (0)	0 (0)	0 (0)	0 (0)	0 (0)	3.2 (1)	1.2 (2)
Other	11.5 (3)	9.5 (2)	0 (0)	0 (0)	3.0 (1)	0 (0)	3.2 (1)	4.2 (7)
Subtotal	46.2 (12)	61.9 (13)	61.5 (8)	43.9 (9)	54.5 (18)	31.8 (7)	45.2 (14)	48.5 (81)
Total	100.0 (26)	100.0 (21)	100.0 (13)	100.0 (21)	100.0 (33)	100.0 (22)	100.0 (31)	100.0 (167)

continues

Table 3.7 Continued

Postscript: G. W. Bush's initial secretaries-designate

Governmental sector	
State, local	6.7 (1)
Members of Congress	6.7 (1)
Noncareer federal	20.0 (3)
Career federal	6.7 (1)
Public service (gen.)	26.7 (4)
Other	6.7 (1)
Subtotal	73.3 (11)
Private sector	
Business, banking	13.3 (2)
Law	6.7 (1)
Education, research	0 (0)
Political party	6.7 (1)
Other	0 (0)
Subtotal	26.7 (4)
Total	100.0 (15)

Loosely grouping the secretaries-designate into the categories of government and private sector service, government service is revealed as the primary career of a slight majority of secretaries-designate in the Democratic administrations, whereas private sector service is the primary career of a majority of secretaries-designate in the Republican administrations.[26] The partisan contrast is only made more notable by the fact that the Democratic administrations entered the Oval Office after years of Republican presidential dominance. Democratic secretaries-designate, therefore, could not build their governmental careers through consecutive presidential administrations. The two Bush administrations are the exceptional cases. In these administrations, higher proportions of secretaries-designate had primary careers in government service. In fact, their percentages are higher than in any of the Democratic administrations.

Looking at the careers in more detail uncovers additional patterns. For the Democratic administrations, within the majority whose primary careers are in government, the largest single category is consistently that of state and local politics. These individuals are typically nominated to the outer cabinet. In the Carter and Clinton administrations, former members of the U.S. Congress were nominated in proportions similar to state and local officials. In the Roosevelt administration, the distribution of primary careers was relatively even, with the second largest career path being tied among members of Congress, noncareer federal positions, and public service throughout the government ("public service, general"). This distribution is also seen among Reagan secretaries-designate with government service careers. This nominee profile could reflect the desire of outsider presidents to gain an entrée for themselves and their policies into the Washington community, a motivation that could cause them to select more representatives from its networks.[27]

The Bush administrations, however, warn against easy distinctions between insider and outsider presidents. George H. W. Bush, with an extensive career in government service, nominated a majority of secretaries-designate whose precabinet careers were also in government service. Members of Congress were the largest single category, followed by those with careers throughout the government. Rather than evidencing a president's need to gain entry to the Washington community, these nominees seem reflective of their president's confidence in that community.[28] They are also indicative of the stress this president placed on selecting nominees with whom he had already worked.[29] George W. Bush selected an even greater proportion of government careerists for his initial cabinet. The largest single category of careers in his initial cabinet, though, were those who had served throughout the federal government, followed by those who had crafted a career of presidential and political appointments. George W. Bush had built a political career outside Washington, as governor of Texas, but he also claimed membership in the Washington community as the son of an insider president. Both factors are evident in his initial nominations, which, department by department, alternatively court favor with and claim membership in the Washington community.

In the remaining Republican administrations, the majority of cabinet secretaries-designate had primary careers centered in the private sector. For the Eisenhower and Reagan administrations, the largest percentage of private sector careers was in business. Business was also the highest proportion among those with private sector careers in the Roosevelt, Carter, and George H. W. Bush administrations. The emphasis upon recruiting businesspeople has been viewed as a product of the Republican platform, which has traditionally been responsive to—and predisposed to represent—business concerns. The fact that business has also predominated among private sector careers in Democratic cabinets, however, suggests that additional factors may be at work. There are departments, such as Treasury, where the business community expects one of its own to lead.[30] There may also be a more generalized sense that, notwithstanding the many differences between public and private sector management, a career spent in large corporate bureaucracies is good preparation for leading large public bureaucracies. Such perceptions create the connections between primary careers and representation that were postulated above.

In the Ford administration, however, the most frequent private sector primary career was in research foundations and education. Though these institutions have contributed secretaries-designate to every administration except Roosevelt's, the numbers are otherwise small. That secretaries-designate with these primary careers would be so disproportionately present in the Ford administration seems further evidence that this president was recruiting individuals whose credentials would be unassailable. In this administration, the Washington community found its representation limited, as the president sought to distance himself and his administration from the corruption associated with "insider politics."

The exceptional administrations notwithstanding, the basic patterns are clear. Government service is the predominant primary career among Democratic secretaries-designate, whereas private sector service predominates among the Republican secretaries-designate. The women's credentials having otherwise been similar to those of the men with whom they were nominated, we would expect their careers to reflect these partisan contrasts. Alternatively, disproportionate numbers of the women secretaries-designate could have primary careers in government service, which would offer demonstrable proof of their political leadership and executive management. At the same time, as their working experiences became more limited, so also would their expertise, their networks, and their capacity to serve as representatives.

In fact, unlike the men secretaries-designate, the women did not evidence partisan differences in their primary careers. Even though the careers of the women and the men were affected by some of the same historical events, such as partisan control of the Oval Office, both the Republican and Democratic women typically had primary careers centered in government service. If women brought a greater background in government to the cabinet, then they also had a more limited set of professional experiences on which to draw as cabinet representatives.

The contrast between the men and women secretaries-designate was, not surprisingly, most evident in Republican administrations. In the Eisenhower, Ford, and Reagan administrations, 58.3 to 60.0 percent of the men secretaries-designate had primary careers in the private sector. These proportions dropped to 31.6 percent in the George H. W. Bush administration and 36.4 percent in the George W. Bush administration. The women among the Eisenhower and Ford secretaries-designate—one in each administration—were also drawn from the private sector. Among the women subsequently nominated by Republican presidents, however, only George H. W. Bush commerce secretary-designate Barbara Franklin had a primary career in the private sector. Cumulatively, then, only three of the twelve Republican women secretaries-designate (25.0 percent) had primary careers in the private sector. In the Reagan, George H. W. Bush, and George W. Bush administrations, women and men secretaries-designate had different precabinet professional experiences and networks. If the men's career experiences were more congruent with presidential priorities, the women secretaries-designate could be at a disadvantage.

The contrasts were less notable in Democratic administrations. Among the men secretaries-designate, a slight majority in the Roosevelt and Carter administrations (52.0 and 52.9 percent, respectively) and a definite majority in the Clinton administration (60.0 percent) had primary careers in the government. Likewise, five of the nine Democratic women secretaries-designate (55.6 percent) had their primary career in government service. Of the remaining five women nominees, four arguably had primary careers in the private sector because their party did not control the presidency from 1981 to 1993.[31] The careers of Clinton secretaries-designate Shalala, O'Leary, Baird, and Albright all suggest that a career outside the national government was a matter of partisan necessity rather than professional choice.[32]

This distribution of primary careers reflects enduring patterns of differential treatment in the private sector, which has historically kept women out of the high-level positions from which cabinet secretaries-designate are routinely recruited. Though the government's record is far from perfect, it has gradually provided women with greater opportunities in a number of policy arenas.[33] Government service, therefore, may have been the career path that provided the women nominees with the credentials and the contacts to be identified as prospective cabinet members.

Career Paths

This demographic, educational, professional, and political survey has confirmed that the secretaries-designate are more similar than different, even across presidential administrations and partisan divides. And yet, the differences between the women and the men secretaries-designate are not insignificant. A sex-based comparison reveals that the women tend to be younger and to have fewer biological children than the men. Several of the women attended schools in which they were in the minority, beginning their careers as "gender outsiders" early. Finally, women more often and more consistently had primary careers in government service; among the men, higher proportions of Democrats had a primary career in governmental service, but higher proportions of Republicans had a primary career in the private sector. The ramifications of these sex-based distinctions for representation in the cabinet cannot be ignored.

As a group, the women secretaries-designate are more similar than are the men secretaries-designate. To the extent that the nominees' performance as representatives will be associated with their career path and life experiences, the congruence of the women's lives may limit their contributions. The women are also younger than the men, and their careers tend to be more coherent and monolithic. This trait may compromise the women's descriptive representation to the extent that they lack the range of credentials and relationships that may be claimed by their male colleagues. As their representation is narrowed, the women may find that they can be more easily subordinated and marginalized within the cabinet. The effect would then be to regender, not to transgender, cabinet nominations.

There are two important provisos to these conclusions, however. First, these comparisons of the women to the men secretaries-designate are likely to be very conservative in their estimations of the potential for change. To the extent that the women's anticipated performance as representatives is measured in reference to historical standards and practices, which are infused with masculinist presumptions, the comparisons will be less indicative of the women's prospective contributions than of their past and present conformity. Second, and related to the first, the women secretaries-designate need to be studied in their own right. The circumstances surrounding the women's nominations as cabinet nominees, as well as their provision of descriptive, substantive, and symbolic representation, can then be more fully appreciated. The innovations effected by women's inclusion among the secretaries-designate may be more evident and the regendering or transgendering of cabinet office more precisely delineated. The next section therefore examines the career paths of the women secretaries-designate in the broader context of studies of women's socialization as political leaders.

THE WOMEN SECRETARIES-DESIGNATE

Rita Mae Kelly, Mary Boutilier, and Mary Lewis observed that women, in pursuing political careers, stepped outside established gender roles. Time and again, their careers raised challenging questions about the connections between personal identity and professional opportunity, and their accomplishments contradicted easy associations of politics with masculinity.[34] As a result, women leaders were often particularly conscious of their gender identity, and their careers were distinguished by self-examination and political initiative. Specifically, Kelly, Boutilier, and Lewis concluded that women leaders had four formative events in common.

(1) As a girl, [the prospective woman leader] must "develop an activist modern sex-role ideology" that will enable her to envision

herself in nontraditional roles, (2) she must attain a sense of personal control over her life, (3) politics must become salient to her, [and] (4) she must experience some political success at crucial points in her life.[35]

Without question, these events are affected by the social, political, and historical context of the women's lives.

The way in which women leaders acquire a "modern" sex-role ideology, for example, is likely to be especially reflective of their circumstances. It may be that, as more women enter politics, aspiring to this career is perceived as less "nontraditional" for women. An anecdote drawn from opening paragraphs of a *New York Times* article about Reagan health and human services secretary-designate Margaret M. Heckler illustrates this point.

> Years ago when Margaret M. Heckler was an elected member of the Massachusetts Governor's Executive Council, her 4-year-old son announced one day, "When I grow up, I am going to be Governor."
> "You can't, silly," his 6-year-old sister Alison informed John Jr. loftily. "You're a boy."[36]

As women hold political office with greater frequency, other women may more easily envision themselves in this profession. The "sex-role ideology" may, accordingly, change. Women may see politics as a constructively challenging and inherently rewarding pursuit. Yet the converse may also occur. If women leaders cannot serve as strong representatives—if their recommendations are dismissed, their credibility is undercut, and their contributions are marginalized—then other women may become politically alienated in their personal and professional lives. In order to explore how the personal, professional, and political intersect in the lives of the women secretaries-designate, the following sections examine their career paths in some detail.

The Personal and the Political

The women nominees' family of origin and their educational opportunities were critical aspects of their personal and professional development, often providing social and economic advantages (see Table 3.8). There was frequently a presumption that the future secretaries-designate would be successful professionals. Thus, in many cases, the nom-

Table 3.8 Family of Origin, Education, Marriage, and Children of the Women Secretaries-Designate

Name	Family of Origin	Education	Marriage	Children
Francis Perkins	Father, businessman; one younger sister	1902, B.A., Mt. Holyoke 1910, M.A., Columbia University	1913, Paul Wilson, NYC mayoral adviser	Two daughters, one surviving childbirth
Oveta Culp Hobby	Mother, suffragist; father, state legislator; seven siblings	Attended Mary Hardin–Baylor Coll. Attended University of Texas Law School	1931, William Pettus Hobby, publisher, former governor	One daughter, one son
Carla Anderson Hills	Father, businessman; one older brother	1955, B.A. *cum laude*, Stanford 1958, Yale Law School degree	1957, Roderick Hills, attorney	Three daughters, one son
Juanita Kreps	Father, mine operator; five older siblings	1942, B.A., Berea College 1944, M.A. Duke University 1946, Ph.D., Duke University	1944, Clifton H. Kreps, Jr., professor	Two daughters, one son
Patricia Roberts Harris	Mother, schoolteacher; father, Pullman porter; one brother	1945, B.A. *summa cum laude*, Howard University 1960, George Washington University Law School degree	1955, William Beasley Harris, professor	None
Shirley M. Hufstedler	Mother, schoolteacher; father, construction foreman; one older brother	1945, B.A., University of New Mexico 1949, Stanford Law School degree	1949, Seth M. Hufstedler, attorney	One son
Elizabeth Hanford Dole	Father, businessman; one older brother	1958, B.A., Duke University 1960, M.A.T., Harvard University 1965, Harvard Law School degree	1975, Robert Dole, senator (R-Kans.), presidential candidate	None, one stepdaughter
Margaret M. Heckler	Father, hotel doorman; no siblings	1953, B.A., Albertus Magnus College 1956, Boston College Law School degree	1953, John Heckler (later divorced), attorney	Three daughters, one son

continues

Table 3.8 Continued

Name	Family of Origin	Education	Marriage	Children
Ann Dore McLaughlin		1963, B.A., Marymount College	1965, William Dore, (later divorced); 1975, John McLaughlin (later divorced) political commentator	None
Lynn Martin	Father, accountant; one older sister	1960, B.A., University of Illinois–Champagne-Urbana	1960, John Martin (later divorced); 1975, Harry D. Leinenweber, judge	Two daughters, five stepchildren
Barbara Hackman Franklin	Mother, schoolteacher; father, school superintendent	1962, B.A. with honors, Pennsylvania State Univ. 1964, M.B.A., Harvard Business School	Two marriages and divorces; 1986, Wallace Barnes, businessman	None
Donna E. Shalala	Mother, teacher, later attorney; father, businessman; one twin sister	1962, B.A. with honors, Western College for Women 1968, MSSC, Maxwell School 1970, Ph.D., Maxwell School	Never married	None
Hazel Rollins O'Leary	Mother, physician; father, physician; stepmother, schoolteacher; one sibling	1959, B.A. *cum laude*, Fisk University 1966, Rutgers University Law School degree	Carl Rollins (later divorced); John O'Leary, energy policy consultant (widowed)	One son
Zoë E. Baird		1972, B.A. with great distinction, Univ. of California–Berkeley 1975, Univ. of California–Berkeley Law School degree	1986, Paul David Gewirtz, professor	One son

continues

Table 3.8 Continued

Name	Family of Origin	Education	Marriage	Children
Janet Reno	Mother, newspaper reporter; father, newspaper reporter; two younger brothers, one younger sister	1960, B.A., Cornell University 1963, Harvard Law School degree	Never married	None; two wards
Madeleine Korbel Albright	Mother, clerk; father, diplomat, later professor; one younger brother, one younger sister	1959, B.A. with honors, Wellesley College 1968, M.A., Columbia University 1976, Ph.D., Columbia University	1959, Joseph M.P. Albright (later divorced), publishing heir	Three daughters
Alexis M. Herman	Mother, reading teacher; father, mortician	1969, B.A. with honors, Xavier University	Never married	None
Ann M. Veneman	Father, gubernatorial and presidential appointee	B.A., University of California–Davis M.P.P., University of California–Berkeley Hastings College of Law degree		
Gale A. Norton		1975, B.A. *magna cum laude*, University of Denver 1978, University of Denver Law School degree	John Hughes, attorney	None
Linda Chavez	Mother, retail clerk; father, housepainter; no living siblings	1970, B.A., University of Colorado attended Ph.D. program, University of California–Los Angeles	1967, Chris Gersten, political consultant	Three sons
Elaine Lan Chao	Father, businessman; five younger sisters	1975, B.A., Mt. Holyoke College 1979, M.B.A., Harvard Business School	Mitch McConnell, senator (R-Ky.)	Three stepchildren

Notes: Several of the women secretaries-designate have declined to discuss their families of origin, their marriages, or their children. This listing is as complete as circumstances permit.

inees' family of origin provided the activist sex role and the sense of personal control that Kelly, Boutilier, and Lewis deem essential to the development of women leaders. Education, sometimes in concert with and sometimes in place of family, similarly often provided the future secretaries-designate with a sense of self-esteem and self-worth that fueled hopes and ambitions.

The women nominees were typically raised in homes of at least middle-class comfort.[37] Six of the women (28.6 percent) came from elite families; they were raised in wealth or with the benefits of other forms of social status. Oveta Culp Hobby, Carla Anderson Hills, and Elizabeth Hanford Dole, for example, came from families known throughout their home state for their standing in social or business communities.[38] Equally notable, twelve of the women secretaries-designate (57.1 percent) had fathers who owned their own business or otherwise controlled the course of their professional lives.[39] The range of enterprises was extraordinary, including sales, manufacturing, and the professions. An entrepreneurial spirit, therefore, was demonstrated more often than not in the nominees' family of origin.

Giving specific impetus to a political career, five women (23.8 percent) came from families in which at least one parent held some form of political office. Oveta Culp Hobby's father was a state legislator; he encouraged her to study law and helped her to get a staff position in the Texas state legislature. Her mother was active in the movement for women's suffrage. Barbara Hackman Franklin's father was a school superintendent. Madeleine Korbel Albright's father was a diplomat and, she believed, one of the greatest influences in her life. Alexis Herman's father was one of the first black ward bosses in Alabama; he confronted great opposition from the Ku Klux Klan throughout her childhood and yet remained constant in his political activism. Ann Veneman's father received gubernatorial appointments to offices in California state government and a presidential appointment to the Department of Health, Education, and Welfare during the Nixon administration. Still other parents gave evidence of being active in their communities, though they do not seem to have held government or party offices. Included in this category are Patricia Robert Harris's father (a Pullman porter) and Donna Shalala's father (owner of a chain of grocery stores). Seven women (33.3 percent), then, came from families in which political leadership was valued as a personal and, often, professional commitment. In the language of Kelly, Boutilier, and Lewis, these parents made politics salient for their children.

No less important, a number of the women secretaries-designate had mothers who were professionals themselves. Though this information is not available for all of the women nominees, it is known that six mothers or stepmothers were teachers.[40] (Donna Shalala's mother was a teacher, and became a lawyer after returning to school.) Two other mothers practiced other professions, namely, medicine (O'Leary) and journalism (Reno), and at least two more held clerical positions (Albright and Chavez). These mothers served, at least potentially, as a support system for their daughter's ambitions. In sum, the parents of the women secretaries-designate were powerful role models of ambition and engagement.

Of course, every generalization invites contradiction, and two brief examples serve to indicate the underlying diversity in the nominees' families of origin. Juanita Kreps was one of six children. Born and raised in Appalachia, where her father was a mine operator, her parents were divorced when she was four. At age twelve, her mother brought her to a church school, where she lived until she left for Berea College. Elizabeth Hanford Dole was the second child in an eminent North Carolina family and was expected to marry well. When she announced that she would be attending Harvard Law School, after earning her teaching degrees and doing some modeling, her parents were shocked. In her autobiography, Dole recorded, she woke up one night to learn that the emotional upheaval created by her decision had made her mother physically ill.[41] The social and economic circumstances of these two women could not be more different, and yet there is a commonalty in the lack of parental support for their ambitions. The women secretaries-designate did have to confront various disadvantages, though these were muted in the greater number of cases.

When the women secretaries-designate married and began to build their own families, they generally married men who encouraged their political ambitions and entrepreneurial abilities.[42] Marriage has often ended a woman's career outside the home because gender role expectations draw her into the private sphere. Yet marriage was a psychological and professional resource for a number of the women secretaries-designate. Eleven women (52.4 percent)—Frances Perkins, Oveta Culp Hobby, Carla Anderson Hills, Juanita Kreps, Shirley Hufstedler, Elizabeth Hanford Dole, Ann Dore McLaughlin, Barbara Hackman Franklin, Hazel O'Leary, Gale Norton, and Linda Chavez—married men in precisely the same profession as themselves. Five others (23.8 percent)—Patricia Roberts Harris, Margaret Heckler, Lynn Martin, Zoë

Baird, and Elaine Chao—married men in related professions.[43] Hills and Hufstedler were members or associates of their husbands' law firms at a time when women could seldom find positions in private law firms. Harris and Heckler both acknowledged the encouragement of their husbands throughout their careers; Heckler's husband served as her campaign manager throughout her career in Massachusetts state politics and for much of her time in the U.S. House of Representatives. Additional examples could be given, but it is enough to say that the women secretaries-designate often had husbands who were active in politics, shared their partisan commitments, and supported their accomplishments. The wives and the husbands in these partnership marriages shared a dedication to the public sphere. In this sense, their personal lives were transgendered. To the extent that this aspect of their marital relationship was made public—and the media coverage of some families was extensive—the symbolic representation of the women secretaries-designate related to the public and the private sphere.

Still, it is important to consider the timing of the marriages, as a number of women only met their husbands after they had established their careers in politics. In these cases—which include Elizabeth Hanford Dole, Hazel O'Leary, Zoë Baird, and Elaine Chao—the husband doubtless reinforced the wife's ambitions but was a less formative influence. In other instances, the husbands did not contribute to the women's advancement. Frances Perkins's husband was in very poor health throughout their married life; she was the sole source of income for their family.[44] Madeleine Albright's political career gained momentum after her divorce. Though husbands were often a source of support for the women secretaries-designate, therefore, the pattern was far from constant or unqualified.

Education also fostered the women's ambitions. College, graduate, and professional degrees are credentials. They testify that an individual has undergone a particular kind of socialization and now claims membership in certain networks. The significance of being educated at an elite institution is found in just these resources. The women nominees have kept pace with the men: nine women secretaries-designate attended prestigious institutions. Yet there is another, less obvious dimension to the women's educational experience.

At its best, education encourages a sense of personal control in its participants. As Kelly, Boutilier, and Lewis explain, a strong sense of self is essential if the woman leader is to withstand the social expectations attributed to her gender and the failures that inevitably accompany a political career. Notably, all the African American women secretaries-designate were educated at historically black colleges or universities.[45] In regard to gender, the majority of the women secretaries-designate (14; 66.7 percent) had the experience of either de jure or de facto single-sex education. "De jure" refers to those women who graduated from women's colleges. By their own rules, these colleges were prohibited from issuing degrees to men. Seven (33.3 percent) of the women attended women's colleges, namely, Perkins, Hobby, Heckler, McLaughlin, Shalala, Albright, and Chao. Additionally, Elizabeth Dole attended Duke University at a time when residence halls, student government associations, and undergraduate courses were single sex. "De facto" refers to those schools that could award a degree to either sex but enrolled an overwhelming preponderance of one sex. Examining the ratio of women to men in their graduating classes, at least ten of the women secretaries-designate (47.6 percent) attended predominantly male professional and graduate programs.[46] Fourteen women secretaries-designate had one or both of these single-sex educational experiences.

The point is not to equate the women's attendance at a women's college with their enrollment in predominantly male graduate or professional program. The two are quite distinct. Yet they are not altogether contradictory. Women's colleges have a long and proud tradition of instilling confidence and strength in their students. Gender is acknowledged, but gender role constraints are not. As a result, a graduate of one of these institutions is likely to be more self-aware, attuned to connections between her identity and her professional development. This same sensitivity is likely to be acquired by women who graduate as minority members of graduate or professional programs. By their presence, these women claim opportunities previously reserved to men. To be successful, these women will have to develop self-esteem and self-reliance and be dedicated to their career goals. By different routes and very different means, therefore, the educational experiences of the women secretaries-designate have instilled a commitment to transgendering personal and professional lives.

Family and education, therefore, contributed to the women nominees' socialization as political leaders. Parents, husbands, and educators, in various combinations, encouraged the women to step outside traditional gender roles, developing their talents and testing their abilities. They presented politics as an important commitment, a viable and rewarding profession. Along the way, the women gained a sense of self-worth and autonomy that was manifested in their professional lives.

Ambition and Opportunity: Precabinet Careers

Kelly, Boutilier, and Lewis note that the resilience of women leaders is constantly tested, obliging them to constantly renew their ambitions and commitments. Success also becomes essential lest the challenges become disheartening. These dynamics are very evident in the precabinet careers of the women secretaries-designate (see Table 3.9). Each has been a "first woman" in countless settings and has repeatedly been promoted through organizational hierarchies. They have been remarkable entrepreneurs, achieving many of their goals.

The vast majority of women began their careers in professions that were predominantly (and sometimes exclusively) male. Five women (23.8 percent) launched their careers through the practice of law, and three (14.3 percent) started in business, two (9.5 percent) in nonprofit organizations, and six (28.6 percent) in government or political office.[47] Five of the women (23.8 percent) were teachers, a profession traditionally ceded to women.[48] Perkins, Dole, and Martin left teaching for politics; Shalala and Kreps were university professors and later presidents and deans. The women secretaries-designate, self-evidently, were not content with traditional careers.

As their lives evolved and their primary careers took shape, there was a pronounced shift into government office. Only Juanita Kreps had not held a full-time government office before receiving her cabinet nomination. Even so, she had been appointed to a number of committees and commissions and had been a policy adviser in the Carter campaign. Eighteen of the women secretaries-designate (85.7 percent) had previously held a full-time position in the national government.[49] Even more indicative of the nominees' precabinet political experience, fifteen (71.4 percent) had served in the executive branch,[50] four (19.0 percent) in the department they were nominated to lead,[51] and six (28.6 percent) on the White House staff or in the Executive Office of the President.[52]

Of course, hindsight makes careers seem far more coherent and certain, disposing of individual uncertainties and dismissing serendipity. The richness of these careers and the complexity of the women's socialization should not, however, be overlooked. Frances Perkins's career path offers insight into some of the difficulties confronted by women nominees. In her case, the progression from interest group leader and legislative lobbyist to labor mediator and state government executive to U.S. cabinet secretary has an appealing linearity. Perkins's contacts among an influential network of social reformers, coupled

continues

Table 3.9 Precabinet Career Chronologies of the Women Secretaries-Designate

Name	Precabinet Career Chronology
Frances Perkins	~1907–1913, social reform organizations, staff member and officer 1913–1918, part-time affiliations with social reform organizations 1918–1932, New York gubernatorial appointments by Al Smith and Franklin D. Roosevelt (brief return to social reform organizations when Smith lost 1920 election) 1933–1945, Secretary of Labor
Oveta Culp Hobby	1925–1931, Texas state legislature, staff member and parliamentarian; Texas State Banking Department, clerk; Houston city attorney's office, assistant 1931–death, Houston *Post*, promoted through the ranks until coeditor and publisher (1952) 1941–1945, War Department, becoming director (colonel) of the Women's Auxiliary Army Corps 1953–1955, Secretary of Health, Education, and Labor
Carla Anderson Hills	1958–1961, Justice Department, assistant U.S. attorney 1962–1974, private practice (associated with husband's law firm) 1974–1975, Justice Department, Civil Division, assistant attorney general 1975–1977, Secretary of Housing and Urban Development
Juanita Kreps	1946–1955, college professor affiliated with various institutions 1955–retirement, Duke University, promoted through the ranks, becoming a chaired professor (also held a variety of administrative posts) Throughout, corporate board member, presidential and congressional commissions member 1977–1979, Secretary of Commerce
Patricia Roberts Harris	1945–1959, women's, African American, and human rights organizations, staff member and officer 1960–1969, Howard Law School faculty member 1969–1976, Fried, Frank, Harris, Shriver, and Kampelman (law firm), partner 1976–1979, Secretary of Housing and Urban Development 1979–1981, Secretary of Health, Education, and Welfare/Health and Human Services Throughout, presidential commissions and advisory committees; first African American ambassador (1965–1967); Democratic National Committee affiliations; and work with the D.C. court system

continues

Table 3.9 Continued

Name	Precabinet Career Chronology
Shirley M. Hufstedler	1950–1960, private practice (solo practitioner)
	1960–1962, Office of the California Attorney General, consultant
	Gubernatorial appointment to fill an unexpired term on the Los Angeles County Superior Court
	1962–1966, Los Angeles County Superior Court, judge (elected)
	1966–1968, California State Court of Appeals for the Second District, judge (gubernatorial appointment)
	1968–1979, U.S. Court of Appeals for the Ninth Circuit, judge (presidential appointment)
	1979–1981, Secretary of Education
Elizabeth Hanford Dole	1967–1968, private practice
	1968–1973, Health, Education, and Welfare Department, staff assistant; White House staff, consumer affairs
	1973–1979, Federal Trade Commission, commissioner
	1980, Dole presidential campaign; later, Voters for Reagan/Bush, chair and Reagan/Bush Truth Squad member
	1981–1983, White House, Office of Public Liaison, director
	1983–1987, Secretary of Transportation
	1987–1988, Dole presidential campaign; later, George H. W. Bush presidential campaign
	1989–1990, Secretary of Labor
Margaret M. Heckler	1958–1960, private practice and Wellesley Republican Town Committee member (elected)
	1962–1966, Massachusetts Governor's Council, member (elected)
	1966–1983, U.S. House of Representatives
	1983–1985, Secretary of Health and Human Services
Ann Dore McLaughlin	1963–1965, ABC-TV, broadcast scheduling supervisor
	1965–1968, Marymount College, director of alumnae relations
	1969–1971, corporate consultant
	1971–1973, Nixon campaign and administration: CREP and inaugural committee communications director, Environmental Protection Agency, office of public affairs
	1974–1978, Union Carbide Corporation, communications manager for state and local government relations
	1979–1980, Robert Dole campaign treasurer; later, Maureen Reagan's press secretary
	1981–1987, Reagan administration: U.S. Treasury Department, assistant secretary, Interior Department, undersecretary
	1987–1989, Secretary of Labor

Table 3.9 Continued

Name	Precabinet Career Chronology
Lynn Martin	1972–1976, Winnebago (Illinois) County Board 1976–1981, Illinois state legislature, House of Representatives (1976–1978) and Senate (1978–1981) 1981–1990, U.S. House of Representatives 1984 and 1988, Reagan/Bush and Bush campaign officer 1991–1993, Secretary of Labor
Barbara Hackman Franklin	1964–1971, corporate officer 1971–1973, White House, staff assistant recruiting women to the administration 1973–1980, U.S. Consumer Product Safety Commission, commissioner 1980–1992, corporate consultant and member of various boards of directors 1992, Bush campaign national finance vice chair 1992–1993, Secretary of Commerce
Donna E. Shalala	1970–1979, college professor, affiliated with Bernard Baruch College and then Teacher's College; also director and treasurer of the Municipal Assistance Corporation (1975–1977) 1977–1979, Housing and Urban Development Department, assistant secretary for policy development and research 1980–1987, Hunter College, president 1987–1993, University of Wisconsin—Madison, chancellor 1993–2001, Secretary of Health and Human Services
Hazel Rollins O'Leary	1966–1968, New Jersey government, legal services program administrator, later assistant attorney general 1972–1974, Cost of Living Council, Public Sector Division, director 1977–1981, Federal Energy Administration/Energy Department posts 1981–1989, founded an energy consulting firm 1989–1993, Northern States Power company, Natural Gas Division, president and CEO 1993–1997, Secretary of Energy

continues

Table 3.9 Continued

Name	Precabinet Career Chronology
Zoë E. Baird	1979–1981, Carter administration, Justice Department, Office of Legal Counsel, staff attorney; White House counsel's office, associate counsel
	1981–1986, Melveny and Myers (law firm), partner
	1986–1993, corporate counsel with General Electric Company and later with Aetna Life and Casualty Insurance Company
Janet Reno	1963–1971, private practice
	1971–1976, Florida state government, legislative staff member, later recruited to the Dade County State Attorney Office
	1976–1993, Dade County State Attorney
	Gubernatorial appointment to fill an unexpired term as Dade County State Attorney, subsequently elected and reelected (four times)
	Throughout, membership in various legal and social issues organizations and on a federal judicial nominating commission (1976–1978)
	1993–2001, Attorney General
Madeleine Korbel Albright	1976–1978, Senator Edmund S. Muskie (D-Maine), chief legislative assistant
	1978–1981, National Security Council staff, congressional liaison officer
	1982–1993, Georgetown University, professor and academic program director; throughout this time, she also served as a foreign policy adviser to Democratic presidential candidates
	1997–2001, Secretary of State
Alexis M. Herman	1969–1977, Recruitment and Training Program (nonprofit organization), becoming director
	1977–1981, Labor Department, Women's Bureau, director
	1981–1989, founded an affirmative action and employment consulting agency
	1989–1993, Democratic National Committee, chief of staff (1989), deputy chairwoman (1989–1991), chief executive officer of the 1992 DNC convention committee (1992)
	1993–1997, White House, Office of Public Liaison, director
	1997–2001, Secretary of Labor

continues

Table 3.9 Continued

Name	Precabinet Career Chronology
Ann M. Veneman	Legal practice as a public defender with the Bay Area Rapid Transit authority 1986–1993, Agriculture Department, rising to the position of deputy secretary 1993–1995, legal practice in Washington, D.C. 1995–1999, California State Department of Food and Agriculture, secretary 1999–2001, legal practice in Sacramento, California 2001–present, Secretary of Agriculture
Gale A. Norton	1978–1979, Colorado Court of Appeals, clerk 1979–1983, Mountain States Legal Foundation, senior attorney 1983–1984, Stanford University, Hoover Institution, national fellow 1984–1987, Reagan administration, U.S. Agriculture Department, deputy secretary (1984–1985), Interior Department, associate solicitor (1985–1987) 1987–1991, private practice 1991–1998, Colorado attorney general 2001–present, Secretary of the Interior
Linda Chavez	1972–1974, Democratic National Committee 1977–1983, *American Educator*, editor 1983–1985, Reagan administration, Commission on Civil Rights, staff director (1983–1985), White House, Office of Public Liaison, director (1985–1986) 1986, campaign for U.S. Senate seat in Maryland (lost to Barbara Mikulski) 1987–1988, U.S. English, president 1992–1996, UN Subcommittee on Human Rights, consultant 1995–2001, Center for Equal Opportunity, founder and president
Elaine Lan Chao	1979–1986, corporate positions (Citicorp and Bank America) and White House Fellow (1983–1984) 1986–1992, Reagan and Bush administrations, Transportation Department, deputy administrator (1986–1988) and deputy secretary (1989–1991), Federal Maritime Commission, chair (1988–1989), Peace Corps, director (1991–1992) 1992–1996, United Way, president and CEO 1996–2001, Heritage Foundation, distinguished fellow 2001–present, Secretary of Labor

with her contributions to key state and national campaigns, seem the crucial elements of her success. Historians have described the time surrounding the passage of the Nineteenth Amendment and extending into the New Deal as one of extraordinary political opportunity for women. For this brief period, it seemed that all the gender barriers would be lowered. Perkins's career, though clearly predicated on her exceptional abilities, shows that this optimism had some basis in reality. Women voters were recognized by the president and represented by a woman with ties to a powerful network of women social reformers.[53] In other words, women voters received descriptive, substantive, and symbolic representation through the Perkins nomination. Formal representation undermined the workings of masculinism.

Without detracting from this conclusion, it is important to remember that Perkins was also driven by her need to have full-time paid employment to support her family. Economic need and family commitments always conditioned her choices. She initially declined the cabinet nomination because she could neither move her husband from New York nor afford to maintain two residences. These difficulties were resolved by sharing Washington accommodations and by taking the train, almost every weekend of the twelve years she spent in the cabinet, to New York to visit her husband.[54] Her life suggests that the sense of personal control and the need for success at crucial moments, both of which Kelly, Boutilier, and Lewis view as essential to the socialization of a woman leader, may be prerequisites for survival, not the luxuries of professional advancement.

Perkins's career path is also illustrative for its intermingling of contexts in which she was a gender outsider with those in which she was a gender insider. Consider the following partial listing of the women nominees' gender insider (women-centered) activities: Perkins's connections to predominantly female networks for social reform; Hobby's leadership of the Women's Auxiliary Army Corps during World War II; Kreps' research on women in the workforce; Dole's commitment to education and consumer issues, the latter shared with O'Leary; Heckler's founding of the Congressional Caucus on Women's Issues; Franklin's recruitment of women for presidential nominations and appointments; Shalala's participation in the Children's Defense Fund; Reno's concern for women and children in criminal justice proceedings; Albright's directorship of the Georgetown Women in Foreign Service Program; and Herman's service as director of the Women's Bureau. Of the ten women who did not have specifically women-centered experiences, three (Hills, McLaughlin, and Martin) were aware of sex discrimination in their own professional lives, one (Hufstedler) perceived herself as a representative of women in her professional life, one (Harris) had a strong commitment to civil rights for people of color, and one (Chao) described herself as being mentored by a woman. Only Baird, Veneman, Norton, and Chavez appeared to lack any of these experiences and associations. The women secretaries-designate therefore typically had precabinet careers that made them generally aware of the differential circumstances of women and men. Thus, they had the knowledge to represent and advance women's interests in the cabinet.

The profiles of two recent secretaries-designate provide more precise evidence of the representation offered by many of the women secretaries-designate, particularly of its transgendering quality. In 1992, President-elect Clinton named Donna E. Shalala as secretary-designate of health and human services. This department had been founded by a woman (Hobby) and had already been led by two other women (Harris and Heckler). Though its clients included such powerful and masculinist organizations as the American Medical Association (AMA), it was also identified with "women's issues" and women's organizations, its jurisdiction including responsibilities traditionally assigned to women.[55] Thus, the Shalala nomination resumed past patterns of regendering in the cabinet. Yet there were also significant elements of transgendering in her selection. Shalala was recruited from a woman's network. She was expected to articulate women's concerns and to provide women with some substantive representation. Rather than merely buffering the president against traditionally powerful interests, Shalala was to bring new perspectives to the department's policymaking. In this sense, Shalala also enhanced women's descriptive representation, because she was known to be a creative and independent decisionmaker. Her nomination was therefore one of promise for women as cabinet officers and as presidential constituents.

Janet Reno's selection as attorney general–designate, announced a few months later, was similarly encouraging. Reno's nomination is often examined in the context of Zoë Baird's legal controversies, but Reno is an interesting nominee in her own right. Throughout her nomination and confirmation, her statements indicated that she would refuse to be marginalized as a gender outsider. At the same time, she insisted that values traditionally attributed to women and devalued by masculinism—such as compassion and nurturing—should be incorporated into the law and legal practice. In doing so, she offered women both descriptive and substantive representation, proving her competence and her commitment to the value of caring for others through policymaking. Reno thereby transgendered cabinet service both descriptively and substantively. Further, because her nomination was to the inner cabinet and because presidents have not been able to end-run their attorneys general, she offered a richer symbolic representation. Reno, like Shalala, pushed the cabinet toward gender integration.

Given the frequency with which women secretaries-designate have been nominated to outer departments with jurisdictions distant from the presidential agenda, they have had more opportunities to protect the president from established interests than to prove their creativity as leaders and managers. Still, the transgendering possibilities of the Clinton administration offer some indication of more constructive possibilities. Whether these trends will continue through the George W. Bush administration are uncertain, especially since the career paths of that administration's women secretaries-designate do not evidence an unequivocal commitment to representation for women.

Though nominated by the same president-elect early in the same administration, the careers of the four women that George W. Bush named to the cabinet were somewhat contrasting. Veneman, Norton, and Chavez each had careers centered in a particular policy area, namely, agricultural trade, public lands, and affirmative action. Earlier women secretaries-designate also had policy-based career paths—Frances Perkins, Juanita Kreps, and Madeleine Albright are the most obvious examples. However, such career paths had not previously predominated among the women secretaries-designate of a single administration. Labor Secretary-Designate Chao's career, in contrast, focused less on policy than on management. She served in a wide array of government and nonprofit organizations, the only constant being her own upward mobility. Among the earlier women secretaries-designate with this career profile was Clinton HHS secretary-designate Donna E. Shalala. Whether policy- or management-based, then, each of the George W. Bush initial women secretaries-designate offered meaningful descriptive representation for women, as each was a presumptively credible and competent departmental executive. In this regard, the Bush women secretaries-designate seemingly continued the Clinton trend toward transgendering.

And yet, these women secretaries-designate have had little contact with women's or "women's issues" organizations. Only Chao attended a women's college, and only Chao views herself as having been mentored by a woman. (She credits Elizabeth Dole with facilitating her appointments to positions in the Department of Transportation.) Thus, the substantive representation that these women secretaries-designate may offer women is open to question. It may be that this administration will provide opportunities to reinterpret "women's issues," broadening the agenda beyond traditional gender roles. If so, the push toward transgendering cabinet office and in favor of the cabinet's gender integration would be continued. Alternatively, this administration may endorse women as officeholders in the presidency, without fully recognizing them as constituents of the president. The uncertain mix of a stronger descriptive representation and a weaker substantive representation would then leave the cabinet caught between gender desegregation and gender integration. Needless to say, George W. Bush's midterm cabinet nominations will be particularly significant to the cabinet's ongoing gender evolution.

The representation offered by secretaries-designate is prospective—the pressures and priorities of office remain unknown, and thus judgments about representation are inherently speculative. Still, secretaries-designate enter office with political relationships and resources, which are often the basis for their recruitment to the cabinet. Accordingly, the career paths of the nominees are among the most helpful indicators of their future performance as representatives. This survey of the women secretaries-designate has demonstrated that they are accomplished in crossing gender boundaries. Precisely because they have so often succeeded in leading and managing organizations that were predominantly male in policy areas typically reserved to men, the women nominees set a powerful example of descriptive representation for women. At the same time, they typically evidence an awareness of women's circumstances, advocating for their interests and thereby broadening the political agenda. Many of the women secretaries-designate, then, have the precabinet experiences to offer women a rich substantive representation as well as a meaningful descriptive representation. Whether these possibilities are realized is determined in part by the president but also in part by the media and the Senate.

SOCIALIZATION AND REPRESENTATION: PRECABINET CAREERS AND CABINET DEVELOPMENTS

Study of the presidents' nomination decisions demonstrated that women's representation is significantly affected by the chief executive's willingness to have a woman secretary-designate serve as a representative *from* women, in addition to being the president's representative *to* women. If a woman secretary-designate is expected (or even allowed) to serve only as a representative *to* women, as in the Reagan administration, then it is unlikely that women will be recognized as the president's constituents. After all, there are no dialogues or conversations in this representation. By serving as the president's representative to women, the secretary's communication is limited, and she mediates a relationship of ruler and subject. If, however, a woman secretary-designate is nominated to serve as a representative *to and from* women, as occurred in several of the nominations, then the ensuing exchanges may allow a thoughtful consideration of women's interests. In the past, this representative role has been determined in part by a president's beliefs and ideologies and in part by a president's electoral needs and concerns.

Yet presidents alone do not determine the representation that is provided by the cabinet. Presidential priorities are interpreted and implemented by the cabinet officers. This chapter therefore examined the precabinet experiences of the secretaries-designate in order to anticipate what representation they might provide in office.

It was first obvious that the secretaries-designate conformed to traditional definitions of elites. Though increasing numbers of people of color and women have been nominated in recent years, white males remain in the majority. Likewise, though some unmarried people have been selected for cabinet service in recent administrations, the secretaries-designate were usually married and had several children. They were often educated at select colleges and universities. Chosen at their "vocational peak," the women and men were recruited from leadership positions in law, business, education, and government. In simple terms, the first qualification for cabinet service, as evidenced by the profiles of the secretaries-designate, was elite status. Though there were underlying contrasts among the nominees, all shared this identity, and all could be expected to at least understand the associated interests.

At the same time, the experience of achieving elite status differed for the women and the men secretaries-designate. There were the differences in the nominees' age at the time of their nomination and in the number of their biological children. There were also more obvious differences in their professional careers; the women regularly had government or political careers, whereas the men's careers were more widely distributed throughout the government and the private sector. Here was preliminary evidence that the women's representation would be more focused than that of the men and potentially narrower, to the extent that life experience could predict policy positions. With shorter precabinet careers evidencing fewer tangents and more coherence, the women presumptively had less diverse professional resources than the men.

Closer study of the women's career paths, however, revealed a more complex dynamic. In their families of origin, their educational experiences, and their marital relationships, the women secretaries-designate typically had strong support for careers that crossed historical gender boundaries. In more instances than not, the women had more than one support system, a redundancy that reinforced their adoption of an "activist modern sex-role ideology" while instilling self-confidence and self-esteem. These same relationships frequently demonstrated the salience of politics, as mothers, fathers, and husbands were active in government, political parties, and community affairs. With few exceptions, the women secretaries-designate had important social and economic advantages.

Throughout their professional lives, the women demonstrated a fluency in masculinist precepts and practices, excelling in organizations that were predominantly male. Time and again, each secretary-designate was the "first woman." Their mentors were therefore often men because there were no women further up the professional or organizational hierarchy. With proven leadership and managerial abilities, the descriptive representation that the women secretaries-designate could offer other women was meaningful and rich. Yet these women also had the credentials to serve as substantive representatives for women and women's interests. A number of the nominees had precabinet relationships with women's and "women's issues" organizations, so their cabinet membership suggested new avenues of access for those political actors. In other instances, the prospect of substantive representation for women rested less on formal associations than on life experiences of discrimination and exclusion. Thus, the women secretaries-designate had career paths that could potentially transgender cabinet representation.

The role of the president in determining whether that potential is realized has already been considered. The chief executive, however, is one actor in a pluralist system. The media are another influential actor. Because they make and publicize judgments about the nominees' competence, the media influence relationships with prospective constituents and affect the credibility of the secretaries-designate as descriptive representatives. By extension, they also affect the nominees' provision of symbolic representation and the extent to which masculinism directs formal representation. Through their informal role in both the nomination and the confirmation proceedings, the media influence the development of the cabinet, whether toward gender desegregation or gender integration.

NOTES

1. On the implications of age for cabinet secretaries-designate, see Jeffrey E. Cohen, *The Politics of the U.S. Cabinet: Representation in the Executive Branch, 1789–1984* (Pittsburgh: University of Pittsburgh Press, 1988), pp. 52–58. For an excellent study of generational effects as manifested by presidential appointees and nominees to a single administration, see Susan Ware, *Beyond Suffrage: Women in the New Deal* (Cambridge, Mass.: Harvard University Press, 1981).

2. On the implications of these roles for conceptions of leadership, see Mark E. Kann, *A Republic of Men: The American Founders, Gendered Language, and Patriarchal Politics* (New York: New York University Press, 1998).

3. David T. Stanley, Dean E. Mann, and Jameson Doig, *Men Who Govern: A Biographical Profile of Federal Political Executives* (Washington, D.C.: Brookings Institution, 1967). On this point, see Janet M. Martin, "Women Who Govern: The President's Appointments," in *The Other Elites, Women, Politics, and Power in the Executive Branch,* ed. MaryAnne Borrelli and Janet M. Martin (Boulder, Colo.: Lynne Rienner Publishers, 1997).

4. For presidential commentary on descriptive representation as more than appearance, see Ruth Marcus, "Clinton Berates Critics in Women's Groups," *Washington Post*, 22 December 1992, p. 1.

5. On the implications of education for the cabinet secretaries-designate, see Joel D. Aberbach and Bert A. Rockman, *In the Web of Politics: Three Decades of the U.S. Federal Executive* (Washington, D.C.: Brookings Institution, 2000), pp. 62–72; Jeffrey E. Cohen, *The Politics of the U.S. Cabinet: Representation in the Executive Branch, 1789–1984* (Pittsburgh: University of Pittsburgh Press, 1988), pp. 59–62. See also David T. Stanley, Dean E. Mann, and Jameson Doig, *Men Who Govern: A Biographical Profile of Federal Political Executives* (Washington, D.C.: Brookings Institution, 1967), pp. 17–25; Linda L. Fisher, "Fifty Years of Presidential Appointments," in *The In-and-Outers: Presidential Appointees and Transient Government in Washington,* ed. by G. Calvin Mackenzie (Baltimore: Johns Hopkins University Press, 1987), pp. 9–10.

6. On the contrasting responsibilities of business CEOs and department secretaries, see "Candid Reflections of a Businessman in Washington," *Fortune* (29 January 1979), p. 37.

7. On the implications of occupation and profession for the cabinet secretaries-designate, see Joel D. Aberbach and Bert A. Rockman, *In the Web of Politics: Three Decades of the U.S. Federal Executive* (Washington, D.C.: Brookings Institution, 2000), pp. 72–78; Jeffrey E. Cohen, *The Politics of the U.S. Cabinet: Representation in the Executive Branch, 1789–1984* (Pittsburgh: University of Pittsburgh Press, 1988), pp. 74–80. See also David T. Stanley, Dean E. Mann, and Jameson Doig, *Men Who Govern: A Biographical Profile of Federal Political Executives* (Washington, D.C.: Brookings Institution, 1967), pp. 31–41; Linda L. Fisher, "Fifty Years of Presidential Appointments," in *The In-and-Outers: Presidential Appointees and Transient Government in Washington*, ed. G. Calvin Mackenzie (Baltimore: Johns Hopkins University Press, 1987), pp. 15–21.

8. David T. Stanley, Dean E. Mann, and Jameson Doig, *Men Who Govern: A Biographical Profile of Federal Political Executives* (Washington, D.C.: Brookings Institution, 1967), p. 25; Linda L. Fisher, "Fifty Years of Presidential Appointments," in *The In-and-Outers: Presidential Appointees and Transient Government in Washington*, ed. G. Calvin Mackenzie (Baltimore: Johns Hopkins University Press, 1987); George C. Edwards III, "Why Not the Best? The Loyalty-Competence Trade-off in Presidential Appointments," in *Innocent Until Nominated: The Breakdown of the Presidential Appointments Process*, ed. G. Calvin Mackenzie (Washington, D.C.: Brookings Institution, 2001). On the implications of party era for the cabinet secretaries-designate, see Jeffrey E. Cohen, *The Politics of the U.S. Cabinet: Representation in the Executive Branch, 1789–1984* (Pittsburgh: University of Pittsburgh Press, 1988), passim.

9. The biographical sources consulted in compiling the database included the following resources for each secretary-designate: confirmation committee hearing reports, *New York Times* biographical articles, *Who's Who* and *Who Was Who*, *Current Biography*, *Politics in America*, and the archival resources of the presidential libraries. Whenever available, the memoirs of the secretaries-designate were also utilized.

10. Jeffrey E. Cohen, *The Politics of the U.S. Cabinet: Representation in the Executive Branch, 1789–1984* (Pittsburgh: University of Pittsburgh Press, 1988), pp. 54, 58.

11. David T. Stanley, Dean E. Mann, and Jameson Doig, *Men Who Govern: A Biographical Profile of Federal Political Executives* (Washington, D.C.: Brookings Institution, 1967), p. 26.

12. There was only one woman secretary-designate in the Ford cabinet, and so the difference in average ages may be reflective of a special case. However, there were three women secretaries-designate in the Reagan cabinet, and the difference in average ages was a still sizable 7.2 years.

13. This sample excludes one African American, HUD secretary Robert C. Weaver, nominated by President Johnson. That administration is not included in this study because there were no women among its cabinet secretaries.

14. Even if adjustments are made for the withdrawn nomination of Linda Chavez, George W. Bush included a significant percentage of women among

his initial cabinet nominations. Of the secretaries-designate confirmed by the Senate, 21.4 percent were women. This is the same percentage seen in the Clinton initial nominations.

15. This term is borrowed from Rosabeth Moss Kanter. See *Men and Women of the Corporation* (New York: Basic Books, 1977).

16. Paul C. Light, *Thickening Government: Federal Hierarchy and the Diffusion of Accountability* (Washington, D.C.: Brookings Institution, 1995).

17. For an excellent discussion of these tensions, see Joel D. Aberbach and Bert A. Rockman, *In the Web of Politics: Three Decades of the U.S. Federal Executive* (Washington, D.C.: Brookings Institution, 2000), pp. 59–62. See also Janet M. Martin, "Women Who Govern: The President's Appointments," in *The Other Elites: Women, Politics, and Power in the Executive Branch,* ed. MaryAnne Borrelli and Janet M. Martin (Boulder, Colo.: Lynne Rienner Publishers, 1997), pp. 53, 62–63.

18. Janet M. Martin, "Women Who Govern: The President's Appointments," in *The Other Elites: Women, Politics, and Power in the Executive Branch,* ed. MaryAnne Borrelli and Janet M. Martin (Boulder, Colo.: Lynne Rienner Publishers, 1997), pp. 53, 62–63.

19. Jeffrey E. Cohen, *The Politics of the U.S. Cabinet: Representation in the Executive Branch, 1789–1984* (Pittsburgh: University of Pittsburgh Press, 1988), pp. 59–64.

20. More generally, Joel D. Aberbach and Bert A. Rockman found that women in the "top administrative elite" are "every bit as educated—in fact slightly more educated—than their male counterparts." *In the Web of Politics: Three Decades of the U.S. Federal Executive* (Washington, D.C.: Brookings Institution, 2000), p. 62.

21. From 1789 to 1984, 19.4 percent of all cabinet secretaries attended either Harvard, Yale, or Princeton Universities. Among those who had undergraduate degrees only, 24.8 percent attended one of these universities. Among those with graduate degrees, 27.5 percent received them from Harvard or Yale. There were no significant partisan differences in these distributions. Jeffrey E. Cohen, *The Politics of the U.S. Cabinet: Representation in the Executive Branch, 1789–1984* (Pittsburgh: University of Pittsburgh Press, 1988), pp. 59–67. On the changing patterns in education and in educational institutions attended, see Joel D. Aberbach and Bert A. Rockman, *In the Web of Politics: Three Decades of the U.S. Federal Executive* (Washington, D.C.: Brookings Institution, 2000), pp. 62–72.

22. U.S. Senate, Committee on Labor and Human Resources, *Nomination* [Shirley M. Hufstedler, of California, to Be Secretary of Education], 96th Cong., 1st sess., pp. 3–17; Phyllis Theroux, "The Judge Goes to Washington," *New York Times Magazine,* 8 June 1980, pp. 41, 102, 104.

23. U.S. Senate, Committee on Finance, *Nominations of Margaret M. Heckler, to Be Secretary of HHS and John A. Svahn, to be Under Secretary of HHS,* 98th Cong., 1st. sess., pp. 4–5. "Margaret M. Heckler," *Current Biography Yearbook 1983.* New York: H. W. Wilson, 1983.

24. Jeffrey E. Cohen, *The Politics of the U.S. Cabinet: Representation in the Executive Branch, 1789–1984* (Pittsburgh: University of Pittsburgh Press, 1988), pp. 76–81.

25. Few cabinet secretaries-designate have had monolithic careers, so it is important to note that this section focuses only on each nominee's "primary career." The following steps were taken in distinguishing between each nominee's primary and secondary careers. First, comprehensive chronologies were compiled for each secretary-designate, revealing the balance of time and the pattern of advancement in each person's career. Where nominees had spent the larger part of their working lives was viewed as preliminarily indicative of their primary careers. Second, each nominee's chronology was placed in a political and historical context. In some cases, opportunities for advancement varied among the professions, but in others, partisan turnover limited access to executive branch service. These and many other factors were considered as part of an effort to understand the more general influences on the nominees' career choices. Third, the writings and oral histories of the secretaries-designate were consulted to see how the future cabinet members explained their career paths. On the basis of this research, a secretary-designate's primary career was identified. This coding was checked several times by the author; the pattern of findings was also compared with those of other scholars. That said, it should be noted that the coding in this study is more likely to understate the proportions of secretaries-designate whose primary career was in the governmental sector because the employment chronology of the secretaries-designate was taken seriously. However much a nominee's ambitions may have been directed toward executive branch service, the primary career was only identified as such if she or he had actually worked in the executive branch. The long twelve-year tenure of Republicans in the White House during the Reagan and Bush administrations unquestionably displaced the career paths of many politically ambitious Democrats. These occurrences, as well as societal patterns of gender and racial exclusion, are acknowledged throughout the text.

26. For a discussion of these patterns from the Truman administration through the first 2.5 years of the Reagan administration, see James D. King and James W. Riddlesperger, Jr., "Presidential Cabinet Appointments: The Partisan Factor," *Presidential Studies Quarterly* 14 (Spring 1984): 231–237. King and Riddlesperger observe similar patterns in the administrations that are not included in this study, namely, Truman, Kennedy, Johnson, and Nixon.

27. On this practice in the Carter administration, see Hedrick Smith, "Overtures of Reassurance," *New York Times*, 4 December 1976, p. 1.

28. James P. Pfiffner, "Establishing the Bush Presidency," *Public Administration Review* (January–February 1990): 64–72; Janet M. Martin, "George Bush and the Executive Branch," in *Leadership and the Bush Presidency*, ed. Ryan J. Barilleaux and Mary E. Stuckey (Westport, Conn.: Praeger, 1992).

29. That the other Republican insider president—Ford—did not follow George H. W. Bush's strategy can be attributed to his concern to appoint individuals distanced from Watergate and any sort of public scandal.

30. This description is well-suited to Robert E. Rubin, head of the Clinton National Economic Council (1993–1994) and secretary of the treasury (1994–1998). Rubin had more than thirty years' experience on Wall Street prior to his service in the administration. He joined the investment firm Goldman Sachs in 1966 and at the time of his White House appointment was its cochairman. It is also interesting to note that Rubin's predecessor, Treasury Secretary Lloyd M. Bentsen, recommended him for this cabinet post. Bentsen's financial portfolio at Goldman Sachs had been partially under Rubin's management. Clay Chandler, "Rubin Stepping into Spotlight at Treasury," *Washington Post*, 7 December 1994, p. F1. The selection of Ford commerce secretary-designate Rogers Morton was defended on these grounds, as well. In Press Secretary Ron Nessen's words, "The President feels it is important to have someone who came from the business community in the Commerce Department to talk to business leaders in their own language." Ben A. Franklin, "Morton, in a Cabinet Shift, Picked for Commerce Job," *New York Times*, 28 March 1975, p. 1.

31. Though the same argument might seem applicable to the Republican nominees, whose party did not control the White House from 1993 to 2001, the patterns and trends in their careers suggest otherwise. Those secretaries-designate in the initial George W. Bush cabinet who had primary careers in the private sector had devoted themselves to working and succeeding in the private sector.

32. Shalala has consistently led public colleges and universities. Education, however, was classified as a "private sector" activity because it did not involve elected or appointed office, as political scientists generally use those terms.

33. See Janet M. Martin, "Women Who Govern: The President's Appointments," in *The Other Elites: Women, Politics, and Power in the Executive Branch,* ed. MaryAnne Borrelli and Janet M. Martin (Boulder: Lynne Rienner Publishers, 1997), pp. 62–64.

34. Rita Mae Kelly, Mary Boutilier, and Mary Lewis, *The Making of Political Women: A Study of Socialization and Role Conflict* (Chicago: Nelson-Hall, 1978).

35. Piper A. Hodson, "Routes to Power: An Examination of Political Change, Rulership, and Women's Access to Executive Office," in *The Other Elites: Women, Politics, and Power in the Executive Branch,* ed. MaryAnne Borrelli and Janet M. Martin (Boulder: Lynne Rienner Publishers, 1997), p. 36. See also Rita Mae Kelly, Mary Boutilier, and Mary Lewis, *The Making of Political Women: A Study of Socialization and Role Conflict* (Chicago: Nelson-Hall, 1978).

36. Marjorie Hunter, "Reagan's Choice for Health Chief," *New York Times*, 13 January 1983, p. D22.

37. Joel D. Aberbach and Bert A. Rockman concluded that "top federal executives" typically had "upper status" families of origin, their fathers holding managerial or professional posts. See *In the Web of Politics: Three*

Decades of the U.S. Federal Executive (Washington, D.C.: Brookings Institution, 2000), pp. 62–63.

38. The other three women who came from elite families were Perkins (a well-established New England family), O'Leary (the daughter of two physicians), and Albright (the daughter of a career diplomat, later university professor).

39. The twelve were Perkins (whose father owned a large share of a manufacturing facility), Hills (whose father was in construction), Hufstedler (whose father was a construction foreman), Dole (whose father was a florist wholesaler), Shalala (whose father owned a chain of grocery stores), O'Leary (whose father was a physician), Reno (whose father was an investigative reporter), Albright (whose father was a diplomat and later university professor), Herman (whose father owned a funeral home), Veneman (whose father owned a fruit farm and held various appointive positions in state and national government), Chavez (whose father was a housepainter), and Chao (whose father owned a shipping business). The occupations of three fathers were unknown, namely, those of McLaughlin, Baird, and Norton.

40. The following secretaries-designate have not disclosed their mother's occupation: Perkins, Hills, Kreps, Dole, Heckler, McLaughlin, Martin, Baird, Veneman, Norton, and Chao. The elite status of the Perkins, Hills, and Dole families suggests that these mothers did not work outside the home; there is some indication that Martin, Baird, Veneman, and Chao also had mothers who were not engaged in paid employment.

The mothers of secretaries-designate Harris, Hufstedler, Franklin, Shalala, and Herman were teachers. The stepmother of secretary-designate O'Leary was also a teacher.

41. Bob Dole and Elizabeth Dole, *The Doles: Unlimited Partners* (New York: Simon and Schuster, 1988). Carla Anderson Hills's father objected to her decision to attend law school on the grounds that she would waste her education after her marriage; she paid her own tuition at Yale Law School until he relented. Irwin Ross, "Carla Hills Gives 'The Woman's Touch' a Brand-New Meaning," *Fortune* 92 (December 1975): 161.

42. Marriage is the norm among the women secretaries-designate, as it is among the men. Only four of the women had not been married before their nomination. The four were Shalala, Reno, Herman, and Veneman. O'Leary (widowed) and Albright (divorced) were not married at the time of their nomination. Heckler underwent a very difficult and very public divorce while she was secretary of health and human services.

43. These circumstances explain the understandable tendency to presume that the women secretaries-designate are "the other half" of the ruling class. After all, the married women secretaries-designate are often members of a "power couple." Elizabeth and Robert Dole are the best-known example, but Barbara Franklin provides the more intriguing anecdote. She met and married Wallace Barnes, her third husband, while both were on the Aetna board of directors. Their marriage was reported in *Fortune*, the Aetna CEO adding,

"When they announced that they were going to get married, I told them I deserved a finder's fee." "Bed and Board," *Fortune* (25 September 1989): 225. Another example of a "power couple" is found in Ann Dore McLaughlin and John McLaughlin. In announcing his nomination of Ann McLaughlin as labor secretary-designate, President Reagan linked McLaughlin's private and public life, suggesting that her accomplishments in one related to her achievements in the other. He stated that "McLaughlin would give the [Labor] department 'decisive and forceful leadership. And besides, if she's handled John McLaughlin this long, she can handle anything.'" William Neikirk, "Reagan Picks Woman as New Labor Secretary," *Chicago Tribune*, 4 November 1987, sec. I, 5.

44. Paul Wilson suffered a nervous breakdown a few years after his marriage to Frances Perkins and was institutionalized for many years. Perkins initially discouraged Roosevelt from offering her the cabinet post because Wilson could not be moved. Similarly, years later, Juanita Kreps left cabinet office to care for her husband, who had allegedly attempted suicide.

45. Harris received her undergraduate degree from Howard University and was later a member of the Howard Law School faculty. O'Leary received her undergraduate degree from Fisk University. Herman received her undergraduate degree from Xavier University, which is the only historically black university that is also Roman Catholic.

46. The ten women for whom this information could be established were Hobby, Hills, Harris, Kreps, Hufstedler, Dole, Heckler, Franklin, Reno, and Chao.

47. Hufstedler, Heckler, Reno, Veneman, and Norton all practiced law; each was the junior partner in a small law firm or a solo practitioner, with the exception of Norton, who was an attorney at the Mountain States Legal Foundation. McLaughlin, Franklin, and Chao all had early positions in the corporate sector. Harris and Herman were in the nonprofit sector. Harris worked for and directed several African American women's organizations and human rights organizations; Herman directed an employment and training organization. The women who began their careers in governmental or political offices were Hobby, parliamentarian and staff member, Texas state legislature; Hills, assistant U.S. attorney; O'Leary, state legal services program administrator and then assistant state attorney general; Baird, staff attorney, U.S. Department of Justice; Albright, congressional staff member; and Chavez, DNC.

48. The five women who were teachers were Perkins, Kreps, Dole, Martin, and Shalala.

49. Perkins, Kreps, and Reno had not had full-time positions in the federal government; only Perkins, however, seems to have entirely lacked precabinet contacts with the national government.

50. Hobby, Hills, Harris, Dole, McLaughlin, Franklin, Shalala, O'Leary, Baird, Albright, Herman, Veneman, Norton, Chavez, and Chao all held full-time positions in the executive branch. Hufstedler was an appellate judge in the federal courts; Heckler and Martin were former members of Congress.

51. O'Leary, Herman, Veneman, and Norton had previously served in the department they were nominated to lead.

52. The six were Dole (public liaison director, White House staff), Franklin (White House staff assistant), Baird (associate counsel, White House Counsel's Office), Albright (National Security Council congressional liaison officer), Herman (public liaison director, White House staff), and Chavez (public liaison director, White House staff).

53. In a letter written in 1961, Perkins described the social work and social reform networks of the Progressive Era as the "forerunners of the New Deal." "In fact, I am sure that it was the humanitarian, active, and effective action of social workers who turned to legislation as a method of overcoming social disabilities, who made possible the effective action and administration under the political New Deal." As quoted in Susan Ware, *Partner and I: Molly Dewson, Feminism, and New Deal Politics* (New Haven: Yale University Press, 1987), pp. 210–211. See also Susan Ware, *Beyond Suffrage: Women in the New Deal* (Cambridge, Mass.: Harvard University Press, 1981); Susan Ware, *Holding Their Own: American Women in the 1930s* (Boston: Twayne Publishers, 1982).

54. On the challenges associated with her personal life and the difficulties posed by accepting the presidential nomination, see Frances Perkins Oral History, Oral History Research Project, Butler Library, Columbia University. For more general biographical information, see also Frances Perkins, *The Roosevelt I Knew* (New York: Viking Press, 1946); Mary W. Dewson, *An Aid to the End,* Molly Dewson Collection of the Arthur and Elizabeth Schlesinger Library on the History of Women, Radcliffe College, Harvard University; Lillian Holmen Mohr, *Frances Perkins: "That Woman in FDR's Cabinet!"* (Great Barrington, Mass.: North River Press, 1979); George Martin, *Madam Secretary: Frances Perkins* (Boston: Houghton Mifflin Company, 1976). On Perkins's professional and political allegiances, see, for example, Kenneth S. Davis, *FDR: Into the Storm, 1937–1940* (New York: Random House, 1993), pp. 595; James A. Farley, *Jim Farley's Story: The Roosevelt Years* (New York: McGraw-Hill, 1948), pp. 328, 364.

55. On the masculinist character of the medical profession and the consequent challenges for women leaders in health care policymaking, see Mary Ellen Guy, "Hillary, Health Care, and Gender Power," in *Gender Power, Leadership, and Governance,* ed. Georgia Duerst-Lahti and Rita Mae Kelly (Ann Arbor: University of Michigan Press, 1995).

4

Media Coverage of the Secretaries-Designate

Politics and the media have always been intertwined, with a free press deemed essential to the preservation of a democratic republic. The details of this relationship, however, are constantly being negotiated. Which media outlets dominate, under which circumstances, and why are matters of great importance to those in government and in the communication industries. Likewise, the interpretations and frames provided in news coverage are strongly contested because these subjective elements shape opinions and policies. Exchanges between government officials and the media, therefore, carry important implications for the daily practice and long-term development of political institutions.[1]

In regard to cabinet nominations, the media report the president's decision and introduce the secretary-designate to the wider public.[2] In doing so, whether in print or broadcast form, they evaluate the nominee's career and character. These judgments, in turn, affect others' judgments of the nominees' likely provision of descriptive representation. Articles about the secretaries-designate are, for example, referenced in their confirmation hearings and included in the hearing reports. Similarly, articles that assess the campaign or governance implications of the nominations influence views of the nominees' likely substantive representation. Cumulatively, the media comment on the symbolic representation that is anticipated from each secretary-designate, as they set out the role each nominee is likely to play in the cabinet and in the administration.

This is a conservative comment about the power of the media. It is not an argument that the media select the secretaries-designate or set the agenda for representation in the cabinet. Nor is it a claim that the media are monolithic. It is, instead, a statement that respects the interpretive power of news reporting. At the same time, there is an appreciation for the "push me–pull you" relationship that often exists between the media and the public, as journalists' and readers' standards interact. Covering the news is about shaping and responding to opinion.[3]

The coverage of the secretaries-designate may be distinctive, however, in that the prospective cabinet members make few public statements until they have been sworn into office. Even when the nomination is announced at a press conference, it is the rare nominee who offers more than a brief and formal acceptance speech.[4] Subsequent public appearances are limited, aside from courtesy calls on confirmation committee members and other decisionmakers.

This restraint is not surprising. Secretaries-designate are petitioners for power. They walk softly in order to avoid alienating those who will determine whether they hold office.[5] Paul Light's *Survivor's Guide for Presidential Nominees* (2000) is unequivocal on this point: "[D]on't say anything at all to the press, on the record or off, while the Senate is considering your nomination."[6] The nominees' silence, however, allows others to frame their reputation and prestige.[7] The media's influence is further magnified by the timing of analysis—the articles assessing the nomination and describing the nominee appear at the most preliminary stage of cabinet service, when uncertainty about the prospective executive is at its height. The coverage and any systematic patterns that might characterize its amount, placement, or content are of corresponding importance.

Scholars analyzing media coverage of Congress members have identified consistent differences in the coverage accorded women and men legislators, which have important implications for their performance as representatives. Linda Witt, Karen M. Paget, and Glenna Matthews, for example, argue that there has been an enduring gender bias against women legislators. They maintain that this differential treatment has not changed since the first woman member of Congress, Representative Jeannette Rankin (R-Mont.), joined with fifty-five male Republican members to vote against the entry of the United States into World War I.

A look back at the coverage of Jeannette Rankin's first vote reveals a virtual template for all aspects of modern-day press coverage that modern-day women politicians have come to loathe: a focus on what she looked like and wore, not what she stood for or had accomplished; an interest only in her presumably aberrant vote and actions, although many of her male colleagues had voted and acted precisely the same way; an inference that Rankin's act was that of Everywoman, in the very face of the fact that women were bitterly divided over her vote; and constant spoofing, which barely veiled hostility, at the notion a woman had either the right or the authority to be a politician. The coverage could not have been better designed, even by conspiracy, to . . . carve into stone the already existing stereotypes of women.[8]

The unusual is news, by definition, and women have yet to become the norm in national politics. Yet the media's bias is so great, these political scientists maintain, that it undercuts the professionalism and the power of women officeholders. In so doing, it compromises their descriptive representation. It also limits the women's ability to participate in the legislative process so that their message as symbolic representatives becomes one of exclusion.

Susan J. Carroll and Ronnee Schreiber's study of the media coverage of women in the 103rd Congress also concluded that the media compromised the women members' provision of descriptive and symbolic representation. However, the Carroll and Schreiber analysis indicated that the media effected this end less through "bias and trivialization" and more through an excessive focus on the women legislators' devotion to "women's issues."[9]

What is missing from general press coverage on women in Congress is any sense that women are important players on legislation other than women's health, abortion, and a handful of other related concerns. There is barely a mention anywhere of women's involvement in foreign affairs, international trade, the appropriations process, or regulatory reform, for example. . . . It certainly is possible for the press to focus on women as a category—to write a story on women— and yet to examine what women in Congress do individually to influence legislation. But stories focusing on the broader and multifaceted contributions of women, as individuals as well as collectively, are not written. The lack of such stories means that press coverage of women in Congress presents a narrow portrayal of what women in Congress can and did accomplish and reinforces, rather than challenges, the perception that women in Congress only do "women's stuff."[10]

Carroll and Schreiber agree with Witt, Paget, and Matthews that the media presents women legislators as outsiders and narrow advocates for women. These political scientists disagree about the media frame and about its further implications. What patterns and biases surface in the coverage of the secretaries-designate, however, is not yet known.

Therefore, this chapter analyzes the *New York Times* coverage of the cabinet nominations. One of the premier media outlets in the United States and the nation's newspaper of record, the *Times'*s news analysis and editorials are reprinted throughout the country. Its circulation is high among political elites.[11] To the extent that the coverage of legislative and executive officeholders is similar, past studies tell us to expect differences in the coverage of women and men secretaries-designate. This investigation will determine whether these differences are present and explore their deeper implications for the regendering or transgendering of cabinet office and for the gender desegregation or gender integration of the cabinet.

REPORTING THE CABINET
NOMINATIONS AND NOMINEES

The cabinet secretaries-designate are typically well-known and well-connected individuals at the apex of their professional careers. Whether they have previously been elected or appointed officials, corporate executives or university presidents, attorneys or party leaders, the secretaries-designate have been visible within their networks and are often personally known to the nominating president. Even so, their names and careers will be unfamiliar to many. The circumstances of their nomination by the president will also be unknown. Media coverage of the secretaries-designate, therefore, is needed both to explain the nomination and to introduce the nominee. The *New York Times* performed these two functions but in distinct articles, one being principally devoted to explanation and the other to introduction.

Nomination articles examined the implications of the presidential nomination decision, weighing programmatic and policy priorities (see Table 4.1). These articles focused on the substantive representation that could be provided by the secretaries-designate and the formal representation provided via the president's exercise of the nomination power. Sources of information were members of the transition team or the White House staff, depending on the nomination's timing. Across the seven administrations with initial and midterm cabinet nominations, a nomination article was provided for 149 of the 167 nominations

Table 4.1 *New York Times* Coverage of Cabinet Nominations: Nomination Articles, by Administration (frequency counts in parentheses)

President	Nominations	Percentage of Nominees with Nomination Articles
Roosevelt	26	65.4 (17)
Eisenhower	21	100.0 (21)
Ford	13	76.9 (10)
Carter	21	100.0 (21)
Reagan	33	93.9 (31)
G. H. W. Bush	22	95.5 (21)
Clinton	31	90.3 (28)
G. W. Bush (initial only)	15	100.0 (15)

(89.2 percent). If the Roosevelt administration, an exceptional case for reasons that will be discussed shortly, is set aside, this percentage increases. In the remaining six administrations, 132 of 141 nominations (93.6 percent) received a nomination article. In the George W. Bush administration, every initial cabinet nomination received a nomination article. Typically, then, the president's cabinet nomination decisions are the subject of a *New York Times* article.

Biographical articles described the nominees' character traits, careers, educational attainments, marriages, and children (see Table 4.2). The nominees' colleagues, friends, and spouses were quoted, as well as transition or White House sources. The biographical articles, therefore, assessed the strength of the descriptive representation and the consequent character of the symbolic representation that each secretary-designate was expected to provide. In the seven administrations

Table 4.2 *New York Times* Coverage of Cabinet Nominations: Biographical Articles, by Administration (frequency counts in parentheses)

President	Nominations	Percentage of Nominees with Biographical Articles
Roosevelt	26	7.7 (2)
Eisenhower	21	85.7 (18)
Ford	13	76.9 (10)
Carter	21	95.2 (20)
Reagan	33	87.9 (29)
G. H. W. Bush	22	81.8 (18)
Clinton	31	90.3 (28)
G. W. Bush (initial only)	15	100.0 (15)

with initial and midterm nominations, a biographical article was published for 125 of the 167 nominations (74.8 percent). Again setting aside the Roosevelt administration, 123 of the 141 nominees (87.2 percent) received a biographical article at the time of their nomination. In the George W. Bush administration, every initial nominee was profiled by a biographical article. Though the credentials of the secretaries-designate therefore seem to be slightly less newsworthy than the presidential nomination decisions, both biographical and nomination articles are provided in most instances. Thus, the *Times* coverage of cabinet nominees and nominations constitutes an ongoing and comprehensive analysis of representation.

Events unique to the Franklin Roosevelt administration complicated the counts for the nomination and biographical articles in that administration. After only a few of the initial nominations had been announced, a complete roster was leaked to the press. This listing appeared on the front page of the *Times,* with abbreviated biographies on page 3, on 23 February 1933.[12] The paper did not provide more extensive biographies when the nominations were formally announced. In fact, the *Times* rarely provided biographies for any of the Roosevelt secretaries-designate.[13] Instead, the nomination articles included a paragraph or two on the nominee's career. Consequently, this administration is an exceptional case relative to others in this study.

Although the *Times* coverage has been extensive, it has also been slightly uneven. Administrations that have been responsible for a notable partisan turnover—bringing a party into the Oval Office after a significant absence—have received higher proportions of nomination articles. These are the administrations of Eisenhower, the first Republican administration in twenty years; Carter, the first Democratic administration in eight years; Clinton, the first Democratic administration in twelve years; and George W. Bush, the first Republican administration in eight years. The proportions of the biographical articles follow a similar pattern, though the Eisenhower administration has a somewhat lower proportion of biographical articles than would otherwise be expected. The promise of greater change, it seems, leads to greater interest in the president's nomination decisions and in the pre-cabinet careers of the secretaries-designate. Precisely because representation is more uncertain, coverage of the representatives increases.

With these general parameters set, a closer examination of the articles, both quantitatively and qualitatively, is in order. Quantitative analysis begins to indicate the paper's response to the secretaries-designate. Which secretaries-designate receive more coverage as measured by the patterns of nomination and biographical articles? Which secretaries-designate receive coverage on the front page and which inside the paper? Do women and men secretaries-designate receive coverage that is similar in amount and placement? Once the quantitative patterns of advantage and disadvantage are determined, qualitative analysis can examine the actual content of the articles, revealing the full implications of this commentary for the representation offered by the secretaries-designate.

THE QUANTITY AND PLACEMENT OF
CABINET NOMINATION COVERAGE

Because they relate to the newsworthiness of a nomination, three factors are likely to affect the *Times*'s coverage of cabinet nominations. First, there is the timing of the nomination. Curiosity and uncertainty are greatest about new administrations, particularly when there is partisan turnover. Initial nominations seem likely, therefore, to receive more extensive coverage—more of the initial nominations may receive both a nomination and a biographical article. Further, articles about the initial nominations are more likely to receive better placement in the paper, appearing on the front page. Midterm nominees enter office after an administration's initiatives and priorities have been set. Accordingly, they may receive less coverage, and the articles may be placed deeper inside the paper. This hypothesis suggests that there will be a relatively consistent relationship between knowledge of the representation offered by the secretary-designate and the media coverage, such that as uncertainty about the representation rises, the *Times* coverage will be more extensive and more prominent. Of course, it is precisely when the least is known that the *Times* articles become the most influential in framing the representation offered by the prospective cabinet member.

Second, there is the status of the nomination. Political observers describe the inner cabinet secretaries-designate—nominated to lead the Departments of State, Treasury, Defense, and Justice—as advising the president on matters of national importance. These nominations would therefore seem likely to receive more extensive coverage, with their nomination articles appearing more frequently on the front page. Because outer cabinet secretaries-designate are generally perceived as representatives of more specialized interests, their nominations might receive less prominent and less extensive coverage. In other words, as the representation becomes more specific, the newsworthiness of the nomination would presumably diminish.

Third, there is the nominee's sex. With three exceptions, the women secretaries-designate have been nominated to lead departments in the outer cabinet. In addition, nine of the women have been midterm nominations. These circumstances suggest that coverage of the women secretaries-designate will be less extensive and that the articles will be placed inside the paper. However, the nomination of a woman (or, for that matter, the nomination of a man of color) as a secretary-designate is still sufficiently unusual that it might be considered newsworthy. Women secretaries-designate would then receive more extensive and more prominent coverage than would the white men nominated to similar posts. Then, the sex of the future cabinet representative would more significantly influence coverage than would the presidential or departmental aspects of the nomination.

Initial Versus Midterm Secretaries-Designate

In each administration except the Ford administration, the cabinet nomination coverage decreases in amount and worsens in placement as the presidential term advances (see Table 4.3). A higher percentage of initial than midterm nominees receive front-page nomination articles or biographical articles. This finding is entirely congruent with expectations. With the administration well established, midterm cabinet nominations are no longer a primary indicator of policy positions and priorities. Cabinet representation is less newsworthy when it is a less prominent indicator of the administration's commitments to political and societal interests.

In the Ford administration, though, it was midterm—not initial—secretaries-designate that received the more extensive, more favorably placed coverage. Still, this administration may be the exception that proves the rule. There was extensive *Times* coverage of the Ford "transition" from late 1974 through early 1975. Changes in the White House staff were reported in detail, undoubtedly because of the Watergate scandal and the continuing investigations. With the exception of the attorney general's office, however, this scandal had little relevance to the cabinet. Early cabinet nominations were therefore neglected, in relative terms, because they were peripheral to the issues that the *Times* had identified as significant. As the Ford administration matured, inter-

Table 4.3 *New York Times* Coverage of Cabinet Nominations: Nomination and Biographical Articles for Initial and Midterm Secretaries-Designate, by Administration (frequency counts in parentheses)

President	Nominations	Percentage of Nominees with Nomination Articles (on page 1)	Percentage of Nominees with Biographical Articles
Roosevelt			
Initial	11	72.7 (8)	9.1 (1)
Midterm	15	60.0 (9)	6.7 (1)
Eisenhower			
Initial	10	100.0 (10)	100.0 (10)
Midterm	11	90.9 (10)	72.7 (8)
Ford			
Initial	5	20.0 (1)	60.0 (3)
Midterm	8	75.0 (6)	87.5 (7)
Carter			
Initial	11	100.0 (11)	100.0 (11)
Midterm	10	90.0 (9)	90.0 (9)
Reagan			
Initial	13	100.0 (13)	100.0 (13)
Midterm	20	90.0 (18)	80.0 (16)
G. H. W. Bush			
Initial	14	92.9 (13)	92.9 (13)
Midterm	8	50.0 (4)	50.0 (4)
Clinton			
Initial	15	100.0 (15)	100.0 (15)
Midterm	16	81.3 (13)	81.3 (13)
G. W. Bush			
Initial	15	100.0 (15)	100.0 (15)

est in the cabinet gradually returned to its more usual levels, and coverage of the cabinet increased. Rather than concluding that Ford's midterm nominations were more newsworthy, it is more accurate to note that coverage of Ford's initial nominations was unusually low. As evidence in support of this contention, note that the proportion of nomination and biographical articles for the initial Ford nominees was much lower than that seen in other administrations, whereas the proportions for midterm Ford nominees were similar.

Inner Cabinet Versus Outer Cabinet Secretaries-Designate

A slightly higher proportion of inner cabinet nominations than outer cabinet nominations received a front-page nomination article and a biographical article (see Table 4.4). However, the differences in cover-

Table 4.4 *New York Times* **Coverage of Cabinet Nominations: Nomination and Biographical Articles for Inner and Outer Cabinet Secretaries-Designate, by Administration (frequency counts in parentheses)**

President	Nominations, by Department	Percentage of Nominees with Nomination Articles (on page 1)	Percentage of Nominees with Biographical Articles
Roosevelt			
Inner	16	75.0 (12)	6.3 (1)
Outer	10	40.0 (4)	10.0 (1)
Eisenhower			
Inner	9	100.0 (9)	88.9 (8)
Outer	12	91.7 (11)	83.3 (10)
Ford			
Inner	3	33.3 (1)	66.7 (2)
Outer	10	60.0 (6)	80.0 (8)
Carter			
Inner	7	100.0 (7)	100.0 (7)
Outer	14	92.9 (13)	92.9 (13)
Reagan			
Inner	10	80.0 (8)	90.0 (9)
Outer	23	87.0 (20)	87.0 (20)
G. H. W. Bush			
Inner	7	85.7 (6)	71.4 (5)
Outer	15	73.3 (11)	86.7 (13)
Clinton			
Inner	11	100.0 (11)	90.9 (10)
Outer	20	68.0 (17)	72.0 (18)
G. W. Bush (initial only)			
Inner	4	100.0 (4)	100.0 (4)
Outer	11	100.0 (11)	100.0 (11)

age were neither consistent nor great across the administrations. In the Reagan administration, for example, approximately equal percentages of inner and outer secretaries-designate were covered by nomination articles. In the Ford and George H. W. Bush administrations, fewer inner cabinet nominees than outer cabinet nominees were covered by a biographical article. Departmental status was therefore less determinative of differences in coverage than was the timing of the nomination.[14]

Coverage for Women and Men Secretaries-Designate

If the coverage patterns described above hold for the women secretaries-designate, they will be among the nominees receiving less extensive and less prominent coverage. The slight majority of the women's nominations have been at midterm, and the great majority have been to the outer

Table 4.5 *New York Times* **Coverage of Cabinet Nominations: The Distribution of Nomination and Biographical Articles for Women and Men Cabinet Secretaries-Designate, Controlling for Timing and Cabinet Department (percentages)**

	Nomination Articles		Biographical Articles	
	Inner Cabinet Nomination	Outer Cabinet Nomination	Inner Cabinet Nomination	Outer Cabinet Nomination
Initial Nominations				
Women	100.0	100.0	100.0	100.0
Men	90.9	97.4	90.9	97.4
Midterm Nominations				
Women	100.0	100.0	0.0	75.0
Men	94.1	88.6	88.2	80.0

cabinet, both categories that have tended to receive poorer coverage. Perhaps mitigating these circumstances, the greater number of the women's nominations have been in administrations—Eisenhower, Carter, Clinton, and George W. Bush—receiving more coverage.

To ensure that comparisons were as accurate as possible, women and men whose nominations were similarly timed (initial or midterm) and to similar departments (inner or outer cabinet) were compared. Surveying the results, the most striking feature is the sheer frequency with which "100.0 percent" appears in Table 4.5. The majority of cabinet nominations are covered by both a nomination article and by a biographical article.[15] That said, there are slight differences in the coverage accorded the women and men secretaries-designate. Every woman secretary-designate—initial and midterm—received a nomination article, though the same could not be said for the men. In other words, every presidential nomination of a woman secretary-designate, though not of a man, merited analysis.

The provision of biographical articles was more uneven. There was a biographical article for every initial woman secretary-designate. There were, however, fewer biographical articles for the women midterm nominees than for the men. The *Times* may deem the career paths of the women of less interest than the president's decision to nominate them. Still, the differences in the coverage granted the women and men are quite small; they do not justify a conclusion that the women secretaries-designate are disadvantaged. Though the identity of the cabinet nominee does seem to have some effect on the coverage, the connection is not one that can be determined through quantitative study alone.

*   *   *

A quantitative survey of the *New York Times* coverage of cabinet nominations and nominees, therefore, yields few surprises. The timing of the nomination seems to have the greatest effect on the extent and placement of the coverage. The departmental status of the nomination also has some influence. The coverage for women and men secretaries-designate evidences slight variations, after controlling for the timing of the nomination and the status of the department, with women more consistently covered by nomination articles and men more consistently by biographical articles. Still, the quantitative differences in coverage accorded the women and the men are slight. More generally, quantitative analysis suggests that the coverage of the cabinet nominations is greatest when there are the most questions about its provision—at the beginning of the presidential term. Whether the secretarial office is perceived as more national or more specialized and whether the representative is male or female were less determinative of the extent or the placement of this coverage. And yet, the numbers suggest only the general patterns; qualitative analysis of the articles' content is needed to uncover the details of the *Times's* judgments about these nominations and nominees.

THE SUBSTANCE OF THE CABINET NOMINATION COVERAGE

Qualitative analysis of the *Times* coverage was narrowed to the six later administrations for three reasons. First, the coverage given the Roosevelt nominations and nominees was quite distinctive. Rather than qualifying a more general investigation at every turn, the Roosevelt case was acknowledged as unusual and set aside. Second, there were also unusual aspects to the nomination, and thus the coverage, of Eisenhower health, education, and welfare (HEW) secretary-designate Oveta Culp Hobby. She was first named administrator of the Federal Security Administration. At that time, Eisenhower promised to submit a reorganization plan to Congress that would create a new cabinet-level department for social programs, which Hobby would lead.[16] Congressional approval of Reorganization Plan No. 1, authorizing the Department of Health, Education, and Welfare, came on 30 March 1953, approximately two months into the administration.[17] Having already presented the cabinet nomination as pending, media coverage of the formal announcement was self-consciously anticlimactic.[18] As a result, comparisons drawn between her media coverage and that of other cabinet secretaries-designate are questionable.[19]

Third, the historical context of the Roosevelt and the Eisenhower administrations is very different from that of the Ford administration and its successors. The emergence of the modern presidency, the establishment of new outer cabinet departments, the increasing size and responsibility of the federal bureaucracy, and the development of the White House staff all had their impact on presidential nominations in the latter quarter of the century. In the interest of advancing accurate comparisons, therefore, the earlier administrations are set aside, though this focus does not preclude appropriate historical references.

The Nomination Articles, 1975–2001

Throughout the presidential term and particularly during the transition, the nomination articles assessed the administration's communication patterns. During the transition, as much attention was given to the administration's contact with the public as to its internal operations.[20] Substantive representation of organized and societal interests, therefore, was a constant concern of these nomination articles. Ford's initial nominations, for example, were described as reassuring the public that there would be stability in executive leadership. Other messages, such as reestablishing popular trust in the chief executive, buttressed this theme. This framing was most powerfully evident in the renomination of Henry Kissinger, announced by Ford on the same day that he entered the presidential office. Kissinger's nomination article appeared on one of the *Times*'s more dramatic front pages. A banner headline declared, "Nixon Resigns: He Urges a Time of 'Healing'; Ford Will Take Office Today." The column 6 article on the front page, which was the lead article, carried the headline, "The 37th President Is First to Quit Post." In matching type over column 1, the headline was "'Sacrifice' Is Praised; Kissinger to Remain." Because this framing was taken from Ford's own statements, the *Times* was *relaying and amplifying* the president's own view of his cabinet nomination decisions.[21]

Campaign promises—and presidential statements, as evidenced in the Ford case—affect the general coverage of cabinet nominations.

Reporters use a theme from campaign, transition, or presidential speeches to bring coherence and unity to the nomination articles. Quite clearly, this coverage has its benefits and its costs. The chief benefit is the clarity and simplicity brought to the nomination coverage by the thematic presentation. However, presidential control over the presentation is uncertain. Presidents-elect sometimes wish to forget their campaign promises and set new standards for themselves. Negotiations—and even disputes—about the meaning and significance of cabinet representation, therefore, begin in the transition and continue throughout the term.

In support of this contention, Janet M. Martin has found that campaign promises to name a more inclusive cabinet have resulted in greater media scrutiny of the nomination process.[22] It was particularly evident during both of the Clinton transitions. In 1992, the *Times* coverage reiterated the president-elect's recent campaign promises of "an administration that looks like America," and inventoried nominees by sex, race, and ethnicity. Clinton sought to shift this standard of evaluation in his 1996 transition, stating that "his Cabinet selections would reflect his view that the election results were a call for him to 'create a vital center.'"[23] The *Times* nomination articles, however, continued to reference the earlier "looks like" theme. In this administration, the paper was *relaying and imposing* a standard of judgment.[24] The nominees' identities continued to be reported as the primary indicators of which constituencies would be represented in the cabinet.

Perhaps in an effort to limit scrutiny and the associated contest for control, President-elect Reagan chose to have most of his initial secretaries-designate presented by a spokesperson.[25] Additionally, the formal announcements articulated neither the president-elect's selection criteria nor the cabinet's anticipated role in the administration.[26] Unfortunately, these strategies also resulted in nomination articles that were, as a group, much less coherent and systematic. When the president pursued similar tactics in his 1984 transition, the coverage became critical. A news analysis article by Hedrick Smith described the administration as "drifting."[27] A *Times* editorial asked, "What, then, is President Reagan up to? . . . How does he expect to govern?"[28] The Reagan transitions, then, demonstrated both the responsiveness and the power of the media. If presidents fail to provide a message about their cabinet nominations that the media may adapt and relay, their administration may be portrayed as lacking purpose and strength. Though presidents may wish to control the way in which the media interprets the representation offered by their cabinet nominees, they cannot do so unilaterally. They must be prepared to negotiate.

As the above references to the "reelection transitions" of Reagan and Clinton demonstrate, the nomination articles examine the midterm nomination decisions for indications of changes in cabinet representation. Replacement cabinet secretaries-designate are assessed for their likely impact on decisionmaking processes.[29] Midterm changes in access to the president were, for instance, a major issue in coverage of the 1979 Carter cabinet "purge." Here again, the coverage reflected and amplified the president's views of the cabinet, with Carter describing the resignations as part of a change in "my life style and my way of working."[30] White House communications routines were also of interest when Reagan chief of staff James A. Baker III and treasury secretary Donald Regan "swapped" positions in 1985.[31]

Substantive representation was an even more obvious concern in the nomination articles that compared the new secretary-designate with her or his predecessor. When the resignation and the replacement nomination were announced on the same day, the resignation often received the more detailed coverage. There would be an analysis of the departing secretary's contributions to the administration, as well as an assessment of her or his limitations. These conclusions were then linked to the selection of the replacement secretary-designate.[32] The resignation of Reagan secretary of state Alexander M. Haig, Jr., and the nomination of Secretary-Designate of State George Schultz, for instance, were both announced on 25 June 1982. The subsequent *New York Times* nomination article for Schultz stressed the unexpected nature of Haig's decision to leave. It also speculated on the implications of this action for White House relations and foreign policymaking.[33] Thus, policy and structural concerns were interwoven, causing these nomination articles to overlap somewhat with the biographical articles and their emphasis on the nominees' likely provision of descriptive representation.

Just as campaign indebtedness, another facet of substantive representation, was part of the calculus of presidential decisionmaking, so also was it addressed in the nomination articles. The connections between a president's campaigning and governing, transitions between them, and the implications for representation were routinely assessed.[34] These themes predominated in the nomination articles for the women secretaries-designate. This seems a reflection of the profile of the cabinet nominees rather than a sex- or gender-bias of the newspaper. Women secretaries-designate have typically been generalists, and their rise in the cabinet has been tied to women's voting patterns. Consequently, an emphasis on the campaign theme in their nomination articles is understandable.[35] The message of the nomination articles, then, seems congruent with the presidential context of the secretary-designate's selection. In this sense, the nomination articles were transgendered in their evaluations of the representation likely to be provided by the secretaries-designate.

Nomination articles assess the presidents' nomination decisions, seeking to determine what substantive representation the future cabinet member will provide. The thematic message of the cabinet nominations, as negotiated by the president and the media, sets the tone for judgments about the substantive representation that is expected of the future secretaries. The implications of each nomination for dialogues and relationships within the administration and with organized and societal interests, in relation to campaigning and governing, are also considered. Still, the precise capabilities—and the anticipated descriptive representation—of the secretaries-designate are not assessed in the nomination articles. That is the subject matter of the biographical articles.

The Biographical Articles, 1975–2001

The compliments and endorsements that the biographical articles provide, when studied systematically, reveal the qualities that the *Times* considers requisite to success as a political leader. Here is the *Times*'s judgment about the descriptive representation that the future cabinet member is likely to provide. The biographical articles detail character traits, outline career paths and political experience, and identify spouses and children, but these pieces are not merely factual presentations. They are, instead, interpretive. They explain the ambitions of the secretaries-designate to the public, drawing connections between the nominees' politics and personalities. In doing so, the articles evaluate the nominees' credibility and capability as political leaders and executive managers.

Because an endorsement from the *Times* is itself a valued credential, its terms merit careful study. For the purposes of this examination, the focus is on the paper's treatment of the nominees' sex and gender identity. Studies of the coverage given women legislators suggest that the media view women as presumptively less capable decisionmakers. Is that pattern observed in connection with the women secretaries-designate? Or, as the quantitative analysis has suggested, are any differences between the women and the men secretaries-designate attributable to the context of their nominations? The more detailed assessments of character and personality offered by the biographical articles allow these sex-based comparisons to be supplemented with a gender-based study. What associations can be drawn between the gender of the secretaries-designate and the *Times*'s assessments of their likely performance as descriptive representatives? Are the *Times*'s standards for success contributing to the regendering or transgendering of cabinet office and to the gender desegregation or integration of the cabinet?

Since men predominate among the secretaries-designate and since their qualifications have set the historical norm for cabinet service, the content of the *Times* coverage of the men secretaries-designate is analyzed first. Any differences in the biographical articles prepared for the men are carefully considered, in preparation for sex-based and gender-based comparisons with the women secretaries-designate. Representative passages are taken from the articles to illustrate and support the author's contentions. These excerpts are drawn from articles about nominees of different generations and administrations, from different parties and to different departments, and with widely varying career paths and political experiences. Though there are some changes in the content of the biographical articles, the *Times* has been remarkably consistent in the standards it uses to evaluate the credentials, and thus the likely descriptive representation, of the secretaries-designate.

The heroic narrative and the women secretaries-designate. Virtually without exception, the biographical articles open with an anecdote about the nominee. From the very beginning of the article, the actions of the secretaries-designate are presented as revelatory of their personality.

> Ten years ago, when President Johnson offered one of this city's most prominent lawyers a United States appellate court judgeship, the answer was no. "Turning down L. B. J. may be the most notable achievement of my life," William Thaddeus Coleman Jr. said today with a chuckle, recalling the late President's legendary powers of persuasion. Despite that disclaimer, there have been considerably more important accomplishments in the career of the 54-year-old Philadelphian whom President Ford nominated today to become the Secretary of Transportation.[36]

From the start, Coleman is depicted as steadfast and enduring, unmoved by the appeals of the powerful. Though brief, this opening offers a political story about an exceptional individual with implications for the president who recruited him. Coleman, after all, could withstand the appeals of Johnson, a legendary lobbyist, but not those of Ford. The anecdote, therefore, applauds the character and lifetime accomplishments of the new secretary-designate while also endorsing the president. The secretary-designate is presented as a valuable addition to the cabinet and the administration, and his descriptive representation is expected to be of high quality.

Time and again, though each article is about a different male secretary-designate, each narrative is about a similar character and set of experiences. However diverse the men's accomplishments, they are cited in support of the same traits. Strength, drive, and determination are celebrated. The nominee is distinguished by his critical sense, though he is also attentive to others' concerns and able to work collaboratively. He possesses the intellect and charisma to resolve complex problems. Reinforcing this characterization are statements from the men's colleagues, former bosses, policy activists, and future departmental clients. At least one testimonial appears in 91 of the 119 biographies (76.5 percent) of the five later administrations with initial and midterm nominations. The message of the biographical articles is therefore as clear as it is unequivocal: The men secretaries-designate have been successful in the past; they can be expected to succeed in the future. Here is a powerful endorsement of the men as descriptive representatives.

The men—the vast majority of whom are white—are being judged as strong descriptive representatives by masculinist standards. Stressing the nominee's singularity, for instance, resonates with the "great man" approach to history and to leadership.

> In this gendered construction of a singular leader, cause and effect are blurred and reinforcing; nevertheless, cultural constructions much more readily accord the possibility of individual accomplishment deserving of greatness—accomplishments earned in one's own right, without regard to connections or support—to men. Gender power gives the advantage to men in terms of the "great man" model of the lone leader at the top.[37]

More specifically, the *Times* articles praise the secretaries-designate for manifesting the traits of "Heroic Men." Historian Mark Kann's description of this role, with its associated assessments of leadership and power, is as applicable to the present day as to the founding.

Adversity not only demanded great leaders and justified powerful ones; it also called forth, tested, and identified the Heroic Man who measured up to the highest standards of manhood.

The standards were diffuse but known. They included preeminence in "ability and virtue" along with disciplined passion, family responsibility, and social civility. John Adams emphasized "exemplary morals, great patience, calmness, coolness, and attention," while Elizur Goodrich highlighted "knowledge, wisdom, and prudence, courage and unshaken resolution, righteousness and justice tempered with lenity, mercy, and compassion, and a steady firmness . . . and a sacred regard to the moral and religious interests of the community." Whatever the particular mix of virtues, the founders felt that great leaders made themselves known by their powerful and positive impact on ordinary men. Zephaniah Swift Moore suggested that great leaders were men of "character and example" who had considerable "influence in forming the public mind."[38]

References to virtue, passion, family responsibility, social civility, coolness, resolution, righteousness, and mercy, among other traits, make it impossible to view masculinity and femininity as mutually exclusive. Many of these qualities have also been historically attributed to women in equally approving tones. What distinguishes the Heroic Man, then, is not merely the traits he evidences but also the goals to which he devotes himself. The Heroic Man is a "leader" who "had considerable 'influence in forming the public mind.'" The congruence between these qualities in the writings of the founders and of the *Times* biographical articles is powerful.

The implications of this similarity need to be given careful thought. The biographical articles in the *Times* are reinforcing a particular tradition and ideology and must be analyzed in reference to that tradition and ideology. The standards employed in evaluating the secretaries-designate are neither ephemeral nor distinctive but long-standing and shared by many in the society. The gender implications are particularly profound. The Heroic Man tradition forges a close connection between the identity and the skill of the leader. The articulation of this ideology in the biographical articles for the men secretaries-designate, then, has a regendering effect. The men are encouraged—and effectively required—to act in accord with traditional conceptions of masculinity. The effect on the women secretaries-designate, however, is less certain. A number of the heroic traits have historically been attributed to women, but women have seldom had the opportunity to exercise a "powerful and positive impact" on men. There is also the question of whether women and men must be perceived in similar terms in order to be recognized as powerful. It may be that women introduce new standards for leadership and management, which are duly applied in assessing men. Such an evolution would facilitate the transgendering of high political office.

In keeping with the Heroic Man tradition, the biographies did not present masculinity and femininity as polar opposites. The founders recommended that leaders exhibit "patience," "calmness," "prudence," and "compassion." Similarly, the articles spoke approvingly of men secretaries-designate who were "contemplative,"[39] "quiet,"[40] and "unpretentious."[41] All these qualities were as traditionally suited to women as to men, and the biographical articles for the women indicated as much. The women were described as "pleasant"[42] and "hardworking,"[43] as exhibiting "politeness" and "cool good humor,"[44] and as being possessed of a "quick mind."[45] In the Heroic Man tradition and in the biographical articles for the men secretaries-designate, however, those traits were in service to the strength, incisiveness, and assertiveness required of leaders in a competitive environment. In the biographical articles for the women, this attribution was lacking. Even though the women had credentials similar to those of the men, they were not described as possessing the traits that distinguish successful leaders. According to the biographical articles, therefore, women and men secretaries-designate shared some traits—but only the men possessed those associated with power and authority. Heroism was reserved to men, masculinism was subtly reinforced, and women's descriptive representation was consistently viewed as being of lesser quality than that of men. The biographical articles, then, were as much about regendering for the women as for the men secretaries-designate.

This message was conveyed even in the articles' opening paragraphs. Functionally, these paragraphs were quite similar for both the women and the men secretaries-designate. In both instances, anecdotes were recounted and the essence of the nominees' character was revealed by reference to particular achievements. The content of the paragraphs, however, was systematically different for the women and for the men.

Dr. Donna E. Shalala, an energetic, exuberant administrator who has never been shy about trumpeting her considerable achievements, is now going to tackle two of the most intractable problems in American society: health care and welfare.

Characteristically, she is almost unnervingly confident that she can make a difference as Secretary of Health and Human Services.[46]

As in the biographical articles for other women secretaries-designate, Shalala received a curiously qualified endorsement. She was described as "almost unnervingly confident," a reference that was not made in regard to any of the men. Indeed, such an expression verged on being an oxymoron by Heroic Man standards.

An even more obvious contrast is seen in the opening paragraphs provided for Carter treasury secretary-designate Michael Blumenthal and George W. Bush labor secretary-designate Elaine Lan Chao. Although both of the paragraphs describe the nominees' early lives and their immigration to the United States, their interpretive frames are very different.

Werner Michael Blumenthal, the 50-year-old chairman, president and chief executive officer of the Bendix Corporation, has not been one to sit back and wait for the good things in life to drop into his lap. He has, instead, pursued them with directness and passion. In his teenage years and early 20s, he scratched to stay alive with his parents in Shanghai after they had left Germany in 1938 to escape Nazi persecution. He recalled buying food by the ounce and cleaning laboratory equipment for $1 a week. When he heard that the Americans were due to arrive he hired a sampan to take him out to the ships so that he would be one of the first to greet them. After much waiting he got a visa in 1947 and sailed for San Francisco. His first job was as a billing clerk with the National Biscuit Company at $34 a week. He did not wait long to quit and begin to study international economics at the University of California, supporting himself with odd jobs such as a janitor, movie ticket taker, armed guard, waiter and as a shill at a gambling casino where he lured customers to gamble with house chips.[47]

Ever since she was 8, and a freighter bearing her family into New York harbor offered a first glimpse of the Statue of Liberty, Elaine L. Chao has concentrated on finding her place in America.

Ms. Chao—Chinese immigrant, Harvard graduate, former head of the Peace Corps and the United Way—reached a new rung today in a fast-rising career, becoming President-elect George W. Bush's choice as secretary of labor.[48]

Blumenthal acted with "directness and passion," whereas Chao "concentrated on finding her place." Blumenthal is depicted as goal-oriented and confident, determined to succeed, and willing to make the associated sacrifices. Chao is presented as lacking direction and uncertain. Feeding into this contrast are racial stereotypes of Asian American women as stoic and silent. The elite educational and professional credentials of both nominees are acknowledged, but Blumenthal is judged the stronger and more powerful. His descriptive representation will be more forceful than hers. Her symbolic representation will carry a message of marginalization.

These contrasts become even more obvious when one considers the attributes that are credited to the women secretaries-designate throughout the body of the biographical articles. The biographical article for Housing and Urban Development (HUD) Secretary-Designate Harris is particularly illustrative.

> "A mind like a steel trap," says one old friend of Patricia Roberts Harris, named today by President-elect Carter to be Secretary of Housing and Urban Development in his Cabinet. "Warm and motherly" were the words used by someone else to describe her. The 52-year-old lawyer, politician and sometime diplomat is the second woman and the first black named to Mr. Carter's Cabinet. Throughout her career, what one friend described as her "duality"—an unusual and generally effective mix of toughness, sharp mind and charm—has been her trademark.[49]

The biographical article presents Harris as combining traditionally masculine and feminine behaviors, namely, command and persuasion.[50] A woman is therefore practicing—in modified form—a masculine style of leadership. Yet no male secretary-designate found his strength qualified, let alone excused, by his "charm."[51] The gender bias is subtle but notable. Also in evidence is a racial bias, as was observed in the biographical article for Chao.[52] In this instance, racial stereotypes of African American women surface in references to Harris's "motherly" nature. Once again, the descriptive representation offered by the women secretaries-designate is presented as less than strong, if not weak, with symbolic representation also compromised.

Thus, the content of the women's and men's biographies overlapped to a certain extent, with similar traits sometimes attributed to the men and the women secretaries-designate. The traits of the women, however, consistently fell short of the Heroic Man standard. It is important to note that this occurred even though the women's and men's pre-cabinet careers and credentials were quite similar. As noted in the previous chapter, both were educated at the same elite institutions and both had similar records of professional accomplishment. Further, the women nominees had frequently crossed traditional gender boundaries, establishing themselves as valued members of predominantly male organizations. Still, the *Times* biographical articles seldom praised the women for their ambition, strength, or self-assurance. The women secretaries-designate were not identified as proactive, powerful, or authoritative leaders.[53] In the judgment of the *Times*, which was premised on a masculinist standard, the women secretaries-designate would provide poorer representation than the men. There was no endorsement of a transgendered standard for cabinet service.

The public implications of the private sphere. In addition to their assessments of the nominees' professional careers, the biographical articles profiled the marriages and children of the secretaries-designate. For the men secretaries-designate, familial relationships were treated as a microcosm of professional partnerships.

> In recent days Moon Landrieu has been engaged in one of his favorite activities, ringing doorbells and canvassing for votes.
>
> This time it is not the former Mayor and reported choice to head the Department of Housing and Urban Development who is running for office. His 23-year-old daughter, Mary, is a candidate for the state legislature, where her father began his political career almost 20 years ago.
>
> The Landrieu name is considered a strong asset to Mr. Landrieu's daughter.[54]

Professional and personal success are a matched set, so much so that children participate in and become extensions of the nominee's political career. Integrity, fidelity, and commitment are highlighted. Testimonials from the nominees' wives reinforce these themes. "'He really, really enjoys Government,' Mrs. Califano said in a telephone interview. 'I think it's his milieu.'"[55] The wife's satisfaction with her marriage is inferred from the state of the nominee's professional life, so that one becomes a reflection of the other. Mrs. Califano supplies the logic of this dynamic by describing politics as her husband's vocation. A job or a career has boundaries, but a vocation is an ongoing expression of one's deeper self. And even though the wife's actions provide a support system for the husband, the husband is viewed as a singular actor. This emphasis on male autonomy surfaces repeatedly throughout the biog raphical articles for the men secretaries-designate.[56] Here is the reinforcement of masculinist standards for capability and success. The credible leader—the representative who provides strong descriptive representation, meeting the polity's prevailing standard for effectiveness—is wholly dedicated to his career and singularly credited with his accomplishments.

To sustain this interpretation of the men secretaries-designate, divorce and family difficulties were skimmed over. Only one biography mentioned any ongoing marital discord.

> A fiercely competitive tennis player, Mr. Carlucci plays on his own court in the backyard of his McLean, Va. home, which a Washington monthly recently assessed at $1 million. Although Marcia, his second wife, is generally regarded as a better player, he is known to publicly criticize her game in their doubles matches.[57]

As a unique statement, the importance of this excerpt should not be overstated. It should not be underestimated, either, as its warnings extend beyond one nominee's private life. The defense secretary-designate is depicted as an individual who has taken good things—competitiveness and ambition—to an extreme. This is a rare reference to a secretary-designate as inferior: Carlucci criticizes those who are more skilled and does so in a disruptive manner. The description of a million-dollar home sets the seal on the depiction of an executive who is self-centered, showy, and self-promoting. This passage cautions the reader about the representation that Secretary-Designate Carlucci might provide.

In general, however, the biographies describe men secretaries-designate as valuing but removed from their families. The nominee's career and family life are discussed separately, with professional accomplishments depicted in greater detail. This treatment is entirely in keeping with the Heroic Man tradition.

> Ultimately, the Heroic Man distinguished himself from the Family Man and the Better Sort by transcending intergenerational time and parochial space. . . . He was exquisitely selfless and supremely public-spirited. . . . He asserted his right to vindicate "the dignity of men" by acting with a higher regard for the public good than for his own family and friends. He could act against both malicious enemies and misguided friends because he sought neither leadership status nor public acclaim. Like Washington, he preferred home life; like Franklin, he accepted the burdens of leadership solely to enlarge his

capacity for doing good; and like history's most memorable heroes, he risked fortune, fame, and immortality to procreate a better future for humankind.[58]

Marriage and children are important. Ironically, however, they are also valued as measures of the leader's self-sacrifice. Marriage and children are so special that setting them aside is a distinguishing feature of a great leader. The Heroic Man relinquishes his duties as a father to individual children so that he can assume paternal responsibilities for the wider polity. The biographies do not articulate quite this level of idealism, but their framing is congruent with such aspirations. The influence of masculinism in *the Times*'s judgments about cabinet representation, with its consequent endorsement of regendering men's behavior to traditionally masculinist standards, is clear.

If women are not readily identified as heroic in the public sphere, they are even less readily identified as such in the private sphere. In this regard as in many others, gender role traditions create a catch-22 for women leaders. A man's public-spiritedness can be measured, to some extent, by his willingness to set aside his family and devote himself to the polity. The same sacrifice by a woman is not viewed with such approbation. The Zoë Baird controversy was significantly about "When Baby Comes In Second to Career," to quote the title of a critical *Washington Post* column.[59]

The women secretaries-designate, as discussed in the previous chapter, do not have traditional marriages. The women are, typically, their husbands' professional equals. In fact, Hobby, Hills, Hufstedler, Dole, Heckler, McLaughlin, Franklin, and O'Leary all worked with their husbands. There are no neat boundaries between private and public spheres, no consistent hierarchies of women and men, in these marriages. These practices, objectively described, challenge expectations that have been historically directed at women.

The biographical articles for the women secretaries-designate reflect these circumstances, presenting husbands and children in the context of the women's careers. Yet this presentation then proceeds to describe the women in terms of their relationships. Pictures of Carla Anderson Hills's children are prominent in her *New York Times* portrait.[60] Patricia Roberts Harris is described as attending law school with the "encouragement" of her husband.[61] Margaret Heckler's husband also provided "encouragement," helping her win election to Congress.[62] Though Elizabeth Hanford Dole had a lengthy political career before marrying Robert Dole, almost half of her biographical article comments on their marriage and her loyal support of his political aspirations.[63] Though the men were doubtless supported by their families, it is the women who are presented as dependent. Men are autonomous; women are heteronomous.

Coverage of the women's husbands and children did, however, gradually alter. In part, it reflected changes in the profiles of the women secretaries-designate. In later administrations, women nominees had fewer children. Several of them were not married when they were selected. During the George W. Bush 2000 transition, the *Times* adopted the practice of putting educational, professional, and family information in boxed graphics, so that the content of the biographical articles became more exclusively professional and political. Though these articles continued to evidence gender bias along other dimensions, this particular aspect of the coverage did become somewhat transgendered.

Still, the biographical articles significantly impaired the women nominees' ability to provide strong descriptive representation. It was not merely that these articles suggested that the women secretaries-designate needed men's endorsement in order to succeed. That much went without saying, since the women worked in predominantly male institutions. Moreover, as the "first women" in various posts, they invariably had men as mentors and supervisors. The bias, instead, was found in the systematic presentation of the women secretaries-designate as depending on relationships, whereas their male colleagues acted unilaterally. In a system that prized autonomy and individualism, these depictions hurt women and helped men. The biographical articles ignored the overwhelming similarity in the nominees' career paths and credentials in order to uphold masculinist expectations of gender role contrasts that supported conclusions that men would be stronger representatives. In their coverage of the professional and personal lives of the secretaries-designate, then, the *Times* biographical articles were strong forces for regendering cabinet offices. Men were presented as the leaders, whereas women received the consolation prize of praise for their thoughtfulness and insightfulness.

NEW YORK TIMES EVALUATIONS OF THE SECRETARIES-DESIGNATE

Notwithstanding the continuing claim of the *New York Times* to provide "all the news that's fit to print," the paper has always had to decide what it would report. And it has done so in such conformity with elite standards that it has established itself as the nation's newspaper of record. In regard to cabinet nominations, the *Times* has extensively covered both presidential decisionmaking (through nomination articles) and the secretaries-designate (through biographical articles). This chapter has quantitatively and qualitatively analyzed these pieces to see how one of the country's most influential media outlets has explained the president's nomination decisions and introduced the secretaries-designate to the public.

Previous research into media coverage of women officeholders has indicated that the media trivializes and marginalizes women officeholders. As evidence, there is the attention given to the women's appearance, the frequency with which they are treated as "Everywoman," and the placement of their coverage in the "Style" sections of the newspapers. Other studies, however, have concluded that the problem lies less with the coverage that is present than with that which is absent. They note, for example, that the media overemphasizes the work of women legislators on "women's issues" while neglecting their dedication to other policy areas. Similarly, women national leaders are described as political newcomers, which may "create false expectations for what the new leader can achieve and, therefore, in the long term may set women leaders on a pedestal from which they can only fall."[64]

The understanding of leadership and gender that surfaces in this study of the *New York Times* falls somewhere between these two perspectives. Women and men secretaries-designate receive nomination coverage that is similar in the number of articles and their placement. Women nominees do not seem to occasion a systematically different perspective on presidential power or presidential decisionmaking, as those events are analyzed in the *New York Times* nomination articles. In this regard, the *Times* coverage contributes to the transgendering of cabinet office by assessing the nominations of women and men in similar terms. Further, the connections drawn between campaigning, women voters, and the women secretaries-designate suggest that the *Times* does see women voters as achieving the status of presidential constituents who have descriptive and substantive representatives in the cabinet.

Turning from the nomination articles to the biographical articles, we move from an analysis of presidential decisions to a study of the secretaries-designate. If we accept that individual nominees significantly influence the institutional development of the cabinet, then we need to understand what influences their reputation and prestige as political actors. Because it comments on the personal attributes, career development, and private lives of the secretaries-designate, the *Times* can have this effect. As we have also seen, its judgments are about the descriptive representation that the nominee will provide as an able and credible leader.

In some ways, the biographical articles, like the nomination articles, deliver a transgendered message. Women and men secretaries-designate are held to a common standard, which is reflective of the Heroic Man tradition of leadership and statesmanship. Further, there is some overlap in the traits for which both women and men secretaries-designate are endorsed as prospective leaders. Yet reliance on this masculinist standard ultimately leads to women being viewed as less qualified than men. Women, according to the biographical articles, lack the strength and self-reliance that typifies heroism. In their professional and their personal lives, they fail to demonstrate the autonomy that is expected of political executives. Can a department afford a leader who is "soft-spoken and gentle"? Can a constituent trust that such an individual will be a strong representative?

The message of the *Times* articles is therefore mixed. Quantitatively, the paper provides coverage that is virtually constant for the women and the men secretaries-designate, in the frequency and placement of the nomination and the biographical articles. Further, qualitative analysis of the nomination articles indicated that the *Times* was assessing the presidential nominations of women and men secretaries-designate by similar standards. Women and men secretaries-designate were therefore similarly valued as substantive representatives. In its judgments about the nomination process, then, the *New York Times* presented formal representation as being transgendered for the cabinet nominees.

This message was contradicted in the biographical articles, which presented women as lacking by the masculinist standards of the Heroic Man. Though women and men shared some character traits—and though the comparisons of the previous chapter demonstrate that women's credentials were more extensive than those of many of the men with whom they were nominated—the women were described as lacking the more dynamic qualities of leadership. There were very few references to the women as confident, aggressive, or competitive, and those few were qualified. Women were presented as dependent; their heteronomy was in marked contrast to men's autonomy. Whether written about women or men secretaries-designate, then, the biographical articles applied the dictates of masculinism, imposing traditional standards of femininity and masculinity. With masculine traits accepted as more useful and valuable, women were presented as presumptively weaker descriptive representatives. With women's lesser competence identifying them as prospectively less effective decisionmakers, the *Times* indicated that women secretaries-designate would be marginal participants in the cabinet. Accordingly, their symbolic representation would speak more to subordination than to inclusivity.

On balance, therefore, the *Times* coverage of the cabinet nominations and nominees suggests that the paper endorses the gender desegregation but not the gender integration of the cabinet. Though the transgendered nature of presidential nomination decisions pushes the cabinet toward gender integration, the *Times*'s evaluations of the nominees suggest that this evolution will be delimited. How can the cabinet be transgendered when its women members are consistently less competent than its men? The only possible organizational evolution is in the direction of regendering, so that the cabinet undergoes nothing more than a qualified gender desegregation. Given the status and readership of the *Times,* this message cannot be ignored. And yet, others may not agree. Their standards and their judgments may be quite different. The Senate, specifically the confirmation committees, directly determines the political fortunes of the secretaries-designate. The standards and assessments of these decisionmakers must be considered, if we are to understand how confirmation decisions, as well as nomination decisions and media coverage, shape the prestige and reputation of the secretaries-designate.

NOTES

1. See, for example: Samuel Kernell, *Going Public: New Strategies of Presidential Leadership,* 3rd ed. (Washington, D.C.: CQ Press, 1999); Michael Baruch and Martha Joynt Kumar, *Portraying the President: The White House and the News Media* (Baltimore: Johns Hopkins Press, 1981); Stephen Hess, *The Government/Press Connection: Press Officers and Their Offices* (Washington, D.C.: Brookings Institution, 1984); Stephen Hess, *Live from Capitol Hill! Studies of Congress and the Media* (Washington, D.C.: Brookings Institution, 1991).

2. Robert Shogan, "The Confirmation Wars: How Politicians, Interest Groups, and the Press Shape the Presidential Appointment Process," in *Obstacle Course: The Report of the Twentieth Century Fund Task Force on the Presidential Appointment Process* (New York: Twentieth Century Fund, 1996).

3. For a discussion of the press as a social institution and an ally of legitimating institutions, see Gaye Tuchman, *Making News: A Study in the Construction of Reality* (New York: Free Press, 1978). The coverage of the nomination of Clinton attorney general–designate Zoë Baird also illustrates these dynamics. The nomination was initially very well received, and the *New York Times* published an editorial that endorsed her without reservation. When news of Baird's illegal actions in hiring household workers broke in a page 1 *New York Times* article on 14 January 1993, the coverage remained generally supportive in the print media, which was more attuned to elite liberal opinion. Meanwhile, talk radio stations were receiving and broadcasting a very different cross-section of public opinion. As Andrew Kohut and Kimberly Parker have demonstrated, "The typical talk radio listener is more conservative, better educated, more antigovernment, more likely to be a male, and more critical of the Clinton administration than the average American." Each of these variables was demonstrably relevant to the Baird case. In this instance as in many others, different media outlets reflected the views of different segments of the population. David Johnston, "Clinton's Choice for Justice Dept. Hired Illegal Aliens for Household," *New York Times,* 14 January 1993, p. A1; Andrew Kohut and Kimberly Parker, "Talk Radio and Gender Politics," in *Women, Media, and Politics,* ed. Pippa Norris (New York: Oxford University Press, 1997), p. 225; Gwen Ifill, "The Baird Appointment: In Trouble from the Start, Then a Firestorm," *New York Times,* 23 January 1993, p. 8; Robert Reinhold, "Fueled by Radio and TV: Outcry Became Uproar," *New York Times,* 23 January 1993, p. 9; Elizabeth Drew, *On the Edge: The Clinton Presidency* (New York: Simon and Schuster, 1994), p. 38; Benjamin I. Page, *Who Deliberates? Mass Media in Modern Democracy* (Chicago: University of Chicago Press, 1996), pp. 81–95; *Obstacle Course: The Report of the Twentieth Century Fund Task Force on the Presidential Appointment Process* (New York: Twentieth Century Fund, 1996), p. 142.

4. The secretary-designate who was perhaps the most outspoken at the announcement of her nomination was Juanita M. Kreps, who criticized the president-elect's personnel search and selection procedures. James T. Wooten, "Bell Is Named Attorney General; Mrs. Kreps Gets Commerce Post," *New York Times,* 21 December 1976, pp. 1, 24. See also Chapter 3 in this book.

5. Richard L. Berke, "For Appointees to Cabinet, a List of Do's and Don't's," *New York Times,* 6 January 1993, p. A14.

6. Paul Light, *A Survivor's Guide for Presidential Nominees* (Washington, D.C.: Brookings Institution, 2000); available online at www.appointee.brookings.org/sg/c6.htm.

7. Richard Neustadt's commentary on the significance of these qualities is of considerable relevance to the secretaries-designate. He writes, "Prestige, like reputation, is a subjective factor, a matter of judgment. It works on power just as reputation does through the mechanism of anticipated reactions. The same men, Washingtonians, do the judging. In the case of reputation they anticipate reactions from the President. In the instance of prestige they anticipate

reactions from the public. Most members of the Washington community depend upon outsiders to support them on their interests. The dependence may be as direct as votes, or it may be as indirect as passive toleration. Dependent men must take account of popular reaction to their actions. What their publics may think of them becomes a factor, therefore, in deciding how to deal with the desires of a President. His prestige enters into that decision; their publics are part of his." As members of the Washington community, the press corps perform perhaps the most extensive and public introductions. Richard E. Neustadt, *Presidential Power and the Modern Presidents: The Politics of Leadership from Roosevelt to Reagan* (New York: Free Press, 1990), p. 73.

8. Linda Witt, Karen M. Paget, and Glenna Matthews, *Running as a Woman: Gender and Power in American Politics* (New York: Free Press, 1993), p. 186.

9. Susan J. Carroll and Ronnee Schreiber, "Media Coverage of Women in the 103rd Congress," in *Women, Media, and Politics,* ed. Pippa Norris (New York: Oxford University Press, 1997), p. 145.

10. Ibid., pp. 145–146.

11. This content analysis is based on careful review of articles published in the *New York Times* that provided coverage of the president's cabinet nominations. As will be seen in this chapter, both quantitative and qualitative analyses were employed to ensure that the findings would be as valid and as reliable as possible. For the quantitative study, the unit of analysis was the articles themselves, classified as either "nomination articles" or "biographical articles." The placement was measured in simple terms, as page 1 or other. These two measures, as explained in the text, revealed the historical patterns of cabinet nomination coverage in clear and simple terms. For the qualitative study, the organizational structure of the articles and their thematic presentation and word choice were each assessed. Sex differences and gender comparisons were conducted. Finally, in presenting the conclusions, representative passages were selected so that the reader might judge the conclusions for herself or himself.

12. "The Roosevelt Cabinet Slate," *New York Times,* 23 February 1933, p. 1; "Public Services of the Ten Prospective Members of Roosevelt's Cabinet," *New York Times,* 23 February 1933, p. 3.

13. All available evidence indicates that only one midterm nominee, Postmaster General-Designate Frank C. Walker, received a biographical article. "Walker Long Aide to Roosevelt Aims," *New York Times,* 1 September 1940, p. 2.

14. To illustrate this point, consider the three Reagan inner cabinet nominations that were made late in the second term. The nominees were Nicholas Brady (Treasury, 1988), Frank Carlucci (Defense, 1987), and Richard Thornburgh (Justice, 1988). Only Brady received a nomination article, which was placed on the front page. Julie Johnson, "Baker Resigns to Work for Bush; Brady Is Named for Treasury Job," *New York Times,* 6 August 1988, p. 1. Timing was also a factor in coverage of the Clinton midterm nominations. Three cabinet nominations were made in 1998, in the midst of the impeachment pro-

ceedings. The three nominees were Treasury Secretary-Designate Lawrence H. Summers, Energy Secretary-Designate Bill Richardson, and Veterans Affairs Secretary-Designate Togo D. West, Jr. Just as campaign events may dominate presidential coverage in the final year of an administration, displacing and limiting the coverage of cabinet nominations, so also may the impeachment have been responsible for the lessened coverage of cabinet nominations.

15. Setting aside the Roosevelt administration for reasons explained previously, only two men—Ford transportation secretary-designate William T. Coleman, Jr., and Reagan agriculture secretary-designate Richard E. Lyng—did not receive a nomination article. Seven secretaries-designate—two women and five men—did not receive a biographical article. Five of these were nominated very late in the presidential term. The two women were Reagan labor secretary-designate Ann Dore McLaughlin and George H. W. Bush commerce secretary-designate Barbara H. Franklin. The five men were Ford labor secretary-designate John T. Dunlop, Carter energy secretary-designate James R. Schlesinger, Reagan commerce secretary-designate C. William Verity, Jr., Reagan transportation secretary-designate James H. Burnley IV, and George H. W. Bush transportation secretary-designate Andrew Card.

16. Leo Egan, "Summerfield Put in Postmaster Job; Posts for 2 Women," *New York Times,* 26 November 1952, p. 1.

17. "FSA Reorganization," *Congressional Quarterly Weekly Report,* 2 April 1953, p. 427.

18. The Hobby cabinet nomination was reported in a brief paragraph, in an article announcing the nomination of the administrator of the Reconstruction Finance Corporation. "Eisenhower Names New Head of R.F.C.," *New York Times,* 3 April 1953, p. 14.

19. The reader might conclude that a comparable case would be that of the Department of Energy reorganization in the Carter administration. That reorganization—and also the nomination of the energy secretary-designate—actually stretched out over considerably more of the president's first year in office than did the HEW reorganization. President Carter did not submit a proposal for the Energy Department reorganization until 1 March 1977. Congressional approval was not received until 4 August 1977, when the department was created, and James R. Schlesinger (assistant to the president and Energy Resources Council chair) was confirmed as its secretary. Thus, in relative terms, the HEW reorganization proposal was receiving final congressional approval at the same point in the presidential term that the Department of Energy received its first consideration in Congress. James T. Wooten, "Secretary of H.E.W., Director of C.I.A. and Chief Assistant for Energy Matters Designated," *New York Times,* 24 December 1976, p. 1; Steven Rattner, "Energy Department: Dust Is Still Settling," *New York Times,* 5 December 1977, p. 61.

20. For example, see Steven R. Weisman, "Reagan Completes Cabinet and Keeps Mansfield as Envoy," *New York Times*, 8 January 1981, p. 1; Steven Greenhouse, "Clinton's Choice of Reich Hints at a Stepped-up Role for Labor Department," *New York Times*, 12 December 1992, p. 10.

21. Bernard Gwertzman, "Ford Promises That He and Kissinger Will Continue Nixon's Foreign Policy," *New York Times*, 15 January 1975, p. 14. See also the following articles, which stress Ford's attentiveness to constituencies ignored or neglected by Nixon: "Dunlop Is Chosen for Labor Office," *New York Times*, 9 February 1975, p. 39; James M. Naughton, "Ford Calls 8 Fit to Run With Him," *New York Times*, 23 January 1976, p. 38.

22. Janet M. Martin, "Women Who Govern: The President's Appointments," in *The Other Elites: Women, Politics, and Power in the Executive Branch*, ed. by MaryAnne Borrelli and Janet M. Martin (Boulder, Colo.: Lynne Rienner Publishers, 1997), pp. 52–57.

23. "Clinton Seeks 'Vital Center' with Cabinet," *New York Times*, 8 November 1996, p. 1; "Groups Press Clinton on Labor Secretary," *New York Times*, 12 December 1996, p. 1. On the 1992 Clinton transition, see Elizabeth Drew, *On the Edge: The Clinton Presidency* (New York: Simon and Schuster, 1994).

24. A similar mixture of adopting and rejecting administration rhetoric was also present in nomination articles during the Carter and George H. W. Bush transition. Carter continued Ford's emphasis on fostering public confidence in the government. Reporters added their assessments of whether the "outsider" motif, so evident during the campaign, would continue during the administration. As with the second Clinton transition, campaign promises were resurrected and sometimes fueled criticism of the nominations. The nomination of Attorney General–Designate Griffin Bell, for example, was described as a long step away from Carter's campaign promises of an independent attorney general. It stimulated memories of Nixon nominees and their associated abuses. In contrast, George H. W. Bush encountered a set of queries that were focused more on governance than on campaigning as he transitioned from the vice presidential to the presidential office. In particular, the *New York Times* coverage evidenced great curiosity about the ways in which his administration would be similar to or different from that of his predecessor. This query was encouraged by Bush's early renomination of those who had entered the cabinet late in Reagan's second term. Other issues raised by the *New York Times* in regard to President-elect Bush's initial secretaries-designate were the nominees' insider qualifications and their past relationships with the president-elect. Charles Mohr, "Vance Is Selected by Carter to Run State Department," *New York Times*, 4 December 1976, p. 1; Hedrick Smith, "A Controversial Nomination," *New York Times*, 21 December 1976, p. 1. See also David E. Rosenbaum, "Choosing a Friend for Attorney General," *New York Times*, 28 December 1976, p. 13. Bernard Weinraub, "Tower Considered for Defense Post in New Bush Move," *New York Times*, 22 November 1988, p. 1; Gerald M. Boyd, "Kemp, Picked as Chief of H.U.D., Pledges to Combat Homelessness," *New York Times*, 20 December 1988, p. 1. See also R. W. Apple, Jr., "Bush's Beltway Team," *New York Times*, 13 January 1989, p. 1.

25. See Steven R. Weisman, "Reagan Designates Eight to Fill Posts At Cabinet Level," *New York Times*, 12 December 1980, p. 1.

26. The *Times* noted that it was "unusual" for the nominees to be formally announced by an administration official other than the chief executive; the president-elect responded that he was seeking to keep the spotlight of attention upon his nominees by absenting himself from these events. Steven R. Weisman, "Reagan Designates Eight to Fill Posts at Cabinet Level," *New York Times*, 12 December 1980, p. 1. Reagan did not personally announce a cabinet nomination until 25 June 1982, when he presented Secretary-Designate George Shultz. Bernard Gwertzman, "Action Is Surprise," *New York Times*, 26 June 1982, p. 1. Reagan appeared at virtually every subsequent announcement of a cabinet nomination, though he rarely conducted a press conference on these occasions.

27. Hedrick Smith, "Shuffle in Administration: Sign of Restlessness, Rather Than of Strategy," *New York Times*, 9 January 1985, p. A19.

28. "The Second-Term Swap," *New York Times*, 9 January 1985, p. A22. Of the seven cabinet nominations made during this transition, four were announced by the president (who took no questions from the press) and three by a presidential spokesman. The subsequent nomination articles assessed only the structural implications of the selections. There was no consideration of the wider cabinet or administration beyond the repeated statement that the changes in cabinet membership were unanticipated. Bernard Weinraub, "President Designates Regan White House Chief of Staff, Switching Him with Baker," *New York Times*, 9 January 1985, p. 1; Gerald M. Boyd, "President Names 3 for His Cabinet in Key Job Shifts," *New York Times*, 11 January 1985, p. 1.

29. For example, see Francis X. Clines, "President Names Watt's Top Aide for Energy Post," *New York Times*, 6 November 1982, p. 1; "Clark Appointment Catches State Department Unawares," *New York Times*, 14 October 1983, p. 1; David E. Sanger, "Choice for Treasury Wins Praise as Clinton Loses Elder Statesman," *New York Times*, 7 December 1994, p. 1.

30. Terence Smith, "Carter Offered Resignations by Cabinet and Senior Staff; Some Going in Days, Aides Say," *New York Times*, 18 July 1979, p. A15; See also David E. Rosenbaum, "New Style Emerging After Shake-Up in the Cabinet," *New York Times*, 13 November 1979, p. A16. Carter's statement was a paraphrase by "a participant" in the cabinet meeting. However, it is reflective of Carter's own account of his deliberations in this period. See Jimmy Carter, *Keeping Faith: Memoirs of a President* (New York: Bantam Books, 1982), pp. 115–117.

31. Bernard Weinraub, "Shift at Treasury," *New York Times*, 9 January 1985, p. 1.

32. For example, see James M. Naughton, "Sweeping Change," *New York Times*, 4 November 1975, p. 1; Steven Rattner, "Energy Head Resigns," *New York Times*, 21 July 1979, p. 1.

33. Bernard Gwertzman, "Action Is Surprise," *New York Times*, 26 June 1982, p. 1.

34. This coverage was sometimes more organizational, sometimes more policy related. The 1975 nomination of Commerce Secretary-Designate C. B.

Morton was described as part of Ford's effort to gain the presidential nomination of the Republican Party. Morton was a close friend of the president and a former Republican National Committee chair. Notwithstanding the administration's objections to depictions of Morton as a campaign officer, the *Times* concluded that the Commerce Department nomination put him "in a position where he could begin organizing the financial base of Mr. Ford's announced 1976 election campaign." As evidence of more policy-based campaign themes, see the following nomination articles: Robert Pear, "Reagan Chooses Ex-Rep. Heckler to Be the New Secretary of Health," *New York Times,* 13 January 1983, p. 1; Gerald M. Boyd, "Elizabeth Dole Chosen by Bush for Labor Dept.," *New York Times,* 25 December 1988, p. 1; Keith Bradsher, "Bush Picks Nominee for Commerce Post," *New York Times,* 27 December 1991, p. 1; Gwen Ifill, "Clinton Completes Cabinet and Points to Its Diversity," *New York Times,* 25 December 1992, p. 1.

35. When women were nominated for their policy expertise, to serve as liaisons in departments central to the presidency or to their administration, the nomination articles addressed the structural and policy implications of their selection. As much was evident in coverage of the Madeleine Albright and Gale Norton nomination decisions. Alison Mitchell, "Albright to Head State Dept.; Republican in Top Defense Job," *New York Times,* 6 December 1996, p. A1; Douglas Jehl, "Interior Choice Sends a Signal on Land Policy," *New York Times,* 30 December 2001, p. A1.

36. James T. Wooten, "Transportation Choice," *New York Times,* 15 January 1975, p. 14.

37. Georgia Duerst-Lahti, "Reconceiving Theories of Power: Consequences of Masculinism in the Executive Branch," in *The Other Elites: Women, Politics, and Power in the Executive Branch,* ed. MaryAnne Borrelli and Janet M. Martin (Boulder, Colo.: Lynne Rienner Publishers, 1997), p. 22.

38. Mark E. Kann, *A Republic of Men: The American Founders, Gendered Language, and Patriarchal Politics* (New York: New York University Press, 1998), p. 141.

39. Philip Taubman, "Benjamin Richard Civiletti," *New York Times,* 20 July 1979, p. A8.

40. David Bird, "Family Doctor for Cabinet," *New York Times,* 8 November 1985, p. B6.

41. David Johnston, "Attorney General Choice with Low-Key Style," *New York Times,* 17 October 1991, p. A20.

42. Linda Charlton, "The Woman Who Is to Be Named to H.U.D. Post: Carla Anderson Hills," *New York Times,* 14 February 1975, p. 15.

43. Linda Charlton, "Patricia Roberts Harris," *New York Times,* 22 December 1976, p. 28; "The New Secretary of Education," *New York Times,* 31 October 1979, p. A12.

44. Linda Charlton, "Juanita Morris Kreps," *New York Times,* 21 December 1976, p. 24. Similarly, the *Washington Post* reported that O'Leary's past colleagues "all described her as knowledgeable, open-minded, approachable

and amiable." Thomas W. Lippman, "An Energetic Networker to Take over Energy," *Washington Post*, 19 January 1993, p. A9.

45. Neil A. Lewis, "For Labor, a Bush Loyalist," *New York Times*, 15 December 1991, p. 11.

46. Susan Chira, "Emphasis on Action: Donna Edna Shalala," *New York Times*, 12 December 1992, p. 11.

47. Agis Salpukas, "Carter's Choices for Treasury and Transportation Posts," *New York Times*, 15 December 1976, p. 12.

48. Christopher Marquis, "Elaine Lan Chao," *New York Times*, 12 January 2001, A15.

49. Linda Charlton, "Patricia Roberts Harris," *New York Times*, 22 December 1976, p. 16.

50. On this characterization of leadership styles and on the transgendering of persuasive leadership, see Malcolm Jewell and Marcia Lynn Whicker, "The Feminization of Leadership in State Legislatures," *PS* 26, no. 4 (December 1993): 705–712.

51. As an example of a secretary-designate who is presented as, perhaps, too ambitious, see David Binder, "Nation's New Defense Chief," *New York Times*, 4 November 1975, p. 25.

52. Commenting on the gender and racial bias that Harris confronted as a secretary, an aide observed, "There're not many people who like to have Black women tell them what to do. In fact, there are not many Whites who like to have Blacks, period, tell them what to do—but certainly not Black women. They will take much more guff from a White male." Alex Poinsett, "Patricia Harris: HUD's Velvet-Gloved Iron Hand," *Ebony* (July 1979): p. 33.

53. This conclusion contrasts somewhat with the Witt, Paget, and Matthews study of media profiles of women national leaders, which identified numerous ways in which those women were marginalized. For example, they were framed as the "first woman," as the unconventional "outsider," or as "agents of change." In the words of former Representative Patricia Schroeder (D-Colo.), women were "novelty acts" rather than authoritative leaders. In contrast, Pippa Norris concluded from her comparative study of women national leaders that these women were often described in terms that suggested they had adopted masculinist precepts to good effect: "As politicians, most of the women are seen as ambitious, effective, and often more confrontational than their rivals." Women secretaries-designate did not receive such a strong masculinist endorsement in their *Times* biographical coverage.

Further study is needed to determine whether these differences are a product of contrasting political cultures or of differing institutional settings. It may be that countries with women as national leaders have gender ideologies that are different from those prevailing in the United States. Alternatively, the standards for endorsing national leaders and U.S. cabinet officers may be different. However, one would expect that the standards for acceptance would be at least slightly lower for a cabinet officer than for a chief executive. Linda Witt, Karen M. Paget, and Glenna Matthews, *Running as a Woman, Gender and Power in*

American Politics (New York: Free Press, 1993), p. 184; Pippa Norris, "Women Leaders Worldwide: A Splash of Color in the Photo Op," in *Women, Media, and Politics*, ed. Pippa Norris (New York: Oxford University Press, 1997), pp. 164, 159.

54. Francis Frank Marcus, "Ex-Mayor Who Left an Imprint," *New York Times*, 28 July 1979, p. 7.

55. Linda Charlton, "Joseph Anthony Califano Jr.," *New York Times*, 24 December 1976, p. 11. Also in this administration, see B. Drummond Ayres, Jr., "Griffin Boyette Bell," *New York Times*, 21 December 1976, p. 25.

56. Georgia Duerst-Lahti, "Reconceiving Theories of Power: Consequences of Masculinism in the Executive Branch," in *The Other Elites: Women, Politics, and Power in the Executive Branch*, ed. MaryAnne Borrelli and Janet M. Martin (Boulder, Colo.: Lynne Rienner Publishers, 1997), p. 22. Once this circumstance is appreciated, the normative strength of the presumptions guiding the *Times* biographical articles begins to be apparent. Yet the Heroic Man ideal has roots that extend further back in history than the founding era. Christine Di Stefano has explained how autonomy, a foundational precept of Western political theory, has repeatedly legitimized political leadership as a masculine endeavor.

[W]e are already in a position to appreciate the ways in which the elements of modern masculine ideology are or might be systematically connected. Heading the list is a combative brand of dualistic thinking, a persistent and systematic amplification of the primal self-other oppositional dynamic and the creation of dichotomously structured polarities with which to describe and evaluate the events, objects, and processes of the natural and social worlds. . . . The explicit or implicit denial of relatedness—to 'fellow' human beings, to women, to nature—would be tied in with an extreme version of modern masculine identity. . . . Because of the tendencies toward a radical individualism built into the masculine differentiation process, we are likely to find versions of a solitary subject immersed in a hostile and dangerous world. Autonomy is likely to figure as a significant theme and ideal. Recapitulating the earlier experience of identity through opposition and negation, we may expect to find versions of knowledge acquired through opposition, tension, and conflict; an antagonistic and distanced relation between the subject and object of knowledge. Finally, we can expect to encounter attitudes of fear, denigration, and hostility toward whatever is identified as female or feminine, along with its idealization and glorification. Both sets of seemingly incompatible attitudes recapitulate the effects of false differentiation from, of unsuccessful rapprochement with, the maternal subject-object. (Christine Di Stefano, *Configurations of Masculinity: A Feminist Perspective on Modern Political Theory* [Ithaca: Cornell University Press, 1991], pp. 60–61.)

To the extent that credibility is presumptively granted on the basis of a "radical individualism," the women secretaries-designate stand indicted as failures by the standards of Western political thought, the ideals of the Heroic Man, and the standards of the *New York Times*. See also Christine Di Stefano, "Autonomy in the Light of Difference," in *Revisioning the Political: Feminist Reconstructions of Traditional Concepts in Western Political Theory,* ed. Nancy J. Hirschmann and Christine Di Stefano (Boulder, Colo.: Westview Press, 1996).

57. Elaine Sciolino, "Carlucci a Tough Pragmatist in Pentagon's Corner," *New York Times,* 6 November 1987, p. A16.

58. Mark E. Kann, *A Republic of Men: The American Founders, Gendered Language, and Patriarchal Politics* (New York: New York University Press, 1998), pp. 141–142.

59. Colman McCarthy, "When Baby Comes in Second to Career," *Washington Post,* 2 February 1993, p. D14.

60. Linda Charlton, "The Woman Who Is to Be Named to H.U.D. Post: Carla Anderson Hills," *New York Times,* 14 February 1975, p. 14.

61. Linda Charlton, "Patricia Roberts Harris," *New York Times,* 22 December 1976, p. 28.

62. Marjorie Hunter, "Reagan's Choice for Health Chief," *New York Times,* 13 January 1983, p. D22.

63. Phil Gailey, "Transit Post Nominee," *New York Times,* 6 January 1983, p. A25.

64. Pippa Norris, "Women Leaders Worldwide: A Splash of Color in the Photo Op," in *Women, Media, and Politics*, ed. Pippa Norris (New York: Oxford University Press, 1997), p. 165.

5

Cabinet Confirmations:
Evaluation and Ideology

In recent decades, the Senate confirmation process has become progressively more complex and contentious.[1] Still, the confirmation hearing remains its centerpiece, publicly inaugurating the secretary-designate's relationship with the Senate. A summit meeting of representatives, the hearing is routinely conducted by the secretary-designate's future authorizations committee. The senators seek commitments that will facilitate their constituent service and policy initiatives, and the secretaries-designate attempt to protect their discretion. The implications for substantive representation are immediate and obvious, with senators commenting on their voters' needs and their own priorities. Yet the implications for descriptive and symbolic representation are equally significant. The committee's judgments about the nominee's abilities and capabilities will affect their future dealings. Likewise, the message sent about the secretary-designate's fitness for office signals the Senate's response to the president's nomination decisions and to broader developments within the cabinet.

More specifically, confirmation hearings relate to three sets of legislative responsibilities. First, the hearings influence the senators' representation of their constituents' concerns. Second, the hearings serve to facilitate the senators' involvement in policymaking. The two are clearly related. One of the legislators' dominant motives in committee service is to advance their constituents' interests. The nomination of a new departmental executive is an opportunity to move those interests onto or up the agenda. That, in its turn, leads to policy-related questions about departmental programs and priorities, with due consideration for their electoral and partisan implications. The selection of a departmental secretary affects the substantive representation that is provided by the legislative as well as the executive branch.

Third, the hearings allow confirmation committee members to assess the nominee's qualifications, judging the descriptive representation that might be offered by the future cabinet member. The character and integrity of the nominee, potential conflicts of interest, and professional competence have each been debated during the confirmation hearings.[2] Presumably, Washington outsiders and generalists would encounter the most difficulties in their confirmation hearings. Lacking prior affiliations with the Washington community or the Senate and lacking knowledge of the policy jurisdiction or clients of their future departments, these individuals are relative unknowns. Logically, therefore, one would expect their credentials to be subject to the most searching review. After all, the secretaries-designate, once confirmed, will be charged with decisions that will affect the senators' own careers and ambitions. Descriptive and substantive representation, therefore, are closely intertwined throughout the confirmation hearing.

To the extent that these hypotheses hold true, the confirmation hearings will be decidedly difficult for the women secretaries-designate. A significant minority (42.1 percent) of the women were Washington outsiders, and the vast majority (84.2 percent) were generalists. To the extent that they were selected to serve as the president's buffers against established departmental clients and networks, the women challenge enduring relationships between the senators and these same clients and networks. Sex and gender only further complicate this dynamic. Media presentations of the women nominees as representatives of women voters could lead to these nominees being perceived as drawing a new group into contention for the resources of the executive and legislative branches. To the extent that the senators embrace the masculinist principles evidenced in presidential decisionmaking and media portrayals, the senators may judge the women to be presumptively less credible than the men with whom they are nominated to the cabinet. Then, the women nominees would both compromise longstanding political relationships with their anticipated substantive representation and offer only a very qualified descriptive representation.

In order to test these hypotheses about the precabinet careers of the secretaries-designate and about the workings of gender in the confirmation process, the hearings of the women and the men nominees were submitted to a careful analysis. As with the media analysis, this examination focused on the six later administrations. None of Franklin D. Roosevelt's initial cabinet nominees received confirmation hearings; the Senate simply voted to confirm. Oveta Culp Hobby's confirmation hearing as Eisenhower's secretary-designate of health, education, and welfare was exceedingly brief. One senator remarked that she had so recently been confirmed as administrator of the Federal Security Administration that a confirmation hearing for the secretarial position was almost gratuitous. Then, too, confirmation hearings at midcentury were typically brief and even cursory, marked by little controversy or, indeed, comment. In the interest of comparing similar events, therefore, only hearings from the Ford administration and later were submitted to study.

In the later six administrations, all the hearings for the women secretaries-designate were studied. Also examined were hearings for the men who preceded and succeeded them in cabinet office. This method of selection controlled for the Senate committees and the departments' status in the inner or outer cabinet. At the same time, it yielded a sample that extended across presidential administrations and congressional sessions that were both Democratic and Republican. Specifically, the sample included fifty-one hearings for thirty-nine nominees to eleven departments. The "extra" hearings resulted from two women each having two cabinet nominations, and from the seven health, education, and welfare (HEW)/health and human services (HHS) secretaries-designate and the two agriculture secretaries-designate each having two confirmation hearings.[3] Of the forty-four nominees, twenty were women, and twenty-four were men. This distribution reflects the fact that some women were preceded or succeeded by other women. Also, some women were in office while the study was being conducted and therefore had no successors. Additionally, Shirley Hufstedler (Carter) was the founding secretary of the Education Department and therefore had no predecessor.

The forty-one secretaries-designate were categorized as insiders or outsiders and as specialists, liaisons, or generalists. The concern was to have some nominees in each category, both as distinct classifications and as a cross-tabulated matrix.[4] In this way, the distinctions between insiders and outsiders and among specialists, liaisons, and generalists could be tested first within and second across the categories. The sample included several secretaries-designate in each of the liaison categories and a significant number in each of the generalist categories. However, the only specialist was Clinton labor secretary-designate

Table 5.1   Classifying the Sampled Secretaries-Designate, 1974–2001

	Insider	Outsider
Policy specialist	None in the six administrations	Edward H. Levi (Justice) John T. Dunlop (Labor) F. Ray Marshall (Labor) Robert Reich (Labor)
Departmental client/ issue network liaison	Joseph A. Califano, Jr. (HEW) Richard S. Schweiker (HHS) Dan Glickman (Agriculture) Madeleine K. Albright (State)	Moon Landrieu (HUD) T. H. Bell (Education) Otis R. Bowen (HHS) Louis W. Sullivan (HHS) James D. Watkins (Energy) Barbara H. Franklin (Commerce) Bruce Babbitt (Interior) Gale A. Norton (Interior)
Policy generalist	James T. Lynn (HUD) Carla Anderson Hills (HUD) Elliot L. Richardson (Commerce) Patricia Roberts Harris (HUD, HEW/HHS) Elizabeth H. Dole (Transportation, Labor) Margaret M. Heckler (HHS) William E. Brock (Labor) James H. Burnley IV (Transportation) Ann Dore McLaughlin (Labor) William P. Barr (Justice) Lynn Martin (Labor) Ron Brown (Commerce) Colin Powell (State)	Juanita M. Kreps (Commerce) Philip M. Klutznick (Commerce) Shirley M. Hufstedler (Education) Andrew L. Lewis, Jr. (Transportation) Robert A. Mosbacher, Sr. (Commerce) Warren Christopher (State) Donna E. Shalala (HHS) Hazel R. O'Leary (Energy) Zoë E. Baird (Justice) Janet Reno (Justice) Alexis Herman (Labor) Ann M. Veneman (Agriculture) Elaine Lan Chao (Labor) John Ashcroft (Justice) Tommy Thompson (HHS) Spencer Abraham (Energy)

Robert Reich, an outsider specialist. Accordingly, the other specialists nominated in these administrations were added to the sample.[5] As Table 5.1 demonstrates, doing so yielded a sample with at least some secretaries-designate in every cell, except for that of insider specialists because none with that profile were nominated in the six administrations. Ultimately, fifty-seven hearings for forty-seven secretaries-designate, nominated to eleven departments, were sampled.

With the sample defined, the content of each segment of the confirmation hearing was carefully analyzed. Though the confirmation committees evidenced subtle differences in their hearing procedures, the basic elements were fairly consistent across the Senate.[6] After the chair called the committee to order, committee members were given an opportunity to make opening statements. These were followed by the introduction of the secretary-designate to the committee, which was typically performed by the nominee's home-state senators. When these speeches were completed, the nominee offered her or his own statement, speaking for the first time on the public record. Once these exchanges were completed, the balance of the hearing was reserved for a question-and-answer session, with the Senators taking turns addressing the nominee.[7]

During their opening statements and introductions, the senators and the secretaries-designate focused on their pending relationship. Qualifications were the principal topic of consideration, which meant that their dialogue focused on descriptive representation. Accordingly, these hearing speeches were studied to determine whether the senators systematically differentiated among the nominees as insiders or outsiders and as women or men.

During the question-and-answer session, the senators and secretaries-designate routinely discussed matters relating to both substantive and descriptive representation. These more complex dialogues offered an opportunity to see how the nominees' precabinet relationships, cumulatively, would affect the senators' judgments about the nominees. They were also indicative of the nominees' own abilities to establish constructive relationships with their future authorization committees. Accordingly, the question-and-answer sessions were reviewed and compared for secretaries-designate in each of the categories listed in Table 5.1.

As always, historical continuities and discontinuities among the hearings were acknowledged. Perhaps the most notable continuity was that of the Senate's own membership, which remained overwhelmingly white and male throughout the years of this study. Though women and people of color did come to hold a higher percentage of seats in later sessions, very few were present or made comments during the hearings. Accordingly, the ways in which women senators might alter the dynamics of the confirmation hearing could not (yet) be determined.

Once more, then, the implications of the nominees' careers for descriptive and substantive representation will be considered, this time from the Senate's perspective. The standards at work in their assessments and the ways in which they mitigate or reinforce those of other actors provide an understanding of the systemic influences that structure cabinet representation.

OPENING THE HEARING

This examination of the opening statements begins with those delivered at the confirmation hearings for the white male secretaries-designate. They are the traditional cabinet nominees, and they are still typically nominated to the higher percentage of cabinet offices. Accordingly, their hearings set a historical and normative baseline for investigations of the Senate's responses to the representation offered by cabinet nominees.[8]

Opening Statements and Introductions for the Men Secretaries-Designate

The opening statements for the men secretaries-designate were reflective of their precabinet relationships with the senators. The male secretaries-designate who were known to the senators, either because they were insiders or because they were specialists or liaisons, were welcomed by the senators. The men who were not known to the senators, because they were Washington outsiders, encountered challenges. Thus, as the senators had greater confidence in the men nominees and in the representation they could be expected to provide, the confirmation hearing opened more smoothly.

In their opening statements to *insider* male secretaries-designate, confirmation committee members listed the nominees' past offices, highlighting their career achievements and successes. In these instances, the members of the confirmation committee seemed to advocate on behalf of the nominee.

> *Chairman Bob Dole* (R-Kans.), opening statement to Reagan HHS secretary-designate Richard Schweiker: [Dole addressed Schweiker after commenting on his own role as the new committee chair.] I can say on a personal note that Dick and I started in the House in 1961. I think Senators Schweiker, Mathias, and I are the survivors of that class of Republicans. But he needs no introduction to the members of this committee.[9]

Time and again, as in this passage, the committee members describe their previous working relationships with the insider men as productive and express their confidence in the nominees' abilities. Accomplishments are attributed to the nominees' independence, strength, and courage, the same qualities heralded in the *Times* biographical articles for the men secretaries-designate. In this instance, however, it is senators who are endorsing the nominees' claims to power. Moreover, the senators' support is extended across party lines and is offered to nominees in different presidential administrations.

Confronted with *outsider* men secretaries-designate, committee members detail the responsibilities and difficulties that the nominees should expect to confront, including policy failures, departmental limitations, and budgetary constraints. The tone is cautionary, and the committee members refrain from expressing great confidence in the nominees. Consider the following opening statement by the ranking minority member to George H. W. Bush energy secretary-designate Admiral James D. Watkins.

> *Senator James A. McClure* (R-Idaho): This is the first of many appearances you will make here. I suspect you do not even have the foggiest notion of how often you are going to be before Congress in one committee or another over the course of the next year, following your confirmation as secretary.
>
> . . . The president, I am sure, looked at your qualifications in this area [of nuclear weapons issues], and one of the reasons you are sitting on that side of the table today is because of your background and expertise in dealing with questions of that kind.
>
> But there are others too. As you are aware, today the United States is more dependent on foreign oil than it was prior to the 1973 Arab oil embargo. Domestic oil production has fallen, and consumption has increased.
>
> The DOE's March 1987 energy security report predicts that by 1990 our dependence could reach 50 percent. If current trends continue, by 1995, only seven years from now, we could be dependent on imports for two-thirds of our oil. And frankly, I am disturbed by that prospect.
>
> As you know, what is at stake is our economic security, our foreign policy flexibility, and our defense preparedness. Such vulnerability must not be allowed to occur.
>
> What is missing is a national energy awareness. I point to a number of factors in my [written] opening statement with respect to where we ought to be going, and why perhaps we ought not get where we are headed right now.[10]

This opening statement makes few references to the nominee's career or character. Instead, it issues numerous warnings about cabinet service and educates the nominee about pending problems. In addressing the outsider men, the senators speak as experts educating the ignorant. The senators establish themselves as the dominant members in their relationship with the future department executive. The equality that characterized exchanges between the insider men and the senators is absent. Quite clearly, the credentials—and thus the descriptive representation—of the outsider men are viewed as comparatively weak.

Communication and relationship are the foundation of the representative's role, and they set the tone of the confirmation hearing in the opening statements. The senators identify themselves as allies of the insider men and as instructors of the outsiders. Insider men are reminded of past occasions when cooperation has secured mutually satisfying outcomes, and they are invited to work again with the senators. Outsider men are relegated to the status of apprentices, who can best serve by accepting the master's guidance. Insider men, therefore, are expected to be stronger representatives than outsider men. In simple terms, the insider men are expected to be better descriptive representatives because they have already demonstrated the leadership qualities that the senators value.

The committee members' opening statements were followed by introductory speeches. Delivered by the nominees' home-state senators and sometimes by other elected officeholders as well, these formally presented and recommended the secretary-designate to the confirmation committee.[11] Given the differences in the opening statements for insider and outsider men, it was not surprising that there were also patterned contrasts in the introductions. After all, the insider and outsider male secretaries-designate needed different endorsements. In their opening statements, the committee members had indicated their approval of the insider secretaries-designate while warning the outsider secretaries-designate of impending problems. Accordingly, the introductions provided for insiders are comparatively brief and may even be waived. Outsider secretaries-designate, however, require strong introductions. The speakers oblige by providing introductions that closely parallel the opening statements with which committee members welcome the insiders. Clearly, senators are in agreement about the skills and traits that the secretaries-designate must possess in order to serve as strong representatives.

The introductions provided for outsider men—just like the opening statements for insider men—detail the nominees' character and professional achievements. Whenever possible, the senator making the introduction also describes the relationship(s) that she or he has previously enjoyed with the nominee.

Senator Dennis DeConcini (R-Ariz.), introducing Interior Secretary-Designate Bruce Babbitt: The Babbitts and the DeConcinis come from a long way back in Arizona; they were pioneer families. Governor Babbitt, as you know, was Governor of the State of Arizona from 1978 to 1986; Attorney General from 1974 to 1978. [Babbitt's accomplishments as governor and as attorney general were listed at this point.] . . . he has not forgotten where his roots are; he has not forgotten his experiences, whether it is in fighting organized crime or land fraud, or developing water projects in the West, or the economic interests that are necessary. . . . And as Secretary of the Interior, that is what you are going to get: what you see, a leader who has been there on issues, and knows how to advocate, knows how to balance, and knows how to negotiate.[12]

In this representative passage, past career experiences, past relationships, and present character traits are each carefully detailed. In regard to the latter, the nominee is expected to be a good leader because he is tough, decisive, strong, intelligent, and energetic. Here again are the traits that were praised by the *New York Times* and that are so integral to the Heroic Man ideal.

In making this connection between the abilities of the men secretaries-designate and their anticipated departmental responsibilities, the senators' opening statements and introductions set out the legislators' standards for political leaders and executive managers. The senators believe that the insider men should govern because they have proven themselves in past relationships and through past governmental achievements. Senators do recommend outsiders for confirmation. However, it is important to note that they have first been assured, through introductions delivered by their Senate colleagues, that the nominees possess the character traits they believe are requisite to effective representation. The ideal of the Heroic Man, so evident in the *Times* assessments, is also part of the confirmation judgments of the U.S. Senate. Tight connections continue to be drawn between gender, power, and governance in each stage of formal representation.

Opening Statements and Introductions for the Women Secretaries-Designate

Whether the women were insiders or outsiders, the senators were markedly less supportive of them than they were of the men. Though a number of the women had achieved insider status, for instance, their

Senate confirmation committees treated them as outsiders. Just as male outsiders were viewed as presumptively less capable representatives than male insiders, so also were the women secretaries-designate viewed as presumptively less capable than their male counterparts.

This differential treatment was particularly evident in the opening statements that greeted Carla Anderson Hills, Patricia Roberts Harris (in 1977), Elizabeth Hanford Dole (in 1983), Ann Dore McLaughlin, and Barbara Hackman Franklin. Prior to being nominated to the cabinet, Hills had been an assistant attorney general in the Justice Department, and McLaughlin had been an undersecretary in the Interior Department. Dole and Franklin each had primary careers in national politics. In their hearings, however, these women received opening statements similar to those that greeted men outsiders. The women insiders who *were* welcomed as insiders were the two former members of Congress, Margaret Heckler and Lynn Martin; the two former cabinet secretaries, Patricia Harris (in 1979) and Elizabeth Dole (in 1989); and the former ambassador to the UN (a position with cabinet rank), Madeleine Korbel Albright. The standards for qualifying as insiders were therefore lower for men than for women: Men qualified as insiders if their primary career was in national politics or if they had held a subcabinet post immediately prior to their cabinet nomination; women qualified as insiders only if their primary career had been in the Congress or if they had held a cabinet or cabinet-rank post immediately prior to their cabinet nomination. Women secretaries-designate thus encountered greater difficulties in establishing themselves as capable and successful leaders before their Senate authorizations committee. They were judged as presumptively weaker descriptive representatives.

Under these circumstances, the women secretaries-designate had an even greater need of strong endorsements from their home-state senators. Yet the introductions given for the women, with few exceptions, were not as strong as those provided for the men outsiders. The introductions for men outsiders listed career achievements, political affiliations, and the nominee's character traits. Only the first two elements were wholly present in the introductions for the women outsiders and insiders-treated-as-outsiders. The third element appeared only in qualified form.

As I have stated elsewhere, "With the exception of the Reno introductions . . . [the senators' introductions] do not go so far as to assert that the women secretaries-designate are competitive, aggressive, or tough—masculinist behaviors that are repeatedly attributed to the men outsiders. Instead, Senators from different parties and generations describe the women as practicing feminine behaviors."[13] The women secretaries-designate are introduced as "intelligent," "committed," "flexible," "youthful," and "honorable" (Hills); as evidencing "fortitude," "discipline," "sensitivity," and "sagacity" (Harris 1977); as "able," "conscientious," and "dedicated" (Kreps); as "dedicated," "cheerful," and "spiritual" (Dole 1983); as "calming," "enthusiastic," and "attentive" (Franklin); and as "respectful," "open," and "responsive" (O'Leary). Similarly, as noted in the previous chapter, the *New York Times* describes the women secretaries-designate as being "pleasant" and "hardworking" while demonstrating "charm" and "cool good humor." In each instance, women are presented as more receptive than proactive, and their symbolic representation is correspondingly qualified.[14] And as was also true for the *Times* biographical analysis, the senators' conclusions are made possible by holding the women to higher standards than the men with whom they are nominated. Thus, the journalists and the senators reassure one another about their judgments. In the media and in the Senate, only men are viewed as possessing the full complement of heroic traits. Only men are presumptively able to lead.

THE NOMINEE STATEMENT AND THE
QUESTION-AND-ANSWER SESSION

Because the question-and-answer sessions emphasize policy, they must be examined in terms of their treatment of insiders and outsiders and of specialists, liaisons, and generalists. The former indicate whether a nominee's career has brought her or him into association with the Senate, either by having a career in national politics or by participating in the confirmation process. The latter describe the nominee's relationship with a department's policy jurisdiction and its traditionally dominant clients and issue networks. Cumulatively, these two classification schemas provide a relatively comprehensive description of the nominees' precabinet political relationships and resources.

Given the senators' responses to the nominees in their opening statements, the committee members could be expected to judge insider specialists and insider liaisons as stronger representatives (see Table 5.2). Both types of secretaries-designate are knowledgeable about their future departments' policies or clients and networks. Accordingly, their substantive representation appears comparatively predictable. Specialists have developed these contacts by mastering policy substance and

Table 5.2   Senate Assessments of the Secretary-Designate's Prospective
             Representation

	Insider	Outsider
Policy specialist	Stronger	Strong
Departmental client/ issue network liaison	Stronger	Strong
Policy generalist	Strong	Less strong

becoming respected as experts. Liaisons have mastered the relationships underlying the policy, becoming facilitators and mediators. Both
specialists and liaisons are essential to the continuance and the health
of policy networks and organizations. Although specialists are guided
by the canons of their profession, liaisons are responsive to the formal
dictates and informal folkways of political organizations and institutions. Their substantive representation and descriptive representation
are thus mutually supportive. When these credentials are combined
with insider status, the senators would presumably consider the secretary-designate as a "stronger" prospective representative. When the
specialist or liaison is an outsider, the confirmation committee would
still have cause to view the nominee as a "strong" representative
because she or he would have some expertise in the department's jurisdiction. At the same time, the lack of a previous relationship with the
senators would slightly compromise the predictability attributed to
their anticipated performance as representatives.

Presumably, insider generalists would also occupy the middle
ground of being "strong" representatives. At first glance, this category
seems paradoxical. Insiders have, during their precabinet careers,
established a reputation with the Senate and the Washington community. (With the notable exceptions of Lewis Strauss and John Tower,
insider nominees have had *constructive* relations with the Senate.) That
shared history confers a degree of substantive expertise and even some
discretionary authority. Generalists, however, are notable for their
dependence on the president. Their career is tied to the chief executive's fortunes. How can the same nominee be viewed as both somewhat autonomous (as an insider) and somewhat dependent on the president (as a generalist)?

In answering this question, it must be remembered that the generalist label described only the secretary-designate's relationship to her or
his department's traditionally dominant clients and networks. For exam-

ple, Labor Secretaries-Designate William Brock (Reagan) and Lynn Martin (George H. W. Bush) were members of Congress whose cabinet nominations were in fields distinct from their areas of legislative expertise. They were therefore (legislative) insiders and (departmental) generalists. Other insider generalists had precabinet careers centered in executive branch service before being named to departments in which they lacked policy expertise. These secretaries-designate included Ford commerce secretary-designate Elliot Richardson and Reagan transportation/Bush labor secretary-designate Elizabeth Dole.

Insider generalists would be expected to be "strong" representatives, then, because they had established a reputation with the Senate, if not with their departmental clients and networks. Senators could use the insider nominee's past performance to judge whether she or he would advance their interests, as related to their own constituents and policy concerns. Of course, that evaluative process would cut both ways. Lewis Strauss was denied confirmation because of his poor legislative relations as a former chair of the Atomic Energy Commission.[15] Substantively and descriptively, there was a measure of predictability to the representation that these secretaries-designate promised.

By this reasoning, the outsider generalists would be the "less strong" representatives. Having a previous relationship neither with the Senate nor with departmental clients and networks, these nominees would have the most to prove about themselves and their capabilities. Descriptively and substantively, their performance as representatives would be the most uncertain. Senators, therefore, would presumably be most inquisitorial about the leadership and managerial credentials and capabilities of these nominees. Each of these hypotheses is tested in the analyses that follow, with a careful attention to the implications for representation.

The Policy Specialists

All the policy specialists nominated in the six administrations studied were outsiders. In the hearings for the *outsider specialists,* Senate committee members readily acknowledged each nominee's policy expertise. Yet they also expressed varying degrees of concern about the nominees' outsider status. Though the substantive representation of the secretaries-designate appeared predictable, their descriptive representation was less certain. These sentiments were particularly in evidence during the hearing for Ford attorney general–designate Edward Levi. Levi's most extended government service had occurred in the 1940s; he was unknown to his nominating president. His hearing consequently focused on his leadership abilities and their relevance to the duties of the attorney general. Levi's claims were buttressed by a strong endorsement from the American Bar Association.[16]

All the labor secretaries-designate, in contrast to Levi, were at least known to their confirmation committee members. In fact, the chair of the confirmation committee for Ford nominee John Dunlop and Clinton nominee Robert Reich was their home-state senator, Edward M. Kennedy (D-Mass.). Dunlop added that he had worked with every president and every secretary of labor since 1938, providing thirty-seven years of consultation to the department he was now nominated to lead.[17] Reich noted that his long-standing relationship with the president (they had attended Oxford University together) would ensure that the Labor Department received Oval Office attention.[18] Finally, each of the labor secretaries-designate had the support of the American Federation of Labor–Congress of Industrial Organizations (AFL-CIO), the traditional client of the Labor Department and an influential player in the Senate committee's network.[19] All of the labor secretaries-designate therefore buttressed their specialist credentials with a "liaison's credential," namely, a constructive relationship with the most influential client of their future department. Such claims implicitly reassured the senators about the descriptive representation that would be provided by the future cabinet members.

These hearings suggest that expertise is an important but not sufficient factor in convincing a confirmation committee that a secretary-designate will function well as a cabinet member and representative. Political experience, particularly in the form of established relationships within the federal government, is also required. Endorsements from influential interest groups within the department's issue network are also valued. Thus the outsider specialists claimed some of the resources of liaisons and insiders to win the senators' approval. More precisely, they claimed the political skills of the liaisons and insiders—their fluency in communication and relationship building—so that the senators would view them as presumptively effective descriptive representatives.

The Departmental Client or Issue Network Liaisons

The ultimate *insider liaisons* must be the secretaries-designate who enter the cabinet from lengthy service on the very committee that conducts their confirmation hearing. Reagan health and human services secretary-designate Richard Schweiker was one such secretary-designate. A twenty-year veteran of the Congress and Reagan's 1976 choice for vice president, he had served on both of the committees that conducted his confirmation hearings.[20] Schweiker did not hesitate to remind his former colleagues of that experience.

Senator Russell B. Long (D-La.): Now my experience has been that the last 20 years around here, whoever was sent over there to that Department of HEW, now HHS, tended to be Gulliver, captured by the Lilliputians. Can we have some assurance that you are not going to be captured by that bureaucracy that was here long before you showed up on the scene?

Health and Human Services Secretary-Designate Richard Schweiker: Senator Long, let me say this: I am fortunate in having spent 10 years not only on the Health Committee but also on the Labor-HEW Appropriations Committee. I sort of know where a lot of bodies are buried. I think people are going to have trouble pulling the wool over my eyes in terms of spending and cost-effectiveness issues, what are the good programs and bad programs and our relative investment in them, just because of my appropriations work. . . .
I cannot take enough people with me to fill all the slots available, Senator, but I assure you that my policies will be implemented and enforced. The policies that I speak to this committee about will be activated; that I assure you.

Long: If you begin to develop a change of heart, would you be willing to come up here and tell us that you are losing faith in your old religion, and give us a chance to reinforce your faith a little bit, so you can continue to forge straight ahead with what you were committed to when you went there?

Schweiker: If I need that kind of moral rearmament, you will be the first to know. I will come back. In addition, I want to say one other thing: I do expect, because I know the subcommittees and the committee have expertise in this area, that I will listen.
I said it in my opening remarks, and I meant it. There is a lot of knowledge and expertise on the Hill that I think has been ignored downtown on some of these really tough problems. . . . I am going to listen before we promulgate something so that we don't find ourselves going in the wrong direction because we didn't get a good reading on the Hill, or didn't understand the program fully.[21]

Schweiker begins by describing the extent of his precabinet service, making clear that he is an expert in the policymaking process. By intertwining his legislative experience with his departmental goals in his first response, he insists that he will be a consultative (as opposed to an independent) secretary. He goes even further in his second response, describing "the Hill" as his ally and support, as a source of "moral rearmament" and "expertise." Each compliment paid to the Senate, of course, reflects well on his own fitness for cabinet office. It is important to note that his rhetoric, with references to confrontation and strength, manifests the masculinist ideal of the Heroic Man. Senator/Secretary-Designate Schweiker is providing his own introduction, insisting that he has the political talents and expertise to be an outstanding representative, responsive to the substantive concerns of the Senate and descriptively aware of proper leadership standards.

Carter HEW secretary-designate Califano and Clinton secretary-designate of state Albright also qualified as insider liaisons. As a member of the Johnson White House, Califano had been associated with a number of the Great Society's innovations in social policy.[22] In or out of government, Califano's career centered on politics, his legal practice including service as general counsel to the Democratic National Committee. Albright was the permanent U.S. ambassador to the United Nations, holding cabinet rank immediately prior to her cabinet nomination. She had been a congressional and National Security Council staff member, a professor, a foundation director, and a campaign policy adviser.[23] Califano and Albright, like Schweiker, stressed their years of serving as policymakers and advisers in asserting their ability to be strong—stronger—representatives. Consider the following exchange from the Albright hearing.

> *Senator Bill Frist* (R-Tenn.): How do you view the role of the U.S. Senate—maybe this committee, but, more broadly, the U.S. Senate— in determining foreign policy?
>
> *Secretary-Designate of State Madeleine Albright:* Senator, my whole background, because I worked here and because my various and previous administration jobs were involved with congressional relations, I believe that we should have close consultations and discussions about how to set priorities in foreign policy. I would hope that you would find, if I am confirmed, that we still spend a lot of time together talking about foreign policy issues and consulting, and that you would not find us wanting in that.
>
> *Frist:* You think that will be different—a change from your predecessor or predecessors?

Albright: I do think having been on both sides of this issue, that members of Congress never think that they get consulted enough, and members of the executive branch always think that they are doing a lot of consulting. I do think that there have been a lot of consultations in the first Clinton term. But I can assure you that, where it is in my power, I will be consulting with you as frequently as possible.[24]

While refusing to criticize her predecessor, Albright sets out her own understanding of legislative-executive relations. Like Schweiker, she praises the Congress as a source of policy expertise and promises to draw on its wisdom. She supports her position by referencing her previous service in the Senate and the presidency, noting that her executive post was as a congressional liaison officer. In this way, Albright brings together her career credentials as an insider and as a liaison. Albright implicitly accepts the standards set by the senators for exercising political leadership and executive management. She also establishes her substantive policy expertise while praising others for their insight. In some ways, Albright (and also Califano) presented themselves as having the intellectual resources of a policy specialist.

Outsider liaisons seemed to face greater challenges in reassuring the senators, who were unsure about the ways in which these future secretaries would capitalize on their past alliances. Like the outsider specialists, the outsider liaisons sought to allay these concerns by stressing their government experience. In other words, the outsiders tried to present themselves as insiders in order to reassure the senators about their policy priorities and their acceptance of political norms.

Reagan education secretary-designate T. H. Bell, for example, identified himself as the former U.S. commissioner of education. Bell had held this post in the former Department of Health, Education, and Welfare from 1974 to 1976, during which time he had had good working relationships with several of the confirmation committee members.[25] At his confirmation hearing, Bell seemed to suggest that he was essentially being renominated to a post that he had already held. This hearing was also interesting for what the nominee did not highlight. Bell had had an extended and distinguished career in local and state educational administration. Senator Orrin Hatch (R-Utah) noted this in his introduction, but it received no further mention. The omission was striking in light of ongoing efforts to acknowledge the education initiatives of local and state governments. It may be that the senators and secretaries-designate are, at some times, less concerned about substantive representation than about descriptive representation.

Those outsiders who did not have national government experience nonetheless emphasized what government experience they did have. Of the sampled outsider liaisons, George H. W. Bush HHS secretary-designate Louis Sullivan is the secretary-designate with the least government and political experience. Sullivan was a former professor of medicine; as president and dean of the Morehouse School of Medicine, he had transformed that medical program into a fully accredited four-year medical school. He had also recruited Barbara Bush for the school's board of trustees and had accompanied Vice President Bush on a state visit to seven African countries. He had served as a consultant or member on various advisory committees associated with the National Institutes of Health and the Veterans Administration. Sullivan's networks therefore extended throughout the medical establishment, higher education, and the African American community. His friendship with Barbara and George H. W. Bush suggested that he would have access to the Oval Office. Here was a powerful claim to being a strong descriptive representative.

Sullivan, however, was the only African American nominated to the George H. W. Bush cabinet. Republican senators, who were resistant to affirmative action policies, rejected the notion that Sullivan was nominated because he was African American. At the same time, they were anxious to present themselves as responsive to the African American community. The result of their crosscutting concerns was a sometimes strained dialogue about Sullivan's responsibilities as a descriptive, substantive, and symbolic representative.

> *Senator Bob Dole* (R-Kans.): Also, I think it is fair to say that you may have learned there are a few cynics in this town, and they are not all in the media. And there are some who say, "Well, the only reason that Dr. Sullivan is going to be approved is he is the only Black appointed by President Bush, and therefore he will get through."
>
> I think it would be very helpful to this committee to know—and I think you do know—why you were chosen by President Bush.
>
> *Health and Human Services Secretary-Designate Louis Sullivan:* Thank you, Senator Dole. I really appreciate your raising that question, because let me say this: First of all, I believe and I hope that I was asked to serve in this position by President Bush because of my qualifications—what I can bring both as a physician and because of my life experiences, and the kinds of concerns and commitments that

I have, to really helping the Department and helping the President and members of the Congress really provide those services to the American people that are owed to them.

I think that the fact that I am Black should be incidental. But I also do represent an important constituency. I believe that we have a Government that, to work best, must have representation of all segments of our society. And certainly, having been very active in the Black community and knowing the concerns and the problems in that community, I think I have a special sensitivity there; but I have a broader sensitivity, which encompasses looking at all segments of our society.

For example, at my medical school, while we say that we are predominantly Black, we have White students, Hispanic students, Native American students, and foreign students as well. The reason that that is important is that our students learn to work with each other. They learn from each other. They learn the different societal and cultural norms, the sensitivities that are important for a physician to relate to his or her patient, the many subtle things that make a big difference to that patient, and the quality of that physician-patient interaction.

So indeed, I believe, and I certainly hope, and I would certainly urge this committee to look at me for the qualifications that I have and that I bring to this position. Certainly I am Black. I am proud of that fact. But I think that I am equally if not more proud of what I have been able to accomplish and what I would hope to accomplish as the Secretary of Health and Human Services if confirmed by this committee.[26]

In this passage, we see a secretary-designate identifying whom he will and will not recognize as his constituents. Even more precisely, the nominee delineates which constituents will receive which type of representation. Sullivan distinguishes between his racial identity ("Certainly I am Black") and his professional identity ("equally if not more proud of what I have been able to accomplish"). His racial identity pertains to his descriptive representation of African Americans as a credible and authoritative decisionmaker. However, his "special sensitivity" to African American concerns is eclipsed by "a broader sensitivity" that "encompasses . . . all segments of our society." Although Sullivan is descriptively an African American cabinet officer, he states that his substantive representation will not be limited to African American interests. In fact, he promises that his service as a descriptive representative will not influence his substantive representation.[27] Sullivan thereby reassures the committee that he will not seek to change the prevailing balance of power among HHS networks and clients. Here we see a liaison secretary-designate adopting his future department's historically dominant constituents as his own, gaining the confidence of confirmation committee members in the process. His symbolic representation is also clearly articulated, with Sullivan presenting himself as a secretary-designate who respects and does not threaten existent institutions—even though his past career has been devoted to effecting significant change on behalf of a marginalized people.

To appreciate the significance of this self-portrayal, consider the way in which Housing and Urban Development (HUD) Secretary-Designate Patricia Roberts Harris defended her presence in the Carter cabinet. Like Sullivan, Harris was the sole African American in the cabinet of her nominating president. Where Sullivan was an outsider and a liaison, however, Harris was an insider and a generalist. The differences between the two nominations mean that comparisons must be drawn carefully. Still, they are illustrative of the complexities of descriptive, substantive, and symbolic representation, especially for "diversity" nominees.

Senator William Proxmire (D-Wis.): We have had in HUD a woman, not a black woman but a woman [Secretary Carla Anderson Hills], who it has been pointed out has great abilities and great competence and yet we have this criticism and I think it's a criticism that has some merit and force, that HUD has not been listening to people who have these problems. Your answer is that you have no problem with this because you're a black woman.

Harris: No; that is not my answer.

Proxmire: Is that right? What is your answer?

Harris: You spoke of the unrepresented and the poor and I said I'm one of them. I started, Senator, not as a lawyer in a prestigious law firm, but as a woman who needed a scholarship to go to college. If you think I have forgotten that, you're wrong. I started as an advocate for a civil rights agency, the American Council on Human Rights, that had to come before this body to ask for access to housing by members of minority groups. If you think I have forgotten that, Senator, you're wrong. I have been a defender of women, of minorities, of those who are the outcasts of this society, throughout my life and if my life has any meaning at all it is that those who start as outcasts may end up being part of the system, and I hope it will mean one other thing, Senator, that by being part of the system one does not forget what it meant to be outside it, because I assure you that while there may be others who forget what it meant to be excluded from the dining rooms of this very building, I shall never forget it.

Proxmire: That's a very reassuring and inspiring answer.[28]

Though nominated to different presidential administrations in different periods of civil rights activism, both Sullivan and Harris were expected to provide outreach to African American voters. In acknowledging this responsibility, the secretaries-designate offered contrasting explanations of how their role as descriptive representatives would affect their performance as substantive representatives. Sullivan limited his representation of African American interests to a descriptive undertaking. Harris, however, takes issue with the senator who would similarly characterize her representation. She insists that her roles as a descriptive and a substantive representative are inseparable. As a symbolic representative, her message is consequently one of presidential inclusivity *and* responsiveness.

In both the specialist and the liaison categories, insiders are clearly in the more advantaged position. They are able to claim the relationships and consequently the experiences that most reassure the senators. Outsiders mimic insiders, highlighting whatever government or political opportunities have been scattered throughout their careers. Whether insider or outsider, however, the liaison secretaries-designate are always careful to comment on their strong connections with the department's traditional clients or issue networks. In this way, the nominees make the crucial points that, first, they and the senators are both representatives and, second, that they have constituents in common. At the same time, the secretaries-designate send a warning, inasmuch as they name their allies should their confirmation become contentious. Substantive and descriptive representation are interconnected throughout all of these dialogues.

The Policy Generalists

Specialists stressed their policy expertise; liaisons stressed their policy relationships. They presented themselves as a prospectively strong—or stronger—representatives by highlighting their defining political resource. If generalists followed this lead, they would defend their claims to be cabinet representatives by emphasizing their relationship with the president, which would presumably allow them to protect and advance their department's interests. As secretaries *cum* presidential surrogates, they would be able to provide the senators with useful insights about the president's policy priorities. This kind of dialogue did occur during several of the generalists' hearings.

> *Senator John Kerry* (D-Mass.): In today's *New York Times*, Mr. Christopher, there is a banner headline and a significant story from the President-elect with respect to Saddam Hussein in which he says he is not obsessed with Hussein and in which he also says that if Saddam Hussein wants a different relationship with the United States, all he has to do is change his behavior.
>
> The newspaper interprets that as an olive branch. I did not necessarily, but clearly I think some clarification would be important. . . . So I ask you if you could tell us today if there is any clarification to that? Is it, in fact, an olive branch? Would a different behavior gain Saddam Hussein a normal relationship or would it simply stop the bombing and stop the response?
>
> *Secretary-Designate of State Warren M. Christopher:* . . . I, of course, saw that story this morning and thought that the writer's interpretation, and particularly the headline, was a mischaracterization of what Governor Clinton had said.
>
> Governor Clinton did emphasize several times in that interview that he would continue to judge the behavior and actions of Saddam Hussein. That the sanctions would be continued in full force, that he would carry out his duties as commander-in-chief, and that he was prepared to use force, indeed perhaps even greater force, to ensure that the U.N. resolutions were carried out. . . .
>
> I do not think it was anything beyond that, except perhaps there was a religious quality about it. He talked about his Baptist belief in redemption. I happen not to be a Baptist and I am not very optimistic about any redemption for Saddam Hussein. . . .
>
> But I do not want to get into a philosophical or religious argument. I would simply say that I see no substantial change in the position, and a continuing total support for what the Bush administration has done.[29]

Having been an influential member of the presidential campaign, Christopher was able to speak with some authority about the priorities that would be assigned to the president-elect's campaign promises. No one could better allay the excitement and anxiety of the partisan transition than a cabinet nominee who was a member of the inner circle.

There were also occasions when the secretaries-designate seemed to be advantaged by their status as outsider generalists. Having some distance from partisan politics and departmental networks benefited both Shirley M. Hufstedler and Janet Reno. Carter education secretary-designate Hufstedler had been a federal judge for eleven years when she was nominated to the cabinet. Her connections with educational networks were also attenuated. Still, the controversies surrounding the establishment of an independent Education Department meant that a specialist or liaison nominee would have been viewed with considerable suspicion.[30] Similarly, Attorney General–Designate Reno had few prior connections with the Clinton campaign or the president-elect.[31] Here was the "independent attorney general" that had been promised in recent presidential campaigns. For Reno, as for Hufstedler, being an outsider generalist was equated with a principled objectivity that would ensure strong representation.

Still, senators did have some reason to doubt the generalists and most especially the outsider generalists. The loyalty of these nominees to the president could, in future consultations, disadvantage the legislature. Even if that danger was avoided, the generalists' lack of understanding in regard to policies and networks could cause them to be ignorant of the stakes and complexities of political battles.

Insider generalists sought to remove these Senate concerns by demonstrating how their government careers gave them a familiarity with the formalities and informalities of policymaking. Thus, these nominees highlighted political processes and de-emphasized policy content. HHS Secretary-Designate Margaret Heckler (Reagan) and Labor Secretaries-Designate William Brock and Lynn Martin all referenced their congressional careers, even though their legislative work was substantively unrelated to their anticipated cabinet service.[32] Transportation/Labor Secretary-Designate Elizabeth Dole and Labor Secretary-Designate Ann McLaughlin (Reagan) did likewise with their executive branch careers.[33] Reagan transportation secretary-designate James Burnley IV and George H. W. Bush attorney general-designate William Barr stated that having previously been deputies in the departments they were now nominated to lead, they had undergone a rigorous apprenticeship.[34] In keeping with their career experience, the nominees presented themselves as effective representatives because they could provide strong descriptive—if not substantive—representation.

Outsider generalist Robert Mosbacher, George H. W. Bush's commerce secretary-designate, had no significant government service prior to his cabinet nomination. He recast his precabinet career, insisting that his business career had introduced him to an extensive and far-flung network and had made him conversant with a wide variety of economic and trade concerns. In essence, Mosbacher claimed to be a liaison. At least one confirmation committee member viewed this strategy with approval.

> *Senator Robert W. Kasten* (R-Wis.): I just want to comment that it has been noted by some that because you have no experience in the government you might have problems in Washington, D.C. I think I would agree with what I understood both Lloyd Bentsen and Phil Gramm to say [in their introductions], and that is that I think it is probably an advantage—I would say an important advantage—that you do not have a whole record of working in the government here, but instead have a strong business career and strong civic and charitable activities.
>
> I think that set of criteria on your resume is more important in your new job than government experience is. And so I applaud your selection. I look forward to your timely confirmation, to your being an active voice on behalf of the private sector within this cabinet, which clearly is going to be made up of a number of people with very strong and distinguished careers in public service. I think your private activities are going to be very helpful in the success of this new administration.[35]

It is also worth noting that both the senator and the secretary-designate were Republicans and that Republican presidents have consistently recruited higher proportions of their secretaries-designate from the private sector. Accordingly, partisanship may well be influencing these judgments about the nominee's likely performance as a representative.

Other outsider generalists presented themselves as specialists. This tactic was very much in evidence among those who had previously worked in a policy area within their future departments' jurisdictions but whose ties were to organizations other than the departments' traditional clients or policy networks. If these nominees presented themselves as liaisons, they would threaten powerful interests and could potentially endanger their own confirmation. They claimed specialist status, instead, and thereby gave a more acceptable tone to their anticipated substantive representation.

Clinton labor secretary-designate Alexis Herman, for example, described her career as a social worker and labor consultant, referencing her past successes in negotiating with unions. She also noted her Carter administration service. Herman had actually specialized in implementing affirmative action plans. Her nomination had raised such concern among organized labor that Carter labor secretary F. Ray Marshall had had to intercede on her behalf.[36] Unable to describe herself as a liaison, she cautiously presented herself as a policy specialist.

Senators, then, viewed generalists as presumptively weaker representatives in comparison with specialists and liaisons. They clearly expected the outsider generalists to be the weakest of these representatives. The senators' responses to the secretaries-designate thus protect the advantaged position of the departments' traditional clients and issue networks. Given the generalists' corresponding willingness to avoid challenging established interests, substantive representation in the cabinet will therefore undergo only incremental change. The nominees are also willing to endorse the senators' standards for credible leadership and management, so descriptive representation will change slowly.

GENDER IN THE CONFIRMATION HEARING

In presidential decisionmaking and confirmation committee deliberations, women are only gradually being recognized as elites and as representatives. Certainly, men are advantaged by the enduring perception that the masculine traits of the Heroic Man are requisite to success as a cabinet officer, and the corresponding willingness to view the men secretaries-designate as heroic men. If comparisons are possible, however, it seems that the Senate's judgments are even more conservative than those of the president. Presidential nominations have sometimes facilitated a transgendering of cabinet offices, but confirmation proceedings have more consistently endorsed only their regendering.

In one confirmation hearing after another, senators resolutely communicated their understanding of the cabinet as a masculine enclave. The ideal of the Heroic Man was upheld, and a masculinist understanding of political life was endorsed. As petitioners for power, the secretaries-designate typically accepted and reinforced these values. In the Hufstedler and Franklin confirmation hearings, the secretaries-designate even appropriated the senators' language to reassure the committee members of their commitment to this political ideology.

Senator Jacob K. Javits (R-N.Y.): You will learn, Judge Hufstedler, as we have learned, that there is nothing that you get around here that you don't fight for like a tiger—even if you are President, I might add. It does not make any difference how eminent you are.

I ask for any viewpoint that you have.

I want to say that the job is good for congratulations immediately after swearing-in, but from there, you are on your own. . . .

Carter education secretary-designate Shirley M. Hufstedler: . . . The length of my claws with respect to any program, I cannot predict until I see how each one fits into another and the extent to which, in a budget I did not make, I can nonetheless possibly make any differences.

Javits: Well, Judge Hufstedler, having identified the weapons, I think you will be very competent.[37]

Senator John C. Danforth (R-Mo.): We want you to be the heavy on behalf of American workers and American jobs and American business.

George H. W. Bush commerce secretary-designate Barbara H. Franklin: Senator, I will be the heavy on behalf of American business and jobs and if the chairman wants to call me the general, that is OK too. I will be the general in charge of American business and jobs.[38]

This is the vocabulary of war, not merely of competitiveness. The contemplative qualities of the Heroic Man are set aside, if not dismissed, as the women insist that they are able to cross traditional gender boundaries and become aggressively heroic leaders.

In other hearings, the women secretaries-designate spoke in deferential terms to the senators. Rather than merely agreeing to work with the legislative branch, the women accepted the lawmakers as their instructors.

George W. Bush labor secretary-designate Elaine Lan Chao: I do need guidance, and I do want to seek counsel from all of you as I begin this new position should I be confirmed, and I will again look forward to your counsel.[39]

Though secretaries-designate routinely acknowledge that they have not yet mastered the policies and programs of their departments, Chao goes further in inviting the Senate to serve as her guide. In doing so, she legitimizes her own marginalization, notwithstanding her precabinet accomplishments as a skilled leader and manager.

During the confirmation process, the senators articulate a consistent and coherent masculinist ideology that is far more fundamental than partisan platforms. The senators define cabinet representation as a masculine activity, delegitimizing the credentials and accomplishments of the women secretaries-designate. In simple terms, the confirmation hearings demonstrate that the senators do not yet view women as equal to men in their capacity for cabinet service. That means that women confront an additional barrier to establishing constructive relations with their Senate authorizations committee, and it is a barrier that exists purely on the basis of gender. It cannot be attributed to differences in the professional qualifications of the secretaries-designate. The regendering character of formal representation is very much in evidence throughout the confirmation hearings.

An exception to this pattern is seen in the Albright confirmation hearing. Albright was a liaison secretary-designate, nominated at the beginning of Clinton's second term to restore the legitimacy of the administration's foreign policy. She was presented to the Senate confirmation committee by her cabinet predecessor, not by her home-state senators. Secretary of State Warren M. Christopher opened his introduction with the following words:

> As far as we can tell from looking at the history books, this is the first time an outgoing Secretary of State has ever had the honor of introducing his nominated successor to the committee. For that particular privilege, I am very grateful to you, Madeleine, for asking me.
>
> Madeleine has been so gracious through this transition period. I am also grateful to the committee for permitting me to do this rather unusual thing.[40]

The introduction was even more "unusual" in light of the long history of disagreements between the confirmation committee chair, Senator Jesse Helms (R-N.C.), and Secretary Christopher.[41] At the conclusion of Christopher's speech, the committee chair responded in kind:

> I was going to do the unnecessary before Secretary Christopher left, which is to tell him that we have enjoyed our relationship with him. I think I speak unanimously for this committee. He is a gracious gentleman and I have enjoyed working with him.[42]

This exchange was highly significant, sending a message that legislative-executive foreign policy relations were entering a new stage. Only the most extraordinary of insider secretaries-designate could script her confirmation hearing in this way. The hearing showcased Albright's exceptionally strong connections in the legislative and executive branches. It also demonstrated that a woman insider liaison may have the discretion, as a descriptive representative, to break with tradition. Albright's actions contributed to transgendering the secretarial office, as she demonstrated that women could be remarkable leaders and thus provided women with a richer descriptive representation.

As more women specialists and liaisons are nominated, it will be necessary to determine whether the women and men secretaries-designate in these categories are being treated similarly. Women liaisons could encounter the questions reserved to generalists if their alliances with departmental clients and networks are deemed insufficient. If that were to occur, women, regardless of their career paths, could find themselves discounted. If so, the senators would then be depreciating the descriptive representation provided by the women specialists and liaisons, just as they already depreciate the descriptive representation of many of the women insiders. Albright's experiences would then be exceptional, encouraging only false hopes of transgendering either political leadership or cabinet representation.

It also seems that women will not soon receive greater or more specialized substantive representation on the cabinet. During their confirmation hearings, the secretaries-designate claim relationships with established departmental clients and issue network members. When nominees have connections to secondary (or tertiary) clients or networks, they are mentioned only in the margins. Though the women secretaries-designate may later seek to advance women's concerns, their lack of consideration at the confirmation hearing does not augur well. The confirmation hearing sets the parameters for future exchanges between the secretary and the Senate authorizations committee, so issues and constituents excluded from consideration at this time are less likely to be on the political agenda.

The masculinist precepts that guide assessments of the secretaries-designate—in the workings of formal representation throughout the confirmation process and in the judgments about the descriptive, substantive, and symbolic representation that the nominees are expected to provide—give little indication that the Senate supports the transgendering of cabinet office. Regendering is far more prevalent. Women and men secretaries-designate are required to manifest heroic traits, even to the point that senators describe policymaking in terms of war. Relationship, representation, and power are all taken as expressive of masculinity, and the ascribed gender identity of the women secretaries-designate precludes their acceptance as authoritative political actors.

By enforcing these strictures, the Senate limits the cabinet's institutional development to gender desegregation.

THE GENDER OF REPRESENTATION

It is easy to overlook the subtleties of the confirmation process, to mistake the symbolic for the merely ceremonial. Yet it is through this process of formal representation that the president and the Senate negotiate the reputation and the prestige accorded the secretary-designate. Judgments about the nominees as prospective substantive and descriptive representatives are closely related to assessments of their symbolic representation. Standards of formal representation are revealed as the confirmation hearings are conducted. The outcome is not merely the vote to confirm but a working agreement about the representation that will be provided by the cabinet members.

In reaching their conclusions about the secretaries-designate, the senators favor those nominees who most resemble themselves. The workings of homosociability advantage men (who endorse masculinist precepts), insiders (with whom the senators have previously had constructive relationships), and specialists or liaisons (possessed of policy or political expertise). Women, outsiders, and generalists are disadvantaged. As symbolic representatives, cabinet members are more (or less) accepted as decisionmakers as they are in more (or less) conformity with these standards. The comments offered by the nominees indicate that they are well aware of their consequent status. Women support masculinist precepts, outsiders stress their political qualifications, and generalists claim substantive knowledge or good relations with department constituents.

Given this information, it seems that senators vote to confirm cabinet nominees because they are reassured that the future secretaries will be appropriately respectful of the status quo. The future cabinet officers are expected to either accept or merely tinker with well-established procedures and relationships. With senators becoming more protective of their programmatic and partisan priorities and the confirmation process becoming increasingly contentious, this standard for legislative approval is only likely to strengthen. The status of women as officeholders or as constituents, therefore, will not change at the behest of the Senate. At best, it seems, women will deliver and receive symbolic rep-

resentation that suggests they are less marginalized and less subordinated within the cabinet—not that they are respected as full participants
in decision- and policymaking.

For these reasons, the Senate's contribution to the processes of formal representation can best be described as accepting the gender desegregation of the cabinet while doing little to further its integration. In contrast, there are elements of transgendering, and of a gender integration
of the cabinet, in the presidents' nomination decisions. In the more
recent administrations, women secretaries-designate have been named
to departments more central to the presidency or to the president's
agenda. Their credentials are recognized through their nomination to
departments in which they have served previously or in which they will
function as liaisons. These include departments that have been more
stringently associated with masculine precepts, as in the case of
Albright's nomination as secretary-designate of state and Gale Norton's
as interior secretary-designate in the George W. Bush administration.
This presidential recognition of women secretaries-designate as presumptively strong descriptive representatives may lead to a similar
endorsement of their substantive representation, either on behalf of traditional "women's issues" or in the interest of new perspectives on
enduring departmental alliances. Though there is nothing inevitable or
inexorable about such a development, the progression seems more likely
in the executive than in the legislative branch, where women and men
secretaries-designate have yet to be viewed as equally able leaders.

NOTES

1. For a critique of the confirmation process, see G. Calvin Mackenzie,
"The State of the Presidential Appointments Process," in *Innocent Until Nomi-
nated: The Breakdown of the Presidential Appointments Process,* ed. G. Calvin
Mackenzie (Washington, D.C.: Brookings Institution, 2001). On the strategies
associated with confirmations, see Burdett Loomis, "The Senate: An 'Obstacle
Course' for Executive Appointments," in *Innocent Until Nominated: The Breakdown of the Presidential Appointments Process,* ed. G. Calvin Mackenzie
(Washington, D.C.: Brookings Institution, 2001); Nolan McCarty and Rose
Razaghian, "Advice and Consent: Senate Responses to Executive Branch Nominations 1885–1996," *American Journal of Political Science* 43, no. 4 (October
1999): 1122–1143; Sharon Lynn Spray, "The Politics of Confirmations: A Study
of Senate Roll Call Confirmation Voting, 1787–1994," Ph.D. diss., Claremont
Graduate School, 1997. On the increasing partisanship and its effects on "diver-

sity" nominees, see Jean Reith Schroedel, Sharon Spray, and Bruce D. Snyder, "Diversity and the Politicization of Presidential Appointments: A Case Study of the Achtenberg Nomination," in *The Other Elites: Women, Politics, and Power in the Executive Branch*, ed. MaryAnne Borrelli and Janet M. Martin (Boulder, Colo.: Lynne Rienner Publishers, 1997).

2. Policy and character concerns fueled the debates about Clinton attorney general-designate Zoë Baird and George W. Bush labor secretary-designate Linda Chavez. In regard to a nominee's civil rights record as an official, public opinion was sharply divided in its assessments of Carter attorney general–designate Griffin Bell. As a judge in the U.S. Court of Appeals for the Fifth Circuit, Bell had a record that some considered too conservative on civil rights. The attorney general–designate was eventually endorsed by several African American leaders and by the Congress on Racial Equality. Still, questions about Bell's record and priorities were raised at his confirmation hearing. In the meantime, Bell had announced that "his choice for Solicitor General" was African American Wade H. McCree, Jr. McCree had an outstanding civil rights record and came to the Justice Department from the U.S. Court of Appeals for the Sixth Circuit. One of those actively critiquing Bell added that "[a] lot of this is tactical, rather than a serious effort to stop him. The interest now is in trying to pressure him and the Carter administration to pick blacks and women and others they approve of for top jobs in the Department of Justice." Anthony Marro, "Studies of Bell's Record as Judge Not Expected to Bar Confirmation," *New York Times*, 29 December 1976, p. 12. William K. Stevens, "Solicitor-General-Designate Wade Hampton McCree, Jr.," *New York Times*, 12 January 1977, p. A14. Conflicts of interest may arise from financial investments or from prior relationships. Clinton commerce secretary-designate Ron Brown, for example, was obliged to promise to recuse himself from all decisions affecting companies that had previously retained him as a lobbyist. His past representation of high-tech companies was judged especially problematic in light of ongoing trade negotiations with Asian nations. Stephen Labaton, "Commerce Nominee's Lobbying Prompts Scrutiny," *New York Times*, 20 December 1992, p. 28; Sara Fritz, "Brown and Kantor Stir Misgivings," *Los Angeles Times*, 1 January 1993, p. D1; "More Questions for Ron Brown," *New York Times*, 13 January 1993, p. A20. Charges of conflict of interest have sometimes been very partisan. When George W. Bush nominated a conservative senator, John Ashcroft (R-Mo.), as attorney general–designate, many legislators wondered if Ashcroft would enforce laws whose passage he had previously sought to overturn or block. *Capitol Hill Hearing Testimony, Senate Judiciary, Testimony for Confirmation for John Ashcroft for U.S. Attorney General*, Federal Documents Clearing House, 2001. On these points, more generally, see Burdett Loomis, "The Senate: An 'Obstacle Course' for Executive Appointments," in *Innocent Until Nominated: The Breakdown of the Presidential Appointments Process*, ed. G. Calvin Mackenzie (Washington, D.C.: Brookings Institution, 2001); G. Calvin Mackenzie, *The Politics of Presidential Appointments* (New York: Free Press, 1981), pp. 97–117.

3. Each HEW/HHS secretary-designate receives a confirmation hearing from her or his authorizations committee (the name has changed several times over the decades) and from the Senate Finance Committee. The agriculture secretaries-designate also had confirmation hearings with two committees, namely, the Committee on Agriculture, Nutrition, and Forestry and the Committee on Energy and Natural Resources.

4. The timing of the nomination as initial or midterm remains a topic for future study. The focus here was on the status of the secretary-designate within the Washington community and within the cabinet. Because these credentials categorized the precabinet relationships of the secretaries-designate with established constituents of the executive branch, they were more strongly associated with the nominees' anticipated descriptive and substantive representation. Though the status of the nominee as an initial or midterm secretary-designate was noted, therefore, it was not submitted to systematic analysis.

5. It is important to note that each specialist served in a department that also had (either before or after their service) a woman secretary. The additional secretaries-designate and their hearing committees therefore still allowed one to control for departmental and committee differences. The three additional specialists were Ford attorney general–designate Edward Levi, Ford labor secretary-designate John Dunlop, and Carter labor secretary-designate F. Ray Marshall.

6. For commentary on the procedural differences among the various Senate committees conducting confirmation hearings, see Christopher J. Deering, "Damned If You Do and Damned If You Don't: The Senate's Role in the Appointments Process," in *The In-and-Outers: Presidential Appointees and Transient Government in Washington*, ed. G. Calvin Mackenzie (Baltimore: Johns Hopkins University Press, 1987); G. Calvin Mackenzie, *The Politics of Presidential Appointments* (New York: Free Press, 1981); see also Terry Sullivan, "Repetitiveness, Redundancy, and Reform: Rationalizing the Inquiry of Presidential Appointees," in *Innocent Until Nominated: The Breakdown of the Presidential Appointments Process,* ed. G. Calvin Mackenzie (Washington, D.C.: Brookings Institution, 2001).

7. Each question-and-answer session reflects the committee's folkways and the chair's preferences. In some committees, senators question the nominee in order of their seniority. In others, senators ask questions in the order in which they arrived for the hearing. There are commonly time limits of five or ten minutes for each senator, which are more or less strictly observed. Committee members participate in several rounds of questions, until every senator has had sufficient opportunity to speak. Senators who are not committee members may also participate in the hearing, expressing the particular concerns of their constituents. As a matter of course, the nominee can expect senators to enter and leave the hearing as they juggle other meetings (sometimes other confirmation hearings) and floor votes. Also routinely, the secretary-designate is allowed or requested to respond to some questions in writing, which gives her or him an opportunity to make a more detailed reply. Meanwhile, senators

hope for a more detailed and strong commitment in accord with their constituency service and policy concerns.

8. For an earlier statement of this research, see MaryAnne Borrelli, "Gender, Credibility, and Politics: The Senate Nomination Hearings of Cabinet Secretaries-Designate, 1975 to 1993." *Political Research Quarterly* 50, no. 1 (March 1997): 171–197.

9. U.S. Senate. Committee on Finance, *Nomination of Richard S. Schweiker,* 97th Cong., 1st sess., p. 3. In Schweiker's Finance Committee hearing, only the chair gave an opening statement.

10. U.S. Senate, Committee on Energy and Natural Resources, *Nomination of James D. Watkins to be Secretary of Energy,* 101st Cong., 1st sess., pp. 9, 13.

11. Typically, introductions are provided by the secretary-designate's home-state senators, even when doing so requires a senator to cross party lines. Similarly, a single nominee may be introduced by senators from both parties, if both parties are in the home-state's delegation.

12. U.S. Senate, Committee on Energy and Natural Resources, *Bruce Babbitt Nomination,* 103rd Cong., 1st sess., pp. 27–28.

13. MaryAnne Borrelli, "Gender, Credibility, and Politics: The Senate Nomination Hearings of Cabinet Secretaries-Designate, 1975 to 1993." *Political Research Quarterly* 50, no. 1 (March 1997): 189.

14. There is some evidence that not all senators consider aggressiveness as requisite to political success. Senator David Durenberger (D-Minn.) introduced Clinton energy secretary-designate Hazel Rollins O'Leary in terms that suggested he identified with and supported a different leadership style. He stated, "And I think you will find . . . in Hazel Rollins O'Leary, an openness, a responsiveness, and a challenge to you and the challenge that she gives to herself to be better at what you do that you are. And that is a typical Minnesotan, and you are going to see that in the nominee." U.S. Senate, Committee on Energy and Natural Resources, *Hearing on the Nomination of Hazel R. O'Leary, to Be Secretary, Department of Energy,* 103rd Cong., 1st sess., p. 23.

15. U.S. Senate, Committee on Interstate and Foreign Commerce, *Nomination of Lewis L. Strauss,* 86th Cong., 1st sess.

16. U.S. Senate, Committee on the Judiciary, *Nomination of Edward H. Levi to Be Attorney General of the United States,* 94th Cong., 1st sess.

17. U.S. Senate, Committee on Labor and Public Welfare, *Nomination of John T. Dunlop, of Massachusetts, to Be Secretary of Labor,* 94th Cong., 1st sess. p. 8.

18. U.S. Senate, Committee on Labor and Human Resources, *Nomination of Robert Reich, of Massachusetts, to Be Secretary, Department of Labor,* 103rd Cong., 1st sess. See especially pp. 6–8, 22, 45.

19. "Dunlop Is Chosen for Labor Office," *New York Times,* 9 February 1975, p. 39; Edward Cowan, "Labor Leader Says Economy Needs Permanent Tax Cut of $25 Billion," *New York Times,* 14 December 1976, p. 29; James T. Wooten, "Carter Names Three to Posts in Cabinet; One a Black Woman," *New*

York Times, 22 December 1976, pp. 1, 16; "Labor Angry over Carter Method," *New York Times,* 22 December 1976, p. 16; James Risen, "Reich May Become New Kind of Labor Secretary," *New York Times,* 12 December 1992, pp. A22, A23.

20. U.S. Senate, Committee on Finance, *Nomination of Richard S. Schweiker to Be Secretary of Health and Human Services,* 97th Cong., 1st sess. See especially pp. 19–20, 22, 24, 27.

21. Ibid., p. 15.

22. In his *New York Times* biographical article, Califano was described as "analyst, referee, prodder, and expediter for much of the Johnson Administration's domestic program, not so much an architect of policy as an efficient contractor in charge of putting up the structure and making sure it would work." Linda Charlton, "Joseph Anthony Califano, Jr.," *New York Times,* 24 December 1976, p. 11.

23. U.S. Senate, Committee on Foreign Relations, *Nomination of Secretary of State,* 105th Cong., 1st sess., passim; see especially pp. 4, 7, 35.

24. Ibid., p. 66.

25. U.S. Senate, Committee on Labor and Human Resources, Nomination of Dr. Terrel H. Bell, of Utah, to Be Secretary, Department of Education, 97th Cong., 1st sess., passim.

26. U.S. Senate, Committee on Finance, Nomination of Louis W. Sullivan, 101st Cong., 1st sess., p. 25.

27. Similar exchanges occurred in both the Carla Anderson Hills and the Patricia Roberts Harris (1977) hearings, but there the questions were distinctly hostile and the responses of the nominee were correspondingly defensive. U.S. Senate, Committee on Banking, Housing, and Urban Affairs, Hearings on the Nomination of Carla A. Hills to Be Secretary of the Department of Housing and Urban Development. 94th Cong., 1st sess.; U.S. Senate, Committee on Banking, Housing, and Urban Affairs, Hearings on the Nomination of Patricia Roberts Harris to Be Secretary of the Department of Housing and Urban Development, 95th Cong., 1st sess.

28. U.S. Senate, Committee on Banking, Housing, and Urban Affairs, *Hearings on the Nomination of Patricia Roberts Harris to Be Secretary of the Department of Housing and Urban Development,* 95th Cong., 1st sess., p. 41.

29. U.S. Senate, Committee on Foreign Relations, *Nomination of Warren M. Christopher to Be Secretary of State.* 103rd Cong., 1st sess., pp. 145–146.

30. One of Hufstedler's home-state senators had actually been a strong opponent of an independent Education Department. Senator S. I. Hayakawa (D-Calif.) noted during the confirmation hearing that "[w]ith President Carter's choice of Judge Hufstedler, I must say that my fears have been laid to rest. I was concerned that this Department of Education would be excessively dominated by products of schools of education. It would be wrong to limit the Department of Education to points of view developed solely from within the discipline of professional education. . . . I hope that the nomination of a person

with a broad intellectual background such as Judge Hufstedler brings to her tasks will mean that the new Department of Education will be staffed by people of many varied interests and backgrounds, as well as by professors of education." U.S. Senate, Committee on Labor and Human Resources, *Nomination* [Shirley M. Hufstedler, of California, to Be Secretary of Education], 96th Cong., 1st sess., p. 20. Later in the hearing, confirmation committee member Senator Claiborne Pell (D-R.I.) echoed these sentiments. He stated, "The fact that you have a first-class mind and are coming into the job not a creature of the individual trade movements or establishments will give that mind free rein." U.S. Senate, Committee on Labor and Human Resources, *Nomination* [Shirley M. Hufstedler, of California, to Be Secretary of Education], 96th Cong., 1st sess., p. 39.

31. U.S. Senate, Committee on the Judiciary, *Nomination of Janet Reno to Be Attorney General of the United States.* 103rd Cong., 1st sess., p. 46.

32. U.S. Senate, Committee on Finance, *Nominations of Margaret Heckler, to Be Secretary of HHS and John A. Svahn, to Be Under Secretary of HHS,* 98th Cong., 1st sess., pp. 12, 21; U.S. Senate, Committee on Labor and Human Resources, *Nomination of William Emerson Brock III, of Tennessee, to Be Secretary of Labor, Department of Labor,* 99th Cong., 1st sess., pp. 1–15; U.S. Senate, Committee on Labor and Human Resources, *Lynn Martin, of Illinois, to Be Secretary, Department of Labor,* 102nd Cong., 1st sess., pp. 3–20.

33. U.S. Senate, Committee on Commerce, Science, and Transportation, *Nomination of Elizabeth H. Dole, to Be Secretary, Department of Transportation,* 98th Cong., 1st sess., pp. 2, 10, 17, 29; U.S. Senate, Committee on Labor and Human Resources, *Ann Dore McLaughlin, of the District of Columbia, to Be Secretary of Labor, U.S. Department of Labor,* 100th Cong., 1st sess., p. 21.

34. U.S. Senate, Committee on Commerce, Science, and Transportation, *Nominations—DOT,* 100th Cong., 1st sess., pp. 1–4; see also p. 23. U.S. Senate, Committee on the Judiciary, *Confirmation Hearings on Federal Appointments—William P. Barr,* 102nd Cong., 1st sess. HHS Secretary-Designate Shalala was particularly careful to present her political credentials. She implicitly described herself as an insider and a liaison—even though she had not served in government for twelve years and her prior nomination was to a different department. In describing her apprenticeship in the subcabinet, Shalala distinguished between lessons learned from a generalist (civil rights lawyer Harris) and from a liaison (former Mayor Landrieu). She then proceeded to endorse the liaison's priorities and to adopt them as her own to present herself as possessing the political abilities to succeed in cabinet service. Later in the hearing, Shalala was praised for her insight, her claim to a relationship with a liaison secretary causing her to be viewed as capable ("tough"). U.S. Senate, Committee on Labor and Human Resources, *Donna E. Shalala, of Wisconsin, to Be Secretary of Health and Human Services.* 103rd Cong., 1st sess., pp. 26, 28.

35. U.S. Senate, Committee on Commerce, Science, and Transportation, *Nomination of Robert A. Mosbacher, to Be Secretary, Department of Commerce,* 101st Cong., 1st sess., p. 19.

36. U.S. Senate, Committee on Labor and Human Resources, *Nomination* [Alexis M. Herman, of Alabama, to Be Secretary of Labor], 105th Cong., 1st sess.; Ronald Smothers, "Social-Worker Roots and Political Experience Lead to Labor Post: Alexis Margaret Herman," *New York Times,* 21 December 1996, p. 10; "AFL-CIO Leaders Pledge Fight to Win Herman's Confirmation for Labor Post," *Wall Street Journal,* 20 February 1997, p. A22.

37. U.S. Senate, Committee on Labor and Human Resources, Nomination [Shirley M. Hufstedler, of California, to Be Secretary of Education], 96th Cong., 1st sess., p. 34.

38. U.S. Senate, Committee on Commerce, Science, and Transportation, *Nomination of Barbara Hackman Franklin to be Secretary of Commerce,* 102nd Cong., 2nd sess., p. 33.

39. U.S. Senate, Committee on Health, Education, Labor, and Pensions, Nomination [Elaine Chao to Be Secretary of Labor], 107th Cong., 1st sess., p. 28.

40. U.S. Senate, Committee on Foreign Relations, *Nomination of Secretary of State,* 105th Cong, 1st sess., pp. 1–2.

41. Albright had served as a mediator between Christopher and Helms throughout much of her tenure as the U.S. ambassador to the United Nations. See David L. Marcus, "The New Diplomacy," *Boston Globe Magazine,* 1 June 1997, pp. 16–17.

42. U.S. Senate, Committee on Foreign Relations, *Nomination of Secretary of State,* 105th Cong, 1st sess. p. 3.

6

Conclusion: Understanding Representation

In identifying representation as one of the principal tasks of a department secretary, this study has echoed the perceptions of presidents, senators, and cabinet members. Time and again, these officeholders have described the cabinet's role in developing relationships with organized and societal interests so that their concerns could be articulated and developed. Political observers have routinely commented on the "balance" among the secretaries-designate, as measured by the variation in their political and partisan affiliations, professional and regional backgrounds, religion, race and ethnicity, and sex. The president's campaign debts and reelection hopes are evident in the alliances that are fostered by the nomination of one secretary-designate over another. Constituency service and policymaking are also dominant themes in the Senate confirmation hearings. Throughout the nomination and confirmation processes, then, participants seek to predict the representation that the secretaries-designate will provide when they enter office.

To better appreciate the complexities of these endeavors, I drew on the intellectual resources of presidency research and gender studies. Presidency scholars have conducted extensive studies of the nomination and confirmation processes, and my analysis has benefited greatly from their work. Their classification schemas—of Washington insiders and outsiders, of policy specialists and liaisons and generalists, among others—have guided this study of representation in the cabinet. Also important have been the discussions of reputation and prestige in the presidency literature, with their attentiveness to the ways in which political actors and the general public influence the status of decisionmakers. Gender scholars have long been interested in the intersections between power and identity, as the normative strength of gender roles has historically influenced the distribution of resources in societies. The distinctions these scholars have drawn between sex and gender, their attentiveness to the gender of men and women, and their concern for the consequences of gender ideologies in the lives of men and of women are the foundation of this investigation. Gender studies also provided the concepts—regendering and transgendering, gender deseg- regation and gender integration—to describe changes in the cabinet offices and in the cabinet itself.

Each of the preceding chapters has studied the nomination and con- firmation processes from the perspective of a different decisionmaker to delineate patterns in their understandings of cabinet representation and their expectations of cabinet representatives. It has repeatedly been demonstrated that women have yet to be perceived as full participants in the cabinet, either as officeholders or as constituents. Their leadership and management skills have been considered inferior to those of the men with whom they were nominated, notwithstanding the similarities in their credentials. The substantive expertise of the women secretaries-designate has been delimited or challenged by presidents and by senators. Too often, the women nominees have contributed more to the image than to the practice of gender inclusivity, the mechanisms for decisionmaking reinforcing the harsh dictates of masculinism. And yet, in the midst of this continuing marginalization, there are important nuances. The gen- dered character of the cabinet is beginning to change. Women secretaries- designate have become routinized tokens among the cabinet nominees. Though their numbers are still limited, their absence would not pass without criticism. In this sense, women are being accorded a qualified membership among presidential elites. This first step taken, it remains to be determined what the second and third steps might be in lifting the con- straints placed on women's representation in the cabinet.

To that end, this concluding chapter looks across the nomination and confirmation processes to draw conclusions, first, about how women sec- retaries-designate have been perceived as representatives and, second, about what those perceptions might signify in the near future.

SUBSTANTIVE REPRESENTATION

Substantive representation is the aspect of political representation that is most familiar to observers. Answering questions about substantive representation involves determining whose programs are established, whose funding is protected, and whose demands are met. To the extent that wins and losses can describe political accomplishments, substantive representation offers a easy measure of success.

Women do seem to be experiencing some success in terms of substantive representation. As presidential constituents, women have more consistently been recognized through the selection of women secretaries-designate. In several administrations, these nominations were directly linked to the power of women voters; presidents felt pressured to select women secretaries-designate either in acknowledgment of women's support in the past or in fear of women's rejection in the future. Likewise, those nominations have been to an increasingly diverse set of departments. A disproportionate number of the women secretaries-designate have been named to departments that were either the "women's seat" in the cabinet (seven labor secretaries-designate) or were congruent with women's traditional gender role (five health, education, and welfare (HEW)/health and human services (HHS) and education secretaries-designate). However, women have also been nominated to departments associated with such male preserves as engineering and the sciences (Transportation and Energy), foreign policy (State), public lands and natural resources (Interior), and business and finance (Commerce). These nominations suggest that women are no longer exclusively identified with traditional "women's issues" and are indicative of a profound shift in understanding women's identity as presidential constituents. In a very real sense, then, perceptions of women as presidential constituents are becoming transgendered, as their interests are no longer defined quite so stringently in terms of traditional gender roles and associated definitions of femininity.

The women secretaries-designate have been perhaps the greatest beneficiaries of these changes, as they have gained access to offices and participated in deliberations that were previously closed to women. The transgendering of women as presidential constituents may also have eased the expectations confronting the women secretaries-designate, insofar as representing women has become a responsibility for each of the cabinet officers and not merely the women. Still, if women secretaries-designate have profited from changing perceptions, they have also paid a price for their opportunities. That price is measured by the regendering that has been so much a part of cabinet nominations and confirmations.

The prospect that the women secretaries-designate might advocate on behalf of women or "women's issues" has caused considerable concern among presidents and senators alike. Though a number of the women secretaries-designate had experience in advancing "women's issues"—oftentimes, in raising awareness of the ways in which women's interests were changing with societal and economic innovations—those credentials have been ignored or dismissed by the presidents or the senators. Presidents have also deliberately recruited women who were unaffiliated with women's or "women's issue" networks. Senators, similarly, have stressed the established roster of departmental clients and networks in querying women's political allegiances. It has been the rare woman secretary-designate who commented on these biases, let alone challenged them.

At the same time that they have been distanced from women-related networks, the women secretaries-designate have been nominated to serve the president as buffers against powerful departmental clients. They have also routinely been nominated to lead departments distant from the president's agenda. And yet, these departments and clients have had strong supporters in the Congress. Of course, every secretary-designate expects to encounter conflict. Substantive representation, in the U.S. government, involves reconciling competing demands for scarce resources. What is notable about the challenges that confront the women secretaries-designate, however, is their consistent and even systematic nature. Many of the men secretaries-designate have encountered these substantive challenges, but virtually every one of the women secretaries-designate has done so.

These are some of the ways in which the transgendering and regendering of cabinet office has affected substantive representation as it has been performed for and by women in the past. What implications have these same developments had for substantive representation as it has been performed for and by men? On the one hand, men's interests have been generally accepted as congruent with those of women. Societal interests have been defined in terms of men, their concerns being so ordinary that the gendered character of the definition passes without notice. Public transportation and urban planning, finance and foreign policy, for example, are discussed in terms of the "public" interest, but the associated professions and networks are predominantly male. At times, these political issues have been explicitly described as "requiring" the exercise of traditionally masculine traits. In all these instances, women have consistently been excluded from the highest ranks of decisionmakers, so that the policies are gender exclusive by definition notwithstanding their presentation as gender inclusive. The nominations and confirmations of the women secretaries-designate are now challenging both these definitions and presentations. Women have been named to lead the Departments of Transportation, Housing and Urban Development, Commerce, and State. Their presence has forced a reconsideration of accepted norms and practices, with uncertain outcomes for men. As women lead these departments with increasing frequency—and if they become secretaries of defense and the treasury—the implications of regendering and of transgendering will become correspondingly more evident for both women and men.

Already, the effects of regendering and transgendering on the men secretaries-designate merit consideration. For the women, regendering within the cabinet has been evidenced in the reinscription of traditionally feminine traits and in their consequent marginalization within a masculinist system. Similarly, for the men, regendering has been evidenced in the reinscription of masculine traits and in the uncertainty of their status within the cabinet hierarchy. Whether in media coverage or in confirmation hearings, men must prove their claims to be "heroic." As one after another male secretary-designate defends his aggressiveness and competitiveness, it becomes clear that masculinism is no less constraining of men than it is of women. In confronting the dictates of masculinism, however, men are aided by presumptions that their gender role will be congruent with their sex. Their identity and substantive representation are expected to be coterminous. This association will become more problematic as the transgendering of cabinet office yields new understandings of masculinity and femininity. Men may then confront few constraints from masculinism, but they will also have fewer guidelines for success.

As emphasized time and again in this analysis, gendered change within the cabinet has been neither unidirectional nor consistent. Regendering and transgendering have each occurred, and movements toward one or another have been contradictory. If regendering has predominated, transgendering has also been evident and may gain more of an impetus in the future administrations. If women secretaries-designate continue to be nominated to a wide array of departments, to departments central to the presidency or to the president's policy agenda, and to departments in which they are policy liaisons, then the gender boundaries of cabinet office will slowly shift. Gender will doubtless continue to exert some influence—it is unlikely that the historical strength of masculinism will be wholly displaced—but substantive representation will become less confined to interests assigned to women and men on the basis of their traditional gender roles.

DESCRIPTIVE REPRESENTATION

As the term suggests, descriptive representation signifies that the representative and the represented share a common identity. A woman secretary-designate is a descriptive representative of women. An African American secretary-designate is a descriptive representative of African Americans. An African American woman secretary-designate is a descriptive representative of African American women. Yet these examples also point to the problematic nature of descriptive representation. Given that each person's identity has many elements, which will be considered most relevant to their performance as a descriptive representative? Or will representation itself be fragmented and fractured until commonalties are lost? Answers to these questions will have to wait for the future, if for no other reason than the questions themselves are only just beginning to be asked in the context of cabinet nominations and confirmations. Still, they set a context for this examination of descriptive representation, which moves from a consideration of identity to an assessment of credibility and competence.

Descriptive representation surfaces repeatedly in political treatises generally and in American political thought specifically. Because it is a democratic republic, there is some expectation that the U.S. government will be reflective of its society. Though this aspiration has yet to be achieved, its appeal is sufficient that presidential candidates repeatedly insist that that they will bring new people and new perspectives to Washington. These campaign promises, in their turn, lead to media assessments of the "balance" provided by the secretaries-designate and by other presidential appointees. Media coverage of the secretaries-designate as descriptive representatives has routinely inventoried the nominees' regional, partisan, racial, and ethnic identities. In the Clinton administration, white males were paired with "diversity" nominees when their nominations were announced to strengthen claims that the cabinet would be responsive to the concerns of all Americans. This development, the product of Clinton's promise to nominate an administration that "looks like America," continued into the George W. Bush transition; it may have become a permanent characteristic of the nomination coverage.

By these standards for descriptive representation, cabinet representation for women is primarily cabinet representation for white women. There have only been five women of color among the twenty-one women secretaries-designate nominated to the cabinet. Three of those nominees have been African American, one was Hispanic (her nomination was withdrawn), and one was Asian American. Quite simply, very few women of color have been nominated to the cabinet, and thus very little descriptive representation has been provided to women of color in the wider society. These women must, it seems, find their representation through white women and through men of color. This dissection of their identity provides little hope of their receiving adequate descriptive representation.

In her seminal work, *The Concept of Representation* (1967), Hanna F. Pitkin concluded that descriptive representation "depends on the representative's characteristics, on what he *is* or is *like*, on being something rather than doing something. The representative does not act for others; he 'stands for' them, by virtue of a correspondence or connection between them, a resemblance or reflection." She continues, "In political terms, what seems important is less what the legislature does than how it is composed." It is not surprising, Pitkin concludes, that conceptions of descriptive representation have been most fully developed by proportional representation theorists.[1]

Pitkin's assertions, however, require careful interpretation. Though the legitimacy of descriptive representation may rest most significantly on qualities shared by the representative and the represented, representation itself is not a static state. As Pitkin subsequently notes, representation is "conduct." Even descriptive representatives must act.

> When the representative is likened to a descriptive representation or a symbol, he is usually seen as an inanimate object and not in terms of any activity; he represents by what he is or how he is regarded. He does not represent by doing anything at all; so it makes no sense to talk about his role or his duties and whether he has performed them. On the other hand, this conception of representing as 'standing for' brings with it another notion—the making or creation of representations or symbols; and that is a kind of activity. In the creating of symbols, the analogy is of doubtful validity, since we do not seem to call symbol-making 'representing.' But if the analogy is nevertheless accepted, it would seem to imply a single rather broad criterion for representative activity: that it be successful in getting accepted, in convincing. In descriptive representation-making . . . the activity is a matter of truthfulness, of accurate rendering of information about something absent.[2]

As descriptive representatives, then, the women cabinet officers must be accepted as faithful representatives of women. Though some would still debate the "proper" political role of women, even those who resist having women lead concede that women have the ability to analyze information, make decisions, and confront the consequences of their actions.[3] If women cabinet officers are to be descriptive representatives of women, then, they must be recognized as practicing these qualities as political actors. Jane Mansbridge develops these points further in her assessments of the benefits derived from meaningful descriptive representation.

> In at least four contexts, for four different functions, disadvantaged groups may want to be represented by "descriptive representatives," that is, individuals who in their own backgrounds mirror some of the more frequent experiences and outward manifestations of belonging to the group. For two of these functions—(1) adequate communication in contexts of mistrust, and (2) innovative thinking in contexts of uncrystallized, not fully articulated, interests—descriptive representation enhances the substantive representation of interests by improving the quality of deliberation. For the other two functions—(1) creating a social meaning of "ability to rule" for members of a group in historical contexts where that ability has been seriously questioned, and (2) increasing the polity's de facto legitimacy in contexts of past discrimination—descriptive representation promotes goods unrelated to substantive representation.[4]

In each of its aspects, therefore, descriptive representation is an important measure of the recognition being extended to a presidential constituency. It cannot be equated with the mere showcasing of individuals.

To systematically assess the descriptive representation offered by and expected of the secretaries-designate, three sets of variables were studied. These were (1) the nominees' demographic profile (race, ethnicity, sex, age, marital status, and children); (2) education (years of schooling, degrees received, and institutions attended); and (3) professional career and political alliances (as centered in the governmental or private sector and as related to partisan, interest group, and issue network affiliations). Patterns in these data revealed the prevailing standards and norms for cabinet nomination. Women and men could be compared and connections drawn between their credentials and their likely credibility as cabinet officers.

Along each of the three dimensions, the women and men secretaries-designate had credentials that were more similar than different. Whether female or male, the typical secretary-designate was white, middle-aged, married, and a parent. She or he had usually been extensively educated, often at prestigious institutions. Democrat or Republican, the nominees had professional records of achievement and success, having experienced rapid promotion into high office. As a group, therefore, the secretaries-designate appeared to be representing a select and mainstream segment of the population, namely, the economically advantaged. As women met the criteria associated with this definition, they seemingly became eligible to serve as descriptive representatives, able to prove women's political competence. This sentiment surfaced in the *New York Times* editorial endorsing the first woman nominated to the inner cabinet. "In a cabinet designed to look like America," it proclaimed, "Zoë Baird, the Attorney General-designate, has the bearing and the credentials of what America would like to look like."[5]

Yet the message of this editorial was qualified by the news articles that covered the cabinet nominations and nominees. Controlling for the timing and status of the nomination and the administration to which the secretary-designate was nominated, women and men received quantitatively equal coverage in the nomination articles. Likewise, the women and men secretaries-designate were each judged by the same heroic, or masculinist, standards. Although the paper acknowledged the strength and resourcefulness of the women, it judged them as lacking the forcefulness, aggressiveness, dedication, and single-minded ambition that distinguished successful leaders and managers. The *Times* questioned the ability of the women nominees to communicate, demonstrate innovative thinking, and prove women's political skills more generally. These circumstances prevailed despite the objective similarities in the women's and men's precabinet careers. The newspaper of record in the United States, therefore, presented the women secretaries-designate as weak descriptive representatives. In brief, the *New York Times* endorsed regendering the cabinet.

Similarly, Senate confirmation committee members held women to a higher standard in awarding the coveted "insider" status. The senators repeatedly questioned the women about their willingness to practice the masculine behaviors that the senators considered requisite to political success. The senators' concerns were undoubtedly heightened by the women's typical status as generalists. These, after all, were the cabinet members least conversant with their departments' issue jurisdiction, clients, and issue networks. Generalists were also the most dependent on the president and might therefore be less responsive to the legislature. In the confirmation hearings, then, gender traditions and legislative-executive tensions were mutually reinforcing. Each rationalized minimizing the prestige and reputation of the women nominees and thus favored regendering cabinet office.

Still there is some transgendering. As noted in regard to substantive representation, presidents have sometimes capitalized on the policy expertise of women secretaries-designate. Presidents have recently named women secretaries-designate to departments important to the presidency and their presidential initiatives, to departments in which they have been liaisons to influential clients and networks, and to departments in which they have previously served as subcabinet officers. Though senators continue to query the "heroic" nature of the women secretaries-designate, some women nominees are granted a measure of credibility and discretion. It is the exceptional woman secretary-designate who is expected to be a strong descriptive representative, but these exceptions are present.

In descriptive representation as in substantive representation, women and men secretaries-designate find that there is strong support for traditional conceptions of femininity and masculinity. With masculinism predisposing decisionmakers to value masculine traits, women and men seek to demonstrate those behaviors to prove their credibility. The present emphasis on regendering imposes a significant burden on the women secretaries-designate, since their gender identities are perceived as precluding their political success. Yet there is also a burden imposed on the men secretaries-designate, as the need to conform to traditional standards causes them to compromise their identity and ignore transformational leadership styles. If the impetus to transgender cabinet office continues, so that the cabinet begins a gendered integration, then both women and men secretaries-designate will benefit. Every step away from historical conceptions of command and control, every consideration of the nominees' distinctive abilities, will only enhance the performance of the cabinet as an institution for representation.

SYMBOLIC REPRESENTATION

Clinton Rossiter described the president as a "father image" sufficient to satisfy even the most skeptical of "political Freudians."[6] More recently, scholars have delineated how this gender identity surfaces in both the nation's founding ideology (the Heroic Man) and in present-day institutions of the presidency (masculinism). In brief, the political traditions of the United States depict the president as an autonomous and wise ruler. The chief executive is repeatedly described as an individual who possesses the strength and the resourcefulness to win in a competitive environment. Additionally, he manifests compassion in caring for others. If recent presidents have fallen short of this standard, the ideal has been kept alive in innumerable popular portrayals of the chief executive. Movies from *Dave* to *Air Force One* endorse a perception of the president as a singular, principled, and heroic leader.

Secretaries-designate are expected to manifest these same qualities. Even as they confront demands to defer to the president and the senators, the cabinet nominees are required to demonstrate political leadership and executive management skills. The question is whether strength, autonomy, and self-reliance, all which are associated with masculinity, will ever be associated with women. This brings us to a discussion of the resistance to and acceptance of women as secretaries-designate.

The nomination power allows presidents to set a personnel and policy agenda. Careful study of this power in the eight administrations that have had women secretaries-designate has indicated that presidents have generally contributed to regendering cabinet office and thus to the gender desegregation of the cabinet. In some administrations, presidents have transgendered cabinet office and thus have somewhat facilitated the gender integration of the cabinet.

Desegregation has taken the form of nominating women to cabinet office while limiting their influence over policy. Thus, women have typically served in the outer cabinet, in the younger departments, and in policy jurisdictions distant from the president's priorities. Women have been nominated as generalists so that they were dependent on the president while protecting the chief executive from powerful interests. Women secretaries-designate have thus been selected to function as caretakers, rather than as innovative leaders or managers. This is a subtle but unmistakable form of regendering, which provides women with a political opportunity while constraining their participation. It is an arrangement that resembles apprenticeship, as the master artisan only gradually allows the student to demonstrate creativity and to assume greater responsibility.

At times, however, presidents have contributed to the gender integration of the cabinet. In these instances, women have been nominated to cabinet offices essential to the success of the administration. They have been nominated as liaisons, signifying that the president found their precabinet alliances with departmental clients useful rather than threatening. In these instances, women have been nominated to serve as representatives *from and to* the president, on behalf of various networks. This role, which is indicative of meaningful substantive and descriptive representation, is an indication of transgendering. Though the effects of gender linger, women and men as secretaries-designate are viewed as equally capable representatives.

In media coverage and Senate hearings, however, women were viewed as presumptively less capable than the men with whom they were nominated. There are two possible interpretations of this judgment. It may be that the *New York Times* and the male senators favor a longer apprenticeship for women, being more hesitant to recognize them as leaders. Given the lengthy tenure of many senators and the corresponding strength of their relationships with established department clients and networks, this response would not be wholly illogical. Any alteration in the relationships that structure the policy process could seriously and negatively affect their political fortunes, giving the senators good reason to favor only the most incremental of changes.

Alternatively, it could be that the male senators are more resistant to the entry of women into politics. For some, this attitude could reflect an ingrained belief that women are more suited to the private sphere; others might expect that the inclusion of these individuals might negatively affect the rationale and dynamic of politics; and still others might fear that the inclusion of this new set of individuals would result in fewer goods being available for themselves and for their constituents. Certainly these views surface in the male senators' confirmation hearing statements and comments. All of them share a common perception of politics as operating in such a fashion that one interest can advance only if another is diminished. Thus, if women enter political office and are recognized as executive/legislative constituents, then others (men) will hold fewer offices and will receive less from the government. This worldview gives scant consideration to the possibility that women and men, as officeholders and as constituents, have many overlapping concerns and interests. It also neglects the reality that gender identities are not exclusive, with some traits possessed only by women and others only by men. Rather, as even the Heroic Man ideal suggests, there is a spectrum of traits that gender traditions assign to women and to men. And, as the pre-cabinet careers of the secretaries-designate demonstrate, the traits requisite to political success—even by the prevailing masculinist and regendered standards—may surface in women as well as in men.

In future hearings, the presence of women in the Senate and on the confirmation committees and the effect of their presence on the gendered evolution of the chamber will merit consideration. The cabinet nominations of George W. Bush suggest that the president will continue to desegregate and even integrate the cabinet. The senators' receptivity to this development is not yet certain. It will be necessary to determine whether women and men secretaries-designate come to be similarly received as insiders. It will also be important to determine whether women and men secretaries-designate are recognized as specialists and liaisons, when their precabinet careers are similarly distinguished. Albright's confirmation suggested that women insider liaisons might have considerable influence in the confirmation process, but her experiences are presently unique.

In the tensions associated with regendering and transgendering cabinet office and also with the gender desegregation and gender integration of the cabinet, it will be most interesting to trace the changes in the normative standards to which the nominees are held. Masculinism may endure. If so, women either will be dismissed for their lack of masculinity or will be obliged to accept its precepts. If masculinism is weakened, however, women and men will be able to demonstrate a more diverse set of political behaviors. Currently, the secretaries-designate and the cabinet are caught in the midst of these possibilities. It may be that resolving this tension will be the final test of women as political apprentices, after which they will assume the full responsibilities of political officeholders and constituents.

FORMAL REPRESENTATION

Nomination and appointment powers did not originate with the Constitution. As historians and political scientists have explained, these executive powers can be traced back to the warrior kings of earlier ages.

> [The Anglo-Saxon] nobleman formed a group of warriors around him in an exclusive relationship known as the *comitatus*. He chose them to protect his lands and acquire new ones; they chose him to protect their lives and acquire status in their own realms. The symbiosis became known as the spirit of the *comitatus:* a special relationship of absolute, to-the-death fealty and archetypal camaraderie.[7]

The debates throughout the constitutional convention revealed considerable respect for this history of executive leadership. Just as the *comitatus* augmented the power of the lord, convention participants viewed the appointment power as a formidable source of influence for the president. Luther Martin argued that the appointment power would enable the chief executive to recruit "a formidable host" of allies, constraining the legislature and even bringing an end to elections.[8] Others rejected these predictions, maintaining that this power would merely aid in building an executive branch able to implement policies and uphold the law.

Senate confirmation was an improvisation. It transformed the "power to appoint" into the more consultative "power to nominate," with the Senate invested with the responsibility of reviewing presidential decisionmaking. The power of the president and of the Senate were leveraged, each against the other, to ensure that the executive branch served the public interest. Moreover, confirmation was assigned to the Senate, rather than the House, so that less populated states could protect their interests.[9]

Thus, the nomination and confirmation processes have been infused with highly gendered conceptions of leadership and power. The *comitatus* and thus today's comity were premised on a conception of loyalty between warriors. Because each warrior trusted the other, the demands of each were honored; because each participant benefited from the relationship, self-interest was exercised constructively and for the good of the whole.[10] Constitutional debates about legislative-executive powers and the present-day exercise of the nomination and confirmation powers evidenced similar principles and goals. Having agreed to a unitary executive—an embodiment of masculinist principles of ambition, strength, and autonomy—the founders proceeded to check that individual by investing other offices with similar traits and with contrary understandings of what was in their self-interest. Competitiveness and aggressiveness, two other qualities prized by masculinism, were thereby drawn into the constitutional order. In theory and in practice, the nomination and confirmation powers—the mechanisms of formal representation for the cabinet—have manifested masculinist precepts. There has never been anything gender neutral about these processes.

As is true of the other three aspects of representation, formal representation testifies to the continuing influence of masculinism. Legislative-executive relations have only become more strained and competitive in recent decades, and the masculinist attentiveness to self-interest and self-advancement have been very much in evidence. At the same time, there has been an underlying continuity, as presidents and senators have each more frequently endorsed regendering than transgendering cabinet office, permitting a gendered desegregation of the cabinet but rarely facilitating its gendered integration. In the midst of so many other political debates, there has been considerable agreement on this point.

*   *   *

The representation promised by the secretaries-designate is extremely complex, in each and every one of its aspects. As substantive representatives, the nominees offer to reconcile different constituencies' competing claims to legitimacy, not merely to provide an accounting of policy wins and losses. As descriptive representatives, they seek to demonstrate leadership and management skills, resisting presidential tendencies to merely showcase "diversity." As symbolic representatives, the secretaries-designate try to secure their roles as advisers and decisionmakers from the earliest moment so that their presence does more than create an image of receptivity to new perspectives. And as they are nominated and confirmed, the nominees reveal the underlying ideologies of identity and power that set the contours of formal representation. As this book goes to press, the cabinet is evidencing regendering and transgendering, gender desegregation and gender integration. Its evolution has not yet settled into a progressive development. Clearly, an opportunity exists to recognize rather than merely require heroism of the secretaries-designate, to expect representation that is both strong and thoughtful. The uncertainty of change in the cabinet may therefore facilitate an extraordinary creativity. Certainly that is what will be required if the past is not to dictate the future of cabinet members and constituents.

NOTES

1. Hanna Fenichel Pitkin, *The Concept of Representation* (Berkeley: University of California Press, 1967), p. 61.
2. Ibid., p. 113.
3. For an overview of conservative perspectives on women's capacities and roles, see Rebecca E. Klatch, *Women of the New Right* (Philadelphia: Temple University Press, 1987).

4. Jane Mansbridge, "Should Blacks Represent Blacks and Women Represent Women? A Contingent 'Yes,'" *Journal of Politics* 61, no. 3 (August 1999): 628.

5. "Looks Like America," *New York Times,* 25 December 1992, p. A30.

6. Clinton Rossiter, *The American Presidency* (New York: Time, 1962), p. 5.

7. Maxine Berman, *The Only Boobs in the House Are Men: A Veteran Woman Legislator Lifts the Lid on Politics Macho Style* (Troy, Mich.: Momentum Books, 1994), p. 1, as quoted in George Duerst-Lahti, "Reconceiving Theories of Power: Consequences of Masculinism in the Executive Branch," in *The Other Elites: Women, Politics, and Power in the Executive Branch* (Boulder, Colo.: Lynne Rienner Publishers, 1997), p. 23.

8. Luther Martin, in *James Madison, Debates of the Federal Constitutional Convention of 1787 Which Framed the Constitution of the United States of America,* vol. 1, ed. Gaillard Hung and James Brown Scott, international ed. (Westport, Conn.: Greenwood Press, 1970), p. 218.

9. Though the unitary executive became a distinguishing feature of the Constitution, checks imposed on that office included the requirement that the Senate confirm presidential nominations. To ensure the Senate's responsible exercise of this power, the Constitution prohibited the appointment or nomination of any legislator to executive office. In James Wilson's words, "if the powers of either branch are perverted, it must be with the approbation of some one of the other branches of government: thus checked on one side, they can do no one act of themselves." When questions arose concerning why the confirmation power had been assigned to the Senate rather than the House of Representatives, W. R. Davie's answer was brief and pointed: "The small states would not agree that the House of Representatives should have a voice in the appointment to offices; and the extreme jealousy of all the states would not give it to the President alone." For commentary on these points, see William Findley in the House of Representatives, 23 January 1798, in James Madison, *Debates of the Federal Constitutional Convention of 1787 Which Framed the Constitution of the United States of America,* vol. 1, ed. Gaillard Hung and James Brown Scott, international ed. (Westport, Conn.: Greenwood Press, 1970), p. 375; James Wilson, in ibid., p. 162; W. R. Davie, in ibid., p. 348; Alexander Hamilton, "Federalist 76," in *The Federalist Papers* (New York: New American Library, 1961). See also Sidney M. Milkis and Michael Nelson, *The American Presidency: Origins and Development, 1776–1998,* 3rd ed. (Washington, D.C.: CQ Press, 1999).

10. John Hart, *The Presidential Branch: From Washington to Clinton,* 2nd ed. (Chatham, N.J.: Chatham House Publishers, 1995), pp. 186–194. See also Eric Uslaner, *The Decline of Comity in Congress* (Ann Arbor: University of Michigan Press, 1993).

Appendix: "Diversity" Secretaries-Designate

Secretary "Diversity" profile	Department	President	Years of Service
Frances Perkins[a] White woman	Labor	Roosevelt	1933–1945
Oveta Culp Hobby White woman	Health, Education, and Welfare	Eisenhower	1953–1955
Robert C. Weaver[b] African American man	Housing and Urban Development	Johnson	1966–1969
William T. Coleman, Jr. African American man	Transportation	Ford	1975–1977
Carla Anderson Hills White woman	Housing and Urban Development	Ford	1975–1977
Patricia Roberts Harris African American woman	Housing and Urban Development	Carter	1977–1979
	Health, Education, and Welfare	Carter	1979–1981
Juanita M. Kreps White woman	Commerce	Carter	1977–1979
Shirley M. Hufstedler White woman	Education	Carter	1979–1981
Samuel R. Pierce, Jr. African American man	Housing and Urban Development	Reagan	1981–1989
Elizabeth Hanford Dole White woman	Transportation Labor	Reagan G. H. W. Bush	1983–1987 1989–1991
Margaret M. Heckler White woman	Health and Human Services	Reagan	1983–1985
Ann Dore McLaughlin White woman	Labor	Reagan	1987–1989
Lauro F. Cavazos Hispanic American man	Education	Reagan G. H. W. Bush	1988–1991

Secretary "Diversity" profile	Department	President	Years of Service
Louis W. Sullivan African American man	Health and Human Services	G. H. W. Bush	1989–1993
Manuel J. Lujan, Jr. Hispanic American man	Interior	G. H. W. Bush	1989–1993
Lynn Martin White woman	Labor	G. H. W. Bush	1991–1993
Barbara H. Franklin White woman	Commerce	G. H. W. Bush	1992–1993
Donna E. Shalala White woman	Health and Human Services	Clinton	1993–2001
Ronald H. Brown African American man	Commerce	Clinton	1993–1996
Henry G. Cisneros Hispanic American man	Housing and Urban Development	Clinton	1993–1997
Hazel R. O'Leary African American woman	Energy	Clinton	1993–1997
Zoë E. Baird[c] White woman	Justice (withdrawn)	Clinton	N.A.
Jesse Brown African American man	Veterans Affairs	Clinton	1993–1998
Mike Espy African American man	Agriculture	Clinton	1993–1994
Federico Peña Hispanic American man	Transportation Energy	Clinton Clinton	1993–1997 1997–1998
Janet Reno White woman	Justice	Clinton	1993–2001
Madeleine Korbel Albright White woman	State	Clinton	1997–2001
Alexis M. Herman African American woman	Labor	Clinton	1997–2001
Rodney E. Slater African American man	Transportation	Clinton	1997–2001
Togo D. West, Jr. African American man	Veterans Affairs	Clinton	1998–1999
Bill Richardson Hispanic American man	Energy	Clinton	1998–2001
Norman Y. Mineta Asian American man	Commerce Transportation	Clinton G. W. Bush	1999–2001 2001–present
Colin L. Powell African American man	State	G. W. Bush	2001–present
Melquiades R. Martinez Hispanic American man	Housing and Urban Development	G. W. Bush	2001–present
Ann M. Veneman White woman	Agriculture	G. W. Bush	2001–present

Secretary "Diversity" profile	Department	President	Years of Service
Gale A. Norton White woman	Interior	G. W. Bush	2001–present
Rod Paige African American man	Education	G. W. Bush	2001–present
Linda Chavez[d] Hispanic American woman	Labor (withdrawn)	G. W. Bush	N.A.
Elaine Lan Chao Asian American woman	Labor	G. W. Bush	2001–present

Notes: Secretaries-designate are listed in the order in which their nomination was announced. When more than one nomination was announced on a single day, the nominees are listed in alphabetical order.

a. Frances Perkins was married to Paul Wilson. She used her married name infrequently and only for social occasions.

b. Robert Weaver is included in this list so that it is comprehensive. However, he is not included in the database for this volume because President Johnson did not nominate any women as secretaries-designate.

c. Zoë E. Baird was married to Paul D. Gewirtz. She did not use her married name. President Clinton withdrew the Baird nomination during the confirmation hearing.

d. Linda Chavez withdrew her nomination when questions were raised about illegalities associated with her offer of housing and support to a woman who was in the country illegally.

References

Aberbach, Joel D., and Bert A. Rockman. *In the Web of Politics: Three Decades of the U.S. Federal Executive*. Washington, D.C.: Brookings Institution, 2000.

Abramson, Rudy. "O'Leary Surprised but Not Unaware." *Los Angeles Times*, 22 December 1992, p. A26.

Ad Hoc Coalition for Women. "Summary of Priority Requests Made by Coalition in Meeting with President Carter and Vice President Mondale at White House Meeting, March 10, 1977." BPW/USA Archives.

"AFL-CIO Leaders Pledge Fight to Win Herman's Confirmation for Labor Post." *Wall Street Journal*, 20 February 1997, p. A22.

"Alexis M. Herman." *Current Biography Yearbook 1998*. New York: H. W. Wilson, 1998.

Anderson, Paul. *Janet Reno: Doing the Right Thing*. New York: John Wiley and Sons, 1994.

"Ann Dore McLaughlin." *Current Biography Yearbook 1988*. New York: H. W. Wilson, 1988.

Anzaldua, Gloria. *La Frontera: The New Mestiza*. San Francisco: Aunt Lute Books, 1987.

Apple, R. W., Jr. "Bush's Beltway Team." *New York Times*, 13 January 1989, p. 1.

Applebome, Peter. "Lauro F. Cavazos." *New York Times*, 22 November 1988, p. A19.

"Assail Woodin and Miss Perkins." *New York Times*, 26 February 1933, p. 12.

Associated Press. "Current Quotes from the 1992 Campaign Trail," 22 May 1992.

Auerbach, Stuart. "Franklin Exhibits Across-the-Board Appeal." *Washington Post*, 27 December 1991, p. D10.

Ayres, B. Drummond, Jr. "Choices for Attorney General and the Agriculture and Commerce Secretary." *New York Times*, 21 December 1976, p. 24.

―――. "Griffin Boyette Bell." *New York Times,* 21 December 1976, p. 25.

"Baird's Letter to Clinton on Nomination." *New York Times*, 22 January 1993, p. A14.

Barringer, Felicity. "Clinton Selects Ex-Mayor for HUD and Ex-Marine for Veterans Affairs." *New York Times,* 18 December 1992, p. 1.

Baruch, Michael, and Martha Joynt Kumar. *Portraying the President: The White House and the News Media.* Baltimore: Johns Hopkins University Press, 1981.

"Bed and Board." *Fortune* (25 September 1989): 225.

Bender, Marylin. "Management." *New York Times*, 14 May 1976, p. D1.

Bennett, Anthony J. *The American President's Cabinet: From Kennedy to Bush.* New York: St. Martin's Press, 1996.

Berke, Richard L. "Clinton Picks Miami Woman, Veteran State Prosecutor, to Be His Attorney General." *New York Times,* 12 February 1993, p. 1.

―――. "For Appointees to Cabinet, a List of Dos and Don'ts." *New York Times,* 6 January 1993, p. A14.

―――. "The Third Choice." *New York Times,* 12 February 1993, p. 1.

Best, James J. "Presidential Cabinet Appointments, 1953–1976." *Presidential Studies Quarterly* 11, no. 1 (Winter 1981): 62–66.

"Best Women Held Too Old For Court." *New York Times,* 25 September 1971, p. 35.

"Bill Clinton's Pragmatists." *New York Times,* 12 December 1992, p. 22.

Binder, David. "Nation's New Defense Chief." *New York Times,* 4 November 1975, p. 25.

Bird, David. "Family Doctor for Cabinet." *New York Times,* 8 November 1985, p. B6.

Blackman, Ann. *Seasons of Her Life.* New York: Scribner's, 1998.

Blackman, Ann, and Tom Curry. "Just Heartbeats Away." *Time,* 1 July 1996, pp. 24–39.

Blood, Thomas. *Madam Secretary: A Biography of Madeleine Albright.* New York: St. Martin's Press, 1997.

Bonafede, Dom. "Reagan and His Kitchen Cabinet Are Bound by Friendship and Ideology." *National Journal,* 11 April 1981, pp. 605–608.

Borrelli, MaryAnne. "Campaign Promises, Transition Dilemmas: Cabinet Building and Executive Representation." In *The Other Elites: Women, Politics, and Power in the Executive Branch,* ed. MaryAnne Borrelli and Janet M. Martin. Boulder, Colo.: Lynne Rienner Publishers, 1997.

―――. "Gender, Credibility, and Politics: The Senate Nomination Hearings of Cabinet Secretaries-Designate, 1975 to 1993." *Political Research Quarterly* 50, no. 1 (March 1997): 171–197.

Bovee, Tim. "Do Clinton Choices Look Like America?" *The Record,* 8 March 1993, p. A1.

Boyd, Gerald M. "Bush Is Reported to Have Chosen Gov. Sununu as His Chief of Staff." *New York Times,* 16 November 1988, p. 1.

———. "Bush Names James Baker as Secretary of State; Hails 40-State Support for 'My Principles.'" *New York Times,* 10 November 1988, p. 1.

———. "Bush Names Tower to Pentagon Post, Ending Long Delay." *New York Times,* 17 December 1988, p. 1.

———. "Bush Picks Doctor Who Was Chided on Abortion Views." *New York Times,* 23 December 1988, p. 1.

———. "Bush Says Talks on Strategic Arms Must Be Delayed." *New York Times,* 15 December 1988, p. 1.

———. "Elizabeth Dole Chosen By Bush for Labor Dept." *New York Times,* 25 December 1988, pp. 1, 23.

———. "In a Cabinet Under New Management, Aggressive Advocacy Is a High Priority." *New York Times,* 6 October 1985, p. E5.

———. "Kemp, Picked as Chief of H.U.D., Pledges to Combat Homelessness." *New York Times,* 20 December 1988, p. 1.

———. "President Names 3 for His Cabinet in Key Job Shifts." *New York Times,* 11 January 1985, p. 1.

———. "President Selects a Leader in House for Defense Post." *New York Times,* 11 March 1989, p. 1.

———. "'Stabilizing Signal.'" *New York Times,* 10 November 1988, p. 1.

———. "Svahn: Moving Up in Power." *National Journal,* 22 February 1985, p. 16.

Bradsher, Keith. "Bush Picks Nominee for Commerce Post." *New York Times,* 27 December 1991, p. D5.

———. "Turning over a Ship Adrift." *New York Times,* 27 December 1991, p. D1.

Brauer, Carl. *Presidential Transitions: Eisenhower Through Reagan.* New York: Oxford University Press, 1986.

Broder, John M. "Trying to Make Labor Work: Can New Secretary Revive a Beleaguered Department?" *New York Times,* 26 August 1997, p. D1.

Bronner, Ethan. *Battle for Justice: How the Bork Nomination Shook America.* New York: W. W. Norton, 1989.

Brown, Lyn Mikel, and Carol Gilligan. *Meeting at the Crossroads.* New York: Ballantine Books, 1992.

Brownell, Herbert. *Advising Ike: The Memoirs of Attorney General Herbert Brownell.* Lawrence: University Press of Kansas, 1993.

———. Papers. Dwight D. Eisenhower Presidential Library, Abilene, Kans.

"Bruce Babbitt." *New York Times,* 25 December 1992, p. A24.

Buchen, Philip. Files. Gerald R. Ford Presidential Library, Ann Arbor, Mich.

Burford, Anne M. *Are You Tough Enough? An Insider's View of Washington Power Politics.* New York: McGraw-Hill, 1986.

Butler, Judith. *Gender Trouble: Feminism and the Subversion of Identity.* New York: Routledge, 1990.

"Cabinet Choices." *New York Times,* 22 December 1976, p. 28.

Califano, Joseph A., Jr. *Governing America: An Insider's Report from the White House and the Cabinet.* New York: Simon and Schuster, 1981.

"Calling Bush a 'Real Fighter,' Martin Nominates President." *Congressional Quarterly Weekly Report,* 22 August 1992, pp. 2552–2553.

"Candid Reflections of a Businessman in Washington." *Fortune* (29 January 1979): 36–49.

Capitol Hill Hearing Testimony, Senate Judiciary, Testimony for Confirmation for John Ashcroft for U.S. Attorney General. Federal Documents Clearing House, 2001.

Carroll, Maurice. "Samuel Riley Pierce, Jr." *New York Times,* 23 December 1980, p. A12.

Carroll, Susan J., and Ronnee Schreiber. "Media Coverage of Women in the 103rd Congress." In *Women, Media, and Politics,* ed. Pippa Norris. New York: Oxford University Press, 1997.

"Carter Accepts Kreps Resignation." *New York Times,* 5 October 1979, sec. 4, p. 16.

"Carter and Secretary Harris." *Christian Science Monitor,* 3 August 1979, p. 24.

Carter, Jimmy. *Keeping Faith: Memoirs of a President.* New York: Bantam Books, 1982.

Carver, Terrell. *Gender Is Not a Synonym for Women.* Boulder, Colo.: Lynne Rienner Publishers, 1996.

Celis, William, III. "An Educator Who Fulfills a Vision." *New York Times,* 18 December 1990, p. B14.

Chandler, Clay. "Rubin Stepping into Spotlight at Treasury." *Washington Post,* 7 December 1994, p. F1.

Charlton, Linda. "Gender and Power: Capital Women Tell How They've Fared." *New York Times,* 15 July 1978, p. 18.

———. "Housing Department: Patricia Roberts Harris." *New York Times,* 22 December 1976, p. 16.

———. "Joseph Anthony Califano, Jr." *New York Times,* 24 December 1976, p. 11.

———. "Juanita Morris Kreps." *New York Times,* 21 December 1976, p. 24.

———. "Patricia Roberts Harris." *New York Times,* 22 December 1976, p. 28.

———. "The Woman Who Is to Be Named to H.U.D. Post, Carla Anderson Hills." *New York Times,* 14 February 1975, p. 14.

Cheney, Richard. Files. Gerald R. Ford Library, Ann Arbor, Mich.

Chira, Susan. "Emphasis on Action: Donna Edna Shalala." *New York Times,* 12 December 1992, p. 11.

"Clark Appointment Catches State Department Unawares." *New York Times,* 14 October 1983, p. 1.

Clark, James A. *The Tactful Texan: A Biography of Governor Will Hobby.* New York: Random House, 1958.

Clay, Lucius D., Sr. Oral History, Conducted 20 February 1967. Dwight D. Eisenhower Library, Abilene, Kans.

Clines, Francis X. "President Names Watt's Top Aide for Energy Post." *New York Times,* 6 November 1982, p. 1.

"Clinton Seeks 'Vital Center' with Cabinet." *New York Times,* 8 November 1996, p. 1.

"Clinton's Latest Cabinet-Level Choices." *Wall Street Journal,* 14 December 1992, p. A4.

Clymer, Adam. "Andrew Lindsay Lewis Jr." *New York Times,* 12 December 1980, p. A29.

————. "A Bipartisan Voice: William Sebastian Cohen." *New York Times,* 6 December 1996, p. A1.

Coalition for Women's Appointments. "Initial List of Recommendations, November 10, 1992." Provided for this author by the National Women's Political Caucus.

————. *The Mirror.* Various dates. Provided for this author by the National Women's Political Caucus.

————. "Project Report, August 1993." Provided for this author by the National Women's Political Caucus.

————. "Statement on Cabinet Appointments to Date by Harriet Woods," December 17, 1992. Provided for this author by the National Women's Political Caucus.

Cohen, Jeffrey E. *The Politics of the U.S. Cabinet: Representation in the Executive Branch, 1789–1984.* Pittsburgh: University of Pittsburgh Press, 1988.

Colman, Penny. *A Woman Unafraid: The Achievements of Frances Perkins.* New York: Atheneum, 1993.

"Common Welfare: Madam Secretary Perkins." *Survey* 69 (March 1933): 110.

Conklin, William R. "A. F. L. Man Is Named Labor Secretary; Weeks Gets a Post." *New York Times,* 2 December 1952, p. 1.

Connor, James E. Files. Gerald R. Ford Presidential Library, Ann Arbor, Mich.

Cooper, Kenneth J. "Espy Steeped in Farm Issues as Lawmaker." *Washington Post,* 25 December 1992, p. A23.

Cowan, Edward. "Labor Leader Says Economy Needs Permanent Tax Cut of $25 Billion." *New York Times,* 14 December 1976, p. 29.

Crawford, Ann Fears, and Crystal Sasse Ragsdale. *Women in Texas: Their Lives, Their Experiences, Their Accomplishments.* Austin: State House Press, 1992.

Crenshaw, Kimberle. "Demarginalizing the Intersection of Race and Sex: A Black Feminist Critique of Antidiscrimination Doctrine, Feminist Theory, and Antiracist Politics." In *Feminist Legal Theory: Foundations,* ed. by D. Kelly Weisberg. Philadelphia: Temple University Press, 1993.

Cronin, Thomas. *The State of the Presidency.* 2nd ed. Boston: Little, Brown, 1980.

Cushman, John H., Jr. "Bush Aide Named Transportation Chief." *New York Times,* 23 January 1992, p. 14.

————. "Carlucci's First Problem Is a Paralyzed Military Budget." *New York Times,* 8 November 1987, sec. 4, p. 4.

Dales, Douglas. "Eisenhower Names Adams as Top Aide; Benson in Cabinet." *New York Times,* 25 November 1952, p. 1.

Davis, James J. *The Iron Puddler: My Life in the Rolling Mills and What Came of It.* Indianapolis: Bobbs-Merrill, 1922.

Davis, Kenneth S. *FDR: Into the Storm, 1937–1940.* New York: Random House, 1993.

————. *FDR: The New York Years, 1928–1933.* New York: Random House, 1985.

De Baca, Fernando E. C. Files. Gerald R. Ford Presidential Library, Ann Arbor, Mich.

Deering, Christopher J. "Damned If You Do and Damned If You Don't: The Senate's Role in the Appointments Process." In *The In-and-Outers: Presidential Appointees and Transient Government in Washington,* ed. G. Calvin Mackenzie. Baltimore: Johns Hopkins University Press, 1987.

"Department of Labor: A Challenge." *The Nation* (22 February 1933): 192.

Dewson, Mary W. *An Aid to the End.* Unpublished autobiography, M-133, Dewson Collection, Schlesinger Library on the History of Women, Radcliffe College, Harvard University.

De Witt, Karen. "Agriculture: John Rusling Block." *New York Times,* 23 December 1980, p. A12.

————. "Patricia Roberts Harris." *New York Times,* 20 July 1979, p. A8.

Di Stefano, Christine. "Autonomy in the Light of Difference." In *Revisioning the Political: Feminist Reconstructions of Traditional Concepts in Western Political Theory,* ed. Nancy J. Hirschmann and Christine Di Stefano. Boulder, Colo.: Westview Press, 1996.

————. *Configurations of Masculinity: A Feminist Perspective on Modern Political Theory.* Ithaca: Cornell University Press, 1991.

Dobbs, Michael. "Albright's Family Tragedy Comes to Light." *Washington Post,* 4 February 1997, pp. 1, A8.

Dole, Bob, and Elizabeth Dole. *The Doles, Unlimited Partners.* New York: Simon and Schuster, 1988.

"Donna Edna Shalala." *Current Biography Yearbook 1991.* New York: H. W. Wilson, 1991.

"Down to the 'Short Lists.'" *Time,* 20 December 1976, pp. 8–11.

Drew, Christopher. "Official's Blending of Duties Questioned." *New York Times,* 3 March 1997, p. A12.

Drew, Elizabeth. *On the Edge: The Clinton Presidency.* New York: Simon and Schuster, 1994.

Duerst-Lahti, Georgia. "Reconceiving Theories of Power: Consequences of Masculinism in the Executive Branch." In *The Other Elites: Women, Politics, and Power in the Executive Branch,* ed. MaryAnne Borrelli and Janet M. Martin. Boulder, Colo.: Lynne Rienner Publishers, 1997.

Duerst-Lahti, Georgia, and Rita Mae Kelly. "On Governance, Leadership, and Gender." In *Gender Power, Leadership, and Governance*, ed. Georgia Duerst-Lahti and Rita Mae Kelly. Ann Arbor: University of Michigan Press, 1995.

Duerst-Lahti, Georgia, and Rita Mae Kelly, eds. *Gender Power, Leadership, and Governance*. Ann Arbor: University of Michigan Press, 1995.

Duke, Lynne, and Barbara Vobejda. "On Justice Nominee, Public Delivered the Opinion." *Washington Post*, 23 January 1993, p. A1.

"Dunlop Is Chosen for Labor Office." *New York Times*, 9 February 1975, p. 39.

Edwards, George C., III. "Why Not the Best? The Loyalty-Competence Trade-Off in Presidential Appointments." In *Innocent Until Nominated: The Breakdown of the Presidential Appointments Process*, ed. G. Calvin Mackenzie. Washington, D.C.: Brookings Institution, 2001.

Egan, Leo. "Dulles and Wilson of G.M. Named State and Defense Secretaries; Westerner Gets Interior Post." *New York Times*, 21 November 1952, p. 1.

———. "G.M. Humphrey to Get Treasury Post and Brownell Attorney Generalship; Stassen Will Direct Mutual Security." *New York Times*, 22 November 1952, p. 1.

———. "Summerfield Put in Postmaster Job; Posts for 2 Women." *New York Times*, 26 November 1952.

"Eisenhower Names New Head of R.F.C." *New York Times*, 3 April 1953, p. 14.

Eisenhower, Dwight D. Pre-Presidential Papers, Principal File, Dwight D. Eisenhower Library, Abilene, Kans.

Evans, Rowland, and Robert Novak. "Shalala: No 'New Democrat,'" *Wall Street Journal*, 8 January 1993, p. A19.

"Excerpts from Bush's News Conference with Elizabeth Dole." *New York Times*, 25 December 1988, p. 22.

"Faculty Record: Dr. Juanita M. Kreps." Biographical File of Juanita M. Kreps, Duke University Archives, Durham, N.C.

Fairlie, John. "The President's Cabinet." *American Political Science Review* (February 1913): 28–44.

Farley, James A. *Jim Farley's Story: The Roosevelt Years*. New York: McGraw-Hill, 1948.

Farrell, William E. "For Top Legal Post." *New York Times*, 15 January 1975, p. 14.

Feder, Barnaby J. "New Energy Chief Has Seen 2 Sides of Regulatory Fence." *New York Times*, 22 December 1992, p. B9.

Fenno, Richard F., Jr. *The President's Cabinet: An Analysis in the Period from Wilson to Eisenhower*. Cambridge, Mass.: Harvard University Press, 1959.

Fiorina, Morris P. *Congress: Keystone of the Washington Establishment*. New Haven: Yale University Press, 1977.

Fisher, Linda L. "Fifty Years of Presidential Appointments." In *The In-and-Outers, Presidential Appointees and Transient Government in Washing-*

ton, ed. G. Calvin Mackenzie. Baltimore: Johns Hopkins University Press, 1987.

Flynn, Jean. *Texas Women Who Dared to Be First.* Austin: Eakin Press, 1999.

Flynn, Sharon. "My Side." *Working Woman* (May 1981): 156.

"Ford Appoints Educator to Head H.E.W." *New York Times,* 27 June 1975, p. 1.

Ford, Gerald R. *A Time to Heal: The Autobiography of Gerald R. Ford.* New York: Harper and Row, 1979.

"Frances Perkins." *New York Times,* 2 March 1933, p. 16.

Frances Perkins Oral History. Oral History Research Project, Butler Library, Columbia University.

Franklin, Ben A. "Morton, in a Cabinet Shift, Picked for Commerce Job." *New York Times,* 28 March 1975, p. 1.

Frankovic, Kathleen A. "Public Opinion in the 1992 Campaign." In *The Election of 1992, Reports and Interpretations,* by Gerald M. Pomper et al. Chatham, N.J.: Chatham House Publishers, 1993.

Frantz, Douglas. "O'Leary Wins Praise Amid Critical Views." *Los Angeles Times,* 28 December 1992, p. A1.

"Fresh Face in a New Job." *New York Times,* 4 November 1979, sec. 4, p. E4.

Friedman, Thomas L. "Clinton Selects Diverse Team of Advisers." *New York Times,* 13 November 1992, p. A18.

———. "Clinton's Cabinet Choices Put Him at Center, Balancing Competing Factions." *New York Times,* 27 December 1992, p. 22.

———. "Clinton's New Foreign-Policy Thinkers: Like-Minded Thinkers, Like-Minded Ex-Carter Teammates." *New York Times,* 23 December 1992, p. A14.

———. "Democratic Leader and Clinton Friend Gain Major Posts." *New York Times,* 13 December 1992, p. 1.

Fritz, Sara. "Brown and Kantor Stir Misgivings." *Los Angeles Times,* 1 January 1993, p. D1.

Fritz, Sara, and Stu Silverstein. "Hiring of Illegal Workers by Baird Sparks Little Uproar." *Los Angeles Times,* 15 January 1993, p. A1.

"FSA Reorganization." *Congressional Quarterly Weekly Report,* 2 April 1953, p. 427.

Gailey, Phil. "Transit Post Nominee." *New York Times,* 6 January 1983, p. A25.

Garland, Susan B., and Hazel Bradford, "Reagan Picks a 'Good Soldier.'" *Business Week,* 16 November 1987, p. 71.

"Gentlewoman." *Washington Post,* 5 November 1979, A22.

"'Getting Things Done,' Philip Morris Klutznick." *New York Times,* 17 November 1979, p. 30.

Gigot, Paul A. "Labor Nomination Illustrates Curse of the Lame Duck." *Wall Street Journal,* 6 November 1987, p. 26.

Gilliam, Dorothy. "Black Women Need a Seat at the Table." *Washington Post,* 19 December 1992, pp. B1, B4.

Gilligan, Carol. *In a Different Voice: Psychological Theory and Women's Development.* Cambridge, Mass.: Harvard University Press, 1982.

Golden, Soma. "Betty Friedan Suggests Women Must Develop Economic Allies." *New York Times,* 3 November 1975, p. 57.

Goshko, John M. "Foreign Service's Painful Passage to Looking More Like America." *Washington Post,* 21 April 1994, p. A29.

Granger, Edmund. Records. Dwight D. Eisenhower Presidential Library, Abilene, Kans.

Gray, Jerry. "After Impasse, Senate Confirms Clinton's Choice for Labor Post." *New York Times,* 1 May 1997, p. 1.

Greenhouse, Linda. "A Career in the Capital." *New York Times,* 25 December 1988, p. 23.

Greenhouse, Steven. "Clinton's Choice of Reich Hints at a Stepped-up Role for Labor Department." *New York Times,* 12 December 1992, p. 10.

Gregg, Gary L., II. "Toward a Representational Framework for Presidency Studies." *Presidential Studies Quarterly* 29, no. 2 (June 1999): 297–305.

"Groups Press Clinton on Labor Secretary." *New York Times,* 12 December 1996, p. 1.

Gruson, Lindsey. "A Novice in Jobs, He Is a Quick Learner." *New York Times,* 14 October 1983, p. 4.

Guy, Mary Ellen. "Hillary, Health Care, and Gender Power." In *Gender Power, Leadership, and Governance,* ed. Georgia Duerst-Lahti and Rita Mae Kelly. Ann Arbor: University of Michigan Press, 1995.

———, ed. *Women and Men of the States: Public Administrators at the State Level.* Armonk, N.Y.: M. E. Sharpe, 1992.

Guy, Mary Ellen, and Georgia Duerst-Lahti. "Agency Culture and Its Effect on Managers." In *Women and Men of the States: Public Administrators at the State Level,* ed. Mary Ellen Guy. Armonk, N.Y.: M. E. Sharpe, 1992.

Gwertzman, Bernard. "Action Is Surprise." *New York Times,* 26 June 1982, p. 1.

———. "Ford Promises That He and Kissinger Will Continue Nixon's Foreign Policy." *New York Times,* 15 January 1975, p. 4.

Hagerty, James A. "Roosevelt Names Farley, Wallace as Cabinet Aides." *New York Times,* 27 February 1933, p. 1.

———. "Roosevelt Names Last of Cabinet." *New York Times,* 1 March 1933, p. 1.

———. "Roosevelt Names Swanson and Ickes." *New York Times,* 28 February 1933, p. 5.

"Hail Miss Perkins for Public Service." *New York Times,* 25 March 1933, p. 32.

Hamilton, Alexander, James Madison, and John Jay. *Federalist Papers.* New York: New American Library, 1961.

"Harold Brown." *New York Times,* 22 December 1976, p. 28.

Harrison, Cynthia. *On Account of Sex: The Politics of Women's Issues.* Berkeley: University of California Press, 1988.

———. "Presidential Appointments and Policy-Making Women." In *The Proceedings of the Third Women's Policy Research Conference: Exploring the Quincentennial: The Policy Challenges of Gender, Diversity, and International Exchange*. Washington, D.C.: Institute for Women's Policy Research, 1992.

Hart, John. *The Presidential Branch: From Washington to Clinton*. 2nd ed. Chatham, N.J.: Chatham House, 1995.

Harwood, John, and David Wessel. "Bush to Nominate Barbara Franklin to Position of Secretary of Commerce." *Wall Street Journal*, 27 December 1991, p. A3.

Hayes, Thomas C. "Robert Adam Mosbacher, Sr." *New York Times*, 7 December 1988, p. B14.

"Hazel O'Leary." *Christian Science Monitor*, 23 December 1992, p. 7.

"Health Nominee Confirmed." *New York Times*, 9 March 1983, p. 20.

Heclo, Hugh. *A Government of Strangers*. Washington, D.C.: Brookings Institution, 1977.

———. "Issue Networks and the Executive Establishment." In *The New American Political System*, ed. Anthony King. Washington, D.C.: American Enterprise Institute, 1978.

"Herman Vote Is Delayed." *New York Times*, 16 April 1997, p. A18.

Hershey, Robert D., Jr. "Working Profile: Elizabeth H. Dole, Transportation Secretary." *New York Times*, 22 August 1983, sec. 2, p. 8.

Hess, Stephen. *The Government/Press Connection: Press Officers and Their Offices*. Washington, D.C.: Brookings Institution, 1984.

———. *Live from Capitol Hill! Studies of Congress and the Media*. Washington, D.C.: Brookings Institution, 1991.

———. *Organizing the Presidency*. Rev. ed. Washington, D.C.: Brookings Institution, 1988.

Hobby, Oveta Culp. Papers. Dwight D. Eisenhower Library, Abilene, Kans.

Hodson, Piper A. "Routes to Power: An Examination of Political Change, Rulership, and Women's Access to Executive Office." In *The Other Elites, Women, Politics, and Power in the Executive Branch*, ed. MaryAnne Borrelli and Janet M. Martin. Boulder, Colo.: Lynne Rienner Publishers, 1997.

Hoffman, David. "2 Lead List of Candidates to Head HHS." *Washington Post*, 6 November 1985, p. A4.

Holsendolph, Ernest. "Purposeful—and Prankish." *New York Times*, 28 July 1979, p. 7.

"Housing Choice Praised by Blacks and Women, Scorned by Mayors." *New York Times*, 22 December 1976, p. 28.

Hufstedler, Shirley M. "Open Letter to a Cabinet Member." *New York Times Magazine*, 11 January 1981, sec. 6, pp. 38–50.

Hull, Gloria T., Patricia Bell Scott, and Barbara Smith, eds. *All the Women Are White, All the Blacks Are Men, But Some of Us Are Brave: Black Women's Studies*. Old Westbury, N.Y.: Feminist Press, 1982.

"Hull and Woodin Named for Cabinet to Speed Action on World Economics: Roosevelt Confers with French Envoy." *New York Times*, 22 February 1933, p. 1.

Hunter, Marjorie. "Congress Approves Dept. of Education; Victory for Carter." *New York Times*, 28 September 1979, p. 1.

———. "Reagan's Choice for Health Chief." *New York Times*, 13 January 1983, p. D22.

Hyatt, James C. "New HEW Head May Be a 'Team Player,' But Legislative Battles Are Sure to Come." *Wall Street Journal*, 20 July 1979, p. 2.

Ifill, Gwen. "The Baird Appointment: In Trouble from the Start, Then a Firestorm." *New York Times*, 23 January 1993, p. 8.

———. "Clinton Chooses 2 and Deplores Idea of Cabinet Quotas." *New York Times*, 22 December 1992, p. 1.

———. "Clinton Completes Cabinet and Points to Its Diversity." *New York Times*, 25 December 1992, p. 1.

———. "Clinton Picks Aspin and Ex-Governor for Cabinet." *New York Times*, 18 December 1992, p. A1.

———. "Clinton Widens His Circle, Naming 4 Social Activists." *New York Times*, 12 December 1992, p. 1.

———. "Clinton's Blunt Reminder of the Mood That Elected Him." *New York Times*, 24 January 1993, sec. 4, p. 3.

———. "Focusing Overseas." *New York Times*, 23 December 1992, p. 1.

"Ike's Staff Fills Out." *U.S. News and World Report* 33 (15 December 1952): p. 40.

"Illusion of Education Reform." *New York Times*, 16 January 1979, p. 14.

Isikoff, Michael, and William Booth. "Miami 'Drug Court' Demonstrates Reno's Unorthodox Approach." *Washington Post*, 20 February 1993, p. 1.

Isikoff, Michael, and Al Kamen. "Baird's Hiring Disclosure Not Seen as Major Block." *Washington Post*, 15 January 1993, p. A14.

Isikoff, Michael, and David von Drehle. "Prosecutor Wins High Marks Battling Miami Vice." *Washington Post*, 12 February 1993, p. A23.

Ivanovich, David. "Richardson Perplexes the Pundits." *Houston Chronicle*, 19 June 1998, p. 1.

Jamieson, Kathleen Hall. *Beyond the Double Bind: Women and Leadership.* New York: Oxford University Press, 1995.

Jarvis, Judy. "To Main Street, It's a Crime." *Los Angeles Times*, 22 January 1993, p. B7.

Jehl, Douglas. "Clinton Names Bentsen, Panetta to Economic Team." *Los Angeles Times*, 11 December 1992, p. 1.

———. "Interior Choice Sends a Signal on Land Policy." *New York Times*, 30 December 2001, p. A1.

———. "Pentagon Deputy Is Clinton's Choice for Defense Chief." *New York Times*, 25 January 1994, p. 1.

Jewell, Malcolm, and Marcia Lynn Whicker. "The Feminization of Leadership in State Legislatures." *PS* 26, no. 4 (December 1993): 705–712.

"Jimmy's Talent File." *Time*, 20 December 1976, p. 14.

Johnson, Dirk. "Federico F. Peña." *New York Times*, 25 December 1992, p. A24.

Johnson, Julie. "Baker Resigns to Work for Bush; Brady Is Named for Treasury Job." *New York Times*, 6 August 1988, p. 1.

———. "Education Chief to Leave Cabinet." *New York Times*, 10 August 1988, p. A12.

Johnston, David. "Attorney General Choice with Low-Key Style." *New York Times*, 17 October 1991, p. A20.

———. "Clinton's Choice for Justice Dept. Hired Illegal Aliens for Household." *New York Times*, 14 January 1993, p. A1.

Jones, William H. "Kreps Resigning; Husband's Health Believed a Factor." *Washington Post*, 4 October 1979, pp. A1, A19.

Jong, Erica. "Conspiracy of Silence." *New York Times*, 10 February 1993, p. A23.

Jordan, Hamilton. Papers. Jimmy Carter Library, Atlanta, Ga.

"Juanita Morris Kreps." *Current Biography* 38 (June 1977): 25–28.

"Judith Lynn Morley Martin." *Current Biography Yearbook, 1989*. New York: H. W. Wilson, 1989.

Kann, Mark E. *A Republic of Men: The American Founders, Gendered Language, and Patriarchal Politics*. New York: New York University Press, 1998.

Kanter, Rosabeth Moss. *Men and Women of the Corporation*. New York: Basic Books, 1977.

Kelly, Rita Mae, Mary Boutilier, and Mary Lewis. *The Making of Political Women: A Study of Socialization and Role Conflict*. Chicago: Nelson-Hall, 1978.

Kendall, William T. Files. Gerald R. Ford Presidential Library, Ann Arbor, Mich.

Kennedy, David M. "Among Friends: Lynn Martin, Jerry Lewis, and the Race for the Chair of the House Republican Conference." In *Gender and Public Policy, Cases and Comments*, ed. by Kenneth Winston and Mary Jo Bane. Boulder, Colo.: Westview Press, 1993.

Kernell, Samuel. *Going Public: New Strategies of Presidential Leadership*. 3rd ed. Washington, D.C.: Congressional Quarterly Press, 1999.

Kernell, Samuel, and Samuel L. Popkin, ed. *Chief of Staff, Twenty-five Years of Managing the Presidency*. Berkeley: University of California Press, 1986.

King, James D., and James W. Riddlesperger, Jr. "Presidential Cabinet Appointments: The Partisan Factor." *Presidential Studies Quarterly* 14 (Spring 1984): 231–237.

———. "Unscheduled Presidential Transitions: Lessons from the Truman, Johnson, and Ford Administrations." *Congress and the Presidency* 22, no. 1 (Spring 1995): 1–17.

Klarr, Albert R. "Bush's Choice of Lynn Martin Brings Tough Fiscal Conservative to Labor Post." *Wall Street Journal*, 17 December 1990, p. B6.

―――. "Labor's Martin Is out to Break 'Glass Ceiling.'" *Wall Street Journal*, 9 August 1991, p. B1.

Klatch, Rebecca E. *Women of the New Right.* Philadelphia: Temple University Press, 1987.

Kohut, Andrew, and Kimberly Parker. "Talk Radio and Gender Politics." In *Women, Media, and Politics*, ed. Pippa Norris. New York: Oxford University Press, 1997.

Labaton, Stephen. "Commerce Nominee's Lobbying Prompts Scrutiny." *New York Times*, 20 December 1992, p. 28.

"Labor Angry over Carter Method." *New York Times,* 22 December 1976, p. 16.

Lacey, Marc. "First Asian-American Picked for Cabinet." *New York Times,* 30 June 2000, p. A15.

Lambie, James M. Files. Dwight D. Eisenhower Library, Abilene, Kans.

Laundry, Donna. "Juanita Kreps a 'No Woman' at Commerce." *Washington Post*, 17 February 1977, p. D1.

Leighton, Frances Spatz. "Washington Whispers: Will Carla Hills Be Vice President?" *Family Weekly*, 29 February 1975, p. 21.

"Letter to the Editor, by Jane Addams." *The Forum* (February 1933): ix–x.

Lewis, Anthony. "If It Were Mr. Baird." *New York Times,* 25 January 1993, p. A17.

Lewis, Neil A. "Clinton Expected to Name Woman Attorney General." *New York Times,* 9 December 1992, p. 1.

―――. "For Labor, a Bush Loyalist." *New York Times*, 15 December 1991, p. 11.

―――. "Getting Things Done, Zoë Baird." *New York Times,* 25 December 1992, pp. 1, A25.

Light, Paul. *A Survivor's Guide for Presidential Nominees.* Washington, D.C.: Brookings Institution, 2000.

Lindsey, Robert. "William French Smith." *New York Times,* 12 December 1980, p. A28.

Lippman, Thomas W. "An Energetic Networker to Take over Energy." *Washington Post*, 19 January 1993, p. A9.

―――. "Energy Nominee Unschooled in Nuclear Weapons Issues." *Washington Post*, 22 December 1992, p. A12.

"Looks Like America." *New York Times,* 25 December 1992, p. A30.

Loomis, Burdett. "The Senate: An 'Obstacle Course' for Executive Appointments." In *Innocent Until Nominated: The Breakdown of the Presidential Appointments Process,* ed. G. Calvin Mackenzie. Washington, D.C.: Brookings Institution, 2001.

Lowi, Theodore J. *The End of Liberalism: Ideology, Policy, and the Crisis of Public Authority.* New York: W. W. Norton, 1969.

―――. *The End of Liberalism: The Second Republic,* 2nd ed. New York: W. W. Norton, 1979.

Lukes, Steven. *Power: A Radical View.* New York: Macmillan, 1974.

Lyons, Richard D. "Caspar Willard Weinberger." *New York Times,* 12 December 1980, p. A28.

MacEachron, David Wells. "The Role of the United States Department of Labor." Ph.D. diss., Harvard University, 1953.

Mackenzie, G. Calvin. *The Politics of Presidential Appointments.* New York: Free Press, 1981.

―――. "The Presidential Appointment Process: Historical Development, Contemporary Operations, Current Issues." In *Obstacle Course: The Report of the Twentieth Century Fund Task Force on the Presidential Appointment Process.* New York: Twentieth Century Fund, 1996.

―――. "The State of the Presidential Appointments Process." In *Innocent Until Nominated: The Breakdown of the Presidential Appointments Process,* ed. G. Calvin Mackenzie. Washington, D.C.: Brookings Institution, 2001.

―――, ed. *Innocent Until Nominated: The Breakdown of the Presidential Appointments Process.* Washington, D.C.: Brookings Institution, 2001.

Macy, John W., Bruce Adams, and J. Jackson Walter. *America's Unelected Government: Appointing the President's Team.* Cambridge, Mass.: Ballinger Publishing, 1983.

"Madeleine Korbel Albright." *Current Biography Yearbook 1995.* New York: H. W. Wilson, 1995.

"Madigan." *New York Times,* 26 January 1991, p. 11.

Madison, James. *The Debates in the Federal Convention of 1787 Which Framed the Constitution of the United States of America,* ed. Gaillard Hung and James Brown Scott. International ed. Westport, Conn.: Greenwood Press, 1970.

Magnusson, Paul. "Competitive, Impatient, Brainy—She May Be a Natural." *Business Week,* 22 January 1990, p. 53.

Manegold, Catherine S. "Clinton Ire on Appointments Startles Women." *New York Times,* 23 December 1992, p. A15.

Mann, Judy. "The Raw Nerve of Child Care." *Washington Post,* 27 January 1993, p. D26.

Mansbridge, Jane. "Should Blacks Represent Blacks and Women Represent Women? A Contingent 'Yes.'" *Journal of Politics* 61, no. 3 (August 1999): 628–657.

Mansfield, Stephanie. "The Heckler Breakup." *Washington Post,* 16 October 1984, p. B4.

Marcus, David L. "The New Diplomacy." *Boston Globe Magazine,* 1 June 1997, p. 16+.

Marcus, Frances Frank. "Ex-Mayor Who Left an Imprint." *New York Times,* 28 July 1979, p. 7.

Marcus, Ruth. "Christopher Picked for State, Aspin for Defense." *Washington Post,* 23 December 1992, pp. 1, A12.
————. "Clinton Berates Critics in Women's Groups." *Washington Post,* 22 December 1992, pp. 1, A12.
————. "Clinton Nominates Reno at Justice." *Washington Post,* 12 February 1993, pp. A1, A23.
Marquis, Christopher. "Elaine Lan Chao." *New York Times,* 12 January 2001, p. A15.
Marro, Anthony. "Bell Defends Acts as Georgia Adviser." *New York Times,* 12 January 1977, p. 1.
————. "Studies of Bell's Record as Judge Not Expected to Bar Confirmation." *New York Times,* 29 December 1976, p. 12.
Martin, George. *Madam Secretary: Frances Perkins.* Boston: Houghton Mifflin, 1976.
Martin, Janet M. "Cabinet Secretaries from Truman to Johnson: An Examination of Theoretical Frameworks for Cabinet Studies." Ph.D. diss., Ohio State University, 1985.
————. "An Examination of Executive Branch Appointments in the Reagan Administration by Background and Gender." *Western Political Quarterly* 44 (1991): 173–184.
————. "Frameworks for Cabinet Studies." *Presidential Studies Quarterly* 18 (Fall 1988): 793–814.
————. "George Bush and the Executive Branch." *Leadership and the Bush Presidency,* ed. Ryan J. Barilleaux and Mary E. Stuckey. Westport, Conn.: Praeger, 1992.
————. *A Place in the Oval Office: Women and the American Presidency.* College Station: Texas A&M Press, forthcoming.
————. "The Recruitment of Women to Cabinet and Subcabinet Posts." *Western Political Quarterly* 42 (1989): 161–172.
————. "Women Who Govern: The President's Appointments." In *The Other Elites: Women, Politics, and Power in the Executive Branch,* ed. MaryAnne Borrelli and Janet M. Martin. Boulder, Colo.: Lynne Rienner Publishers, 1997.
McCarthy, Colman. "When Baby Comes in Second to Career." *Washington Post,* 2 February 1993, p. D14.
McCarty, Nolan, and Rose Razaghian. "Advice and Consent: Senate Responses to Executive Branch Nominations 1885–1996." *American Journal of Political Science* 43, no. 4 (October 1999): 1122–1143.
McGlen, Nancy E., and Meredith Reid Sarkees. *Women in Foreign Policy: The Insiders.* New York: Routledge, 1993.
McGrory, Mary. "Confirmation Shalalacking." *Washington Post,* 17 January 1993, p. C1.
————. "Why Zoe Got Zapped." *Washington Post,* 24 January 1993, p. C1.
Melich, Tanya. *The Republican War Against Women: An Insider's Report from Behind the Lines.* New York: Bantam Books, 1996.

Milkis, Sidney M., and Michael Nelson. *The American Presidency: Origins and Development, 1776–1998.* 3rd ed. Washington, D.C.: CQ Press, 1999.

Miller, Bill. "Espy Acquitted in Gifts Case." *Washington Post,* 3 December 1998, p. A1.

Miller Center Oral History Interview with Zbigniew Brzezinski and National Security Council Staff Members [including Congressional Liaison Officer Madeleine Albright]. Jimmy Carter Library, Atlanta, Ga.

Mills, C. Wright. *The Power Elite.* New York: Oxford University Press, 1957.

"Miss Perkins Cool Under [AFL President William] Green's Fire." *New York Times,* 3 March 1933, p. 2.

"Miss Perkins Ready for Cabinet Duties." *New York Times,* 24 February 1933, p. 2.

Mitchell, Alison. "Albright to Head State Dept.; Republican in Top Defense Job." *New York Times,* 6 December 1996, p. A1.

Moe, Terry. "The Politicized Presidency." In *The New Direction in American Politics,* ed. John E. Chubb and Paul E. Peterson. Washington, D.C.: Brookings Institution, 1985.

Mohr, Charles. "Interior: James Gaius Watt." *New York Times,* 23 December 1980, p. A12.

———. "Vance Is Selected by Carter to Run State Department." *New York Times,* 4 December 1976, p. 1.

Mohr, Lillian Holmen. *Frances Perkins: "That Woman in FDR's Cabinet!"* Great Barrington, Mass.: North River Press, 1979.

Molotsky, Irvin. "Dick Thornburgh." *New York Times,* 22 November 1988, p. A19.

———. "Dole Resigns Transportation Post to Join Her Husband's Campaign." *New York Times,* 15 September 1987, p. 1.

———. "Reagan Nominates Transport Chief." *New York Times,* 9 October 1987, p. 1.

Moran, Terence. "It's Not Just Zoe Baird." *New York Times,* 23 January 1993, p. A21.

"More Questions for Ron Brown." *New York Times,* 13 January 1993, p. A20.

"Mrs. Heckler's Record." *New York Times,* 21 January 1983, p. 16.

"Mrs. Kreps Goes Home." *New York Times,* 7 October 1979, p. 16.

"Mrs. Oveta Hobby May Win Rank in Ike's Cabinet." *Sulphur Springs News Telegram,* 26 November 1952.

Myers, Steven Lee. "Albright Learns that She Lost 3 Ancestors in the Holocaust." *New York Times,* 4 February 1997, p. A13.

Naff, Katherine C. *To Look Like America: Dismantling Barriers for Women and Minorities in Government.* Boulder, Colo.: Westview Press, 2001.

Nathan, Richard P. *The Administrative Presidency.* New York: Macmillan, 1986.

National Women's Political Caucus Collection. Schlesinger Library on the History of Women, Radcliffe College, Harvard University.

Naughton, James M. "The Change in Presidents: Plans Began Months Ago." *New York Times*, 26 August 1974, p. 1.

———. "Ford Calls 8 Fit to Run with Him." *New York Times*, 23 January 1976, p. 38.

———. "Sweeping Change." *New York Times*, 4 November 1975, p. 1.

Neikirk, William R. "Reagan Picks Woman as New Labor Secretary." *Chicago Tribune*, 4 November 1987, sec. 1, p. 5.

Neustadt, Richard. *Presidential Power and the Modern Presidents: The Politics of Leadership from Roosevelt to Reagan.* New York: Free Press, 1990.

"New Secretary of Education." *New York Times*, 31 October 1979, p. A12.

"1996 Catalyst Census of Women Corporate Officers and Top Earners," www.wwork.com/Work/catalyst.htm.

"Nomination of Peña Advances to Full Senate." *New York Times*, 7 March 1997, p. A20.

"Nominees of Carter Differ on Club Role." *New York Times*, 25 December 1976, p. 14.

Norris, Pippa. "Women Leaders Worldwide: A Splash of Color in the Photo Op." In *Women, Media, and Politics*, ed. Pippa Norris. New York: Oxford University Press, 1997.

Obstacle Course: The Report of the Twentieth Century Fund Task Force on the Presidential Appointment Process. New York: Twentieth Century Fund, 1996.

"On Changing Academic Culture from the Inside: An Interview with Donna Shalala." *Change* 21 (January–February 1989): 20–29.

Orth, Maureen. "Profile: Elizabeth Dole." *Vogue* (October 1984): 110.

"Our Next Cabinet." *The Forum* (January 1933): 11–12.

Page, Benjamin I. *Who Deliberates? Mass Media in Modern Democracy.* Chicago: University of Chicago Press, 1996.

Pear, Robert. "A Caretaker Nominated to Oversee the Brock Legacy." *New York Times*, 8 November 1987, sec. 4, p. E4.

———. "Mrs. Heckler Disputes 'Token' Woman Label." *New York Times*, 15 January 1983, p. 24.

———. "New Chief's Deputy Is Used to Running the Show." *New York Times*, 11 March 1983, p. 20.

———. "Reagan Chooses Ex-Rep. Heckler to Be the New Secretary of Health." *New York Times*, 13 January 1983, p. 1.

———. "Softening Some Images, If Not Policies." *New York Times*, 26 June 1983, p. E4.

"People and Business." *New York Times,* 17 August 1974, p. 33.

"People and Business." *New York Times*, 21 November 1975, p. 69.

Perkins, Frances. "The Cost of a Five-Dollar Dress." *Survey Graphic* 22 (February 1933): 75–78.

———. Oral History. Oral History Research Project, Butler Library, Columbia University, New York, N.Y.

———. *The Roosevelt I Knew.* New York: Viking Press, 1946.

Pfiffner, James P. "Establishing the Bush Presidency." *Public Administration Review* (January–February 1990): 64–72.

———. "Presidential Appointments: Recruiting Executive Branch Leaders." In *Innocent Until Nominated: The Breakdown of the Presidential Appointments Process,* ed. G. Calvin Mackenzie. Washington, D.C.: Brookings Institution, 2001.

Pitkin, Hanna Fenichel. *The Concept of Representation.* Berkeley: University of California Press, 1967.

Poinsett, Alex. "Patricia Harris: HUD's Velvet-Gloved Iron Hand," *Ebony* (July 1979): 33.

Polsby, Nelson W. "Presidential Cabinet Making: Lessons for the Political System." *Political Science Quarterly* 93, no. 1 (Spring 1978): 15–25.

Poussaint, Alvin F. "To Get and to Get Not." *New York Times,* 13 March 1977, p. 23.

"Public Services of the Ten Prospective Members of Roosevelt's Cabinet." *New York Times,* 23 February 1933, p. 3.

Quint, Michael. "The Financier Who Knows What Is Going On." *New York Times,* 6 August 1988, p. 8.

Raskin, A. H. "The Labor Scene." *New York Times,* 8 November 1976, p. 52.

Rattner, Steven. "Energy Department: Dust Is Still Settling." *New York Times,* 5 December 1977, p. 61.

———. "Energy Head Resigns." *New York Times,* 21 July 1979.

"Reagan Appoints an Ardent Prolifer to a Cabinet Position." *Christianity Today,* 8 April 1983, pp. 48–50.

"Reagan to Nominate Former Interior Aide as Labor Secretary." *New York Times,* 3 November 1987, p. A22.

"Reforms Begun by Miss Perkins." *New York Times,* 22 March 1933, p. 22.

Reinhold, Robert. "Fueled by Radio and TV, Outcry Became Uproar." *New York Times,* 23 January 1993, p. A24.

———. "Mrs. Harris Is Expected to Alter H.E.W. Subtly." *New York Times,* 21 July 1979, p. 17.

"Richard Shultz Schweiker." *New York Times,* 12 December 1980, p. A29.

Riche, Martha Farnsworth. "The Bean Count Is In!" *Washington Post,* 23 January 1994, p. C2.

Richter, Paul, and David Lauter. "Clinton Appoints Cisneros and Brown to Cabinet Posts." *Los Angeles Times,* 18 December 1992, p. A24.

———. "Education, Energy Picks Appear Set." *Los Angeles Times,* 21 December 1992, A1.

Risen, James. "Reich May Become New Kind of Labor Secretary." *New York Times,* 12 December 1992, pp. A22, A23.

Robards, Terry. "The Big Board's Nominees." *New York Times,* 11 June 1972, sec. 3, p. 21.

Robbins, William. "Robert Selmer Bergland." *New York Times,* 21 December 1976, p. 24.

Roberts, Steven V. "Reagan Names Ex-Government Aide to Labor Post." *New York Times*, 4 November 1987, p. 31.

———. "Reagan Selects Pennsylvanian for Justice Job." *New York Times*, 13 July 1988, p. A14.

"Roderick Hills Chosen as Counsel to Ford." *New York Times*, 2 April 1975, p. 36.

Rohter, Larry. "Tough, 'Front-Line Warrior.'" *New York Times*, 12 February 1993, pp. 1, A22.

"Roosevelt Cabinet Slate." *New York Times*, 23 February 1933, p. 1.

Roosevelt, Eleanor, and Lorena A. Hickok. *Ladies of Courage*. New York: G. P. Putnam's Sons, 1954.

Rosenbaum, David E. "Choosing a Friend for Attorney General." *New York Times*, 28 December 1976, p. 13.

———. "Diligent Politician with a Quick Temper." *New York Times*, 30 August 1980, p. A14.

———. "Freddie Ray Marshall." *New York Times*, 22 December 1976, p. 28.

———. "New Style Emerging After Shake-Up in the Cabinet." *New York Times*, 13 November 1979, p. A16.

———. "Steely Veteran of Nixon Days." *New York Times*, 17 December 1980, p. 1.

Rosenbaum, David E., and Robert Reinhold. "Bell Reported Carter's Choice from the Start." *New York Times*, 24 December 1976, p. 1.

Rosenthal, Andrew. "Bush Nominates Deputy as Head of Justice Dept." *New York Times*, 17 October 1991, p. 1.

———. "Lawmaker Selected as Labor Secretary." *New York Times*, 15 December 1990, p. 11.

Ross, Irwin. "Carla Hills Gives 'The Woman's Touch' a Brand-New Meaning." *Fortune* 92 (December 1975): 120–123.

Rossiter, Clinton. *The American Presidency*. New York: Time, 1962.

Rowen, Hobart. "Kreps: Introspective Farewell." *Washington Post*, 3 November 1979, p. A1.

Saddler, Jeanne. "McLaughlin Nominated as Labor Chief." *Wall Street Journal*, 4 November 1987, p. 72.

Salpukas, Agis. "Carter's Choices for Treasury and Transportation Posts." *New York Times*, 15 December 1976, p. 12.

———. "Werner Michael Blumenthal." *New York Times*, 15 December 1976, p. 12.

Sanger, David E. "Choice for Treasury Wins Praise as Clinton Loses Elder Statesman." *New York Times*, 7 December 1994, p. 1.

———. "Lessons of a Swift Exit." *New York Times*, 10 January 2001, A1.

Schneider, Keith. "Influential Illinois Congressman Is Named Secretary of Agriculture." *New York Times*, 26 January 1991, p. 11.

Schorr, Burt. "Former Rep. Margaret Heckler Is Picked by Reagan for Top Post at Health Agency." *Wall Street Journal*, 13 January 1983, p. 2.

———. "HHS's Mrs. Heckler: A Leader for the Poor or Just a Poor Leader?" *Wall Street Journal*, 29 February 1984, p. 1.

Schroedel, Jean Reith, Sharon Spray, and Bruce D. Snyder. "Diversity and the Politicization of Presidential Appointments: A Case Study of the Achtenberg Nomination." In *The Other Elites: Women, Politics, and Power in the Executive Branch*, ed. MaryAnne Borrelli and Janet M. Martin. Boulder, Colo.: Lynne Rienner Publishers, 1997.

Sciolino, Elaine. "Carlucci, a Tough Pragmatist in Pentagon's Corner." *New York Times*, 6 November 1987, p. A16.

———. "Madeleine Albright's Audition." *New York Times Magazine*, 22 September 1996, pp. 63–67.

———. "An Operator for the Pentagon." *New York Times*, 17 December 1993, p. 1.

"Second-Term Swap." *New York Times*, 9 January 1985, p. A22.

"Secretary of Collision." *New York Times*, 3 October 1984, p. 26.

"Secretary of Health and Human Services Donna Shalala." *Christian Science Monitor*, 21 December 1992, p. 9.

Shabecoff, Philip. "Donald Paul Hodel." *New York Times*, 11 January 1985, p. B6.

———. "Ford Bids Cabinet and Agency Heads Remain in Posts." *New York Times*, 11 August 1974, p. 1.

———. "Ford Will Name a Woman to Be Secretary of H.U.D." *New York Times*, 14 February 1975, p. 1.

———. "George William Miller." *New York Times*, 20 July 1979, p. A8.

Shanahan, Eileen. "Ford Sets up Unit on Women's Year." *New York Times*, 10 January 1975, p. 15.

Shipler, David K. "Pentagon's Style Likely to Change After Weinberger." *New York Times*, 4 November 1987, p. 6.

"Shirley M. Hufstedler." *New York Times*, 31 October 1979, p. A12.

Shogan, Robert. "The Confirmation Wars: How Politicians, Interest Groups, and the Press Shape the Presidential Appointment Process." In *Obstacle Course: The Report of the Twentieth Century Fund Task Force on the Presidential Appointment Process*. New York: Twentieth Century Fund, 1996.

"The Shuffle: New Faces, Old Cards." *New York Times*, 20 July 1979, p. 24.

Silk, Leonard. "Candid Academic at Commerce." *New York Times*, 8 May 1977.

Simpson, Peggy. "Reagan's Answer to the Gender Gap." *Ms.* (March 1988): 53.

Smith, Hedrick. "Carter Urges Aides to Find a Broad 'Mix' for Posts in Cabinet." *New York Times*, 19 November 1976, p. 1.

———. "A Controversial Appointment." *New York Times*, 21 December 1976, p. 24.

———. "A Neatly Balanced Cabinet." *New York Times*, 24 December 1976, p. A10.

————. "Overtures of Reassurance." *New York Times*, 4 December 1976, p. 1.

————. "Reshaping of Carter's Presidency: 16 Days of Shifts and Reappraisals." *New York Times*, 22 July 1979, p. 1.

————. "Shuffle in Administration: Sign of Restlessness, Rather Than of Strategy." *New York Times*, 9 January 1985, p. A19.

Smith, Terence. "Carter Asserts He Has No Apologies to Make over Cabinet Changes." *New York Times*, 22 July 1979, pp. 1, 31.

————. "Carter Offered Resignations by Cabinet and Senior Staff; Some Going in Days, Aides Say." *New York Times*, 18 July 1979, p. A15.

————. "Carter Replaces Bell, Blumenthal, Califano; Miller Goes to Treasury." *New York Times*, 20 July 1979, p. 1.

————. "Home State Labor Backs Kennedy; Education Group Supports Carter." *New York Times*, 29 September 1979, p. 1.

————. "No Staff Shifts Yet." *New York Times*, 21 July 1979, p. 1.

————. "President Asks for Public Support and Promises Orderly Transition." *New York Times*, 21 July 1979, pp. 1, 8.

————. "2 Nominations End Shuffle of Cabinet." *New York Times*, 28 July 1979, p. 1.

Smothers, Ronald. "Dr. Louis Wade Sullivan." *New York Times*, 23 December 1988, p. A25.

————. "Social-Worker Roots and Political Experience Lead to Labor Post: Alexis Margaret Herman." *New York Times*, 21 December 1996, p. 10.

Solomon, Burt. "Bush Promised Fresh Faces but He's Hiring Old Friends." *National Journal*, 21 January 1989, pp. 142–143.

————. "Bush's Laggard Appointment Pace May Not Matter All That Much." *National Journal* (2 December 1989): 2952–2953.

"Some Cabinet Diversity, But . . . ," *San Francisco Examiner*, 22 December 1996, p. C16.

Spray, Sharon Lynn. "The Politics of Confirmations: A Study of Senate Roll Call Confirmation Voting, 1787–1994." Ph.D. diss., Claremont Graduate School, 1997.

Stanley, David, Dean E. Mann, and Jameson W. Doig. *Men Who Govern: A Biographical Profile of Federal Political Executives*. Washington, D.C.: Brookings Institution, 1967.

"Starting to Look a Bit More Like America." *Los Angeles Times*, 12 December 1992, p. B7.

Stence, Mark. "Those Who Withdrew." *New York Times*, 23 January 1993, p. A10.

Stevens, William K. "Solicitor-General-Designate Wade Hampton McCree, Jr." *New York Times*, 12 January 1977, p. A14.

Stuart, Peter C. "Education Post: Tough Assignment." *Christian Science Monitor*, 1 November 1979, p. 3.

Stumbo, Bella. "Dukakis Aide Estrich: She's More Than Most Can Manage." *Los Angeles Times*, 4 June 1988, p. 1.

Sullivan, Terry. "Repetitiveness, Redundancy, and Reform: Rationalizing the Inquiry of Presidential Appointees." In *Innocent Until Nominated: The Breakdown of the Presidential Appointments Process,* ed. G. Calvin Mackenzie. Washington, D.C.: Brookings Institution, 2001.

"Summerfield Rise Dates to Wilkie." *New York Times*, 26 November 1952, p. 11.

Swoboda, Frank. "Bush Picks Rep. Lynn Martin to Head Labor Department." *Washington Post*, 15 December 1990, p. A2.

———. "Labor Secretary Martin Finds Criticism Is Par for the Political Course." *Washington Post*, 9 March 1992, p. A15.

———. "Martin Holds Back Endorsement of Dole's 'Glass Ceiling' Initiative." *Washington Post*, 21 February 1991, p. C12.

———. "McLaughlin in Line for Labor Post." *Washington Post*, 31 October 1987, p. A8.

———. "McLaughlin Tapped for Labor Post." *Washington Post*, 5 November 1987, p. A22.

———. "McLaughlin to Be Named as Secretary of Labor." *Washington Post*, 3 November 1987, p. A22.

———. "Organized Labor May Find Martin to Be Influential but Not Compliant." *Washington Post*, 4 January 1991, p. A15.

Taubman, Philip. "Benjamin Richard Civiletti." *New York Times,* 20 July 1979, p. A8.

Taylor, Charles. *Multiculturalism and "The Politics of Recognition."* Princeton: Princeton University Press, 1992.

Tenpas, Kathryn Dunn. "Women on the White House Staff: A Longitudinal Analysis (1939–1994)." In *The Other Elites: Women, Politics, and Power in the Executive Branch*, ed. MaryAnne Borrelli and Janet M. Martin. Boulder, Colo.: Lynne Rienner Publishers, 1997.

"Tentative List of Roosevelt Cabinet Includes Miss Perkins of New York, Ickes, Roper, Dern, and Wallace." *New York Times*, 23 February 1933, p. 1.

"Texas Ex-WAC Boss Gets Post Near Ike's Cabinet." *San Angelo* (Texas) *Standard*, 26 November 1952.

"Text of President's Letter to Zoë Baird." *New York Times*, 22 January 1993, p. A14.

Theroux, Phyllis. "The Judge Goes to Washington." *New York Times Magazine*, 8 June 1980, p. 41.

Thomas, Sue. *How Women Legislate.* New York: Oxford University Press, 1994.

Tolchin, Martin. "Manuel Lujan, Jr." *New York Times,* 23 December 1988, p. A25.

"Tonic for a Tired Department?" *New York Times*, 30 December 1991, p. A14.

"Tough, Charming Cabinet Woman." *Time,* 24 February 1975, p. 14.

"Transcript of Remarks Made by Vice President Ford." *New York Times,* 9 August 1974, p. 3.

Tronto, Joan. *Moral Boundaries: A Political Argument for an Ethic of Care.* New York: Routledge, 1993.

"Two for One Deal." *Time,* 3 January 1977, p. 44.

Tuchman, Gaye. *Making News: A Study in the Construction of Reality.* New York: Free Press, 1978.

Tugwell, Rexford G. *The Democratic Roosevelt.* Garden City, N.Y.: Doubleday and Company, 1957.

Tumulty, Karen, and John M. Broder. "Ron Brown Failed to Pay Employer Tax." *Los Angeles Times,* 8 February 1993, p. A1.

Uchitelle, Louis. "A Crowbar for Carla Hills." *New York Times Magazine,* 10 June 1990, p. 51.

Ulrich, Laurel Thatcher. "Harvard's Womanless History." *Harvard Magazine* 102, no. 2 (November–December 1999).

U.S. Senate. Committee on Agriculture, Nutrition, and Forestry. *Nomination Hearing of Ann M. Veneman.* 107th Cong., 1st sess.

———. Committee on Agriculture, Nutrition, and Forestry. *Nomination Hearing of Daniel R. Glickman.* 104th Cong., 1st sess.

———. Committee on Armed Services. *Nomination of John G. Tower to Be Secretary of Defense.* 101st Cong., 1st sess.

———. Committee on Armed Services. *Nominations of Robert T. Herres . . . Frank C. Carlucci. . . .* 100th Cong., 1st sess.

———. Committee on Banking, Housing, and Urban Affairs. *Hearings on the Nomination of Carla A. Hills to Be Secretary of the Department of Housing and Urban Development.* 94th Cong., 1st sess.

———. Committee on Banking, Housing, and Urban Affairs. *Hearings on the Nomination of Patricia Roberts Harris to Be Secretary of the Department of Housing and Urban Development.* 95th Cong., 1st sess.

———. Committee on Banking, Housing, and Urban Affairs. *The Nomination of Moon Landrieu to Be Secretary of the Department of Housing and Urban Development.* 96th Cong., 1st sess.

———. Committee on Commerce. *Hearings—Secretaries, Departments of Transportation and Commerce.* 95th Cong., 1st sess.

———. Committee on Commerce. *Nominations—Secretaries, Departments of Transportation and Commerce.* 95th Cong., 1st sess.

———. Committee on Commerce, Science, and Transportation. *Nomination of Barbara Hackman Franklin to Be Secretary of Commerce.* 102nd Cong., 2nd sess.

———. Committee on Commerce, Science, and Transportation. *Nomination of Elizabeth H. Dole to Be Secretary, Department of Transportation.* 98th Cong., 1st sess.

———. Committee on Commerce, Science, and Transportation. *Nomination of Robert A. Mosbacher to Be Secretary, Department of Commerce.* 101st Cong., 1st sess.

———. Committee on Commerce, Science, and Transportation. *Nominations—DOT.* 100th Cong., 1st sess.

———. Committee on Commerce, Science, and Transportation. *Nominations—Department of Commerce.* 101st Cong., 1st sess.

———. Committee on Energy and Natural Resources. *Bruce Babbitt Nomination.* 103rd Cong., 1st sess.

———. Committee on Energy and Natural Resources. *Dan Glickman Nomination.* 104th Cong., 1st sess.

———. Committee on Energy and Natural Resources. *Gale Norton Nomination.* 107th Cong., 1st sess.

———. Committee on Energy and Natural Resources. *Hearing on the Nomination of Hazel R. O'Leary to Be Secretary, Department of Energy.* 103rd Cong., 1st sess.

———. Committee on Energy and Natural Resources. *Nomination of James D. Watkins to be Secretary of Energy.* 101st Cong., 1st sess.

———. Committee on Energy and Natural Resources. *Spencer Abraham Nomination.* 107th Cong., 1st sess.

———. Committee on Finance. *Anticipated Nomination of Donna E. Shalala.* 103rd Cong., 1st sess.

———. Committee on Finance. *Anticipated Nomination of Governor Tommy G. Thompson.* 107th Cong., 1st sess.

———. Committee on Finance. *Nomination of Dr. Otis R. Bowen.* 99th Cong., 1st sess.

———. Committee on Finance. *Nomination of Louis W. Sullivan.* 101st Cong., 1st sess.

———. Committee on Finance. *Nomination of Patricia Harris to Be Secretary of Health, Education, and Welfare.* 96th Cong., 1st sess.

———. Committee on Finance. *Nomination of Richard S. Schweiker to Be Secretary of Health and Human Services.* 97th Cong., 1st sess.

———. Committee on Finance. *Nominations of George M. Humphrey, Secretary of the Treasury–Designate, Oveta Culp Hobby, Federal Security Administrator–Designate.* 83rd Cong., 1st sess.

———. Committee on Finance. *Nominations of Joseph A. Califano, Jr., and Lawrence N. Woodworth.* 95th Cong., 1st sess.

———. Committee on Finance. *Nominations of Margaret Heckler, to Be Secretary of HHS and John A. Svahn, to Be Under Secretary of HHS.* 98th Cong., 1st sess.

———. Committee on Foreign Relations. *Nomination of Secretary of State.* 105th Cong., 1st sess.

———. Committee on Foreign Relations. *Nomination of Warren M. Christopher to Be Secretary of State.* 103rd Cong., 1st sess.

———. Committee on Health, Education, Labor, and Pensions. *Nomination [of Governor Tommy G. Thompson].* 107th Cong., 1st sess.

———. Committee on Interstate and Foreign Commerce. *Nomination of Lewis L. Strauss.* 86th Cong., 1st sess.

——. Committee on Labor and Human Resources. *Additional Considera-tion of Margaret M. Heckler, of Massachusetts, to be Secretary, Depart-ment of Health and Human Services.* 98th Cong., 1st sess.

——. Committee on Labor and Human Resources. *Ann Dore McLaughlin, of the District of Columbia, to be Secretary of Labor, U.S. Department of Labor.* 100th Cong., 1st sess.

——. Committee on Labor and Human Resources. *Lynn Martin, of Illinois, to Be Secretary, Department of Labor.* 102nd Cong., 1st sess.

——. Committee on Labor and Human Resources. *Nomination Hearing, Elizabeth Hanford Dole, of Kansas, to Be Secretary of Labor.* 101st Cong., 1st sess.

——. Committee on Labor and Human Resources. *Nomination* [of Alexis M. Herman, of Alabama, to be Secretary of Labor]. 105th Cong., 1st sess.

——. Committee on Labor and Human Resources. *Nomination* [Donna E. Shalala, of Wisconsin, to Be Secretary of Health and Human Services]. 103rd Cong., 1st sess.

——. Committee on Labor and Human Resources. *Nomination* [of Elaine Chao to be Secretary of Labor]. 107th Cong., 1st sess.

——. Committee on Labor and Human Resources. *Nomination* [Shirley M. Hufstedler, of California, to Be Secretary of Education]. 96th Cong., 1st sess.

——. Committee on Labor and Human Resources. *Nomination of Dr. Terrel H. Bell, of Utah, to Be Secretary, Department of Education.* 97th Cong., 1st sess.

——. Committee on Labor and Human Resources. *Nomination of Robert Reich, of Massachusetts, to Be Secretary, Department of Labor.* 103rd Cong., 1st sess.

——. Committee on Labor and Human Resources. *Nomination of William Emerson Brock III, of Tennessee, to Be Secretary of Labor, Department of Labor.* 99th Cong., 1st sess.

——. Committee on Labor and Public Welfare. *Additional Consideration of Joseph A. Califano, Jr., to Be Secretary of Health, Education, and Welfare.* 95th Cong., 1st sess.

——. Committee on Labor and Public Welfare. *F. David Mathews to Be Sec-retary of Health, Education, and Welfare—Additional Consideration.* 94th Cong., 1st sess.

——. Committee on Labor and Public Welfare. *Nomination of Dr. F. Ray Marshall, of Texas, to Be Secretary of Labor.* 95th Cong., 1st sess.

——. Committee on Labor and Public Welfare. *Nomination of John T. Dun-lop, of Masschusetts, to Be Secretary of Labor.* 94th Cong., 1st sess.

——. Committee on the Judiciary. *Confirmation Hearings on Federal Appointments—William P. Barr.* 102nd Cong., 1st sess.

——. Committee on the Judiciary. *The Confirmation of Edwin Meese III to Be Attorney General of the United States.* 99th Cong., 1st sess.

————. Committee on the Judiciary. *Nomination of Edward H. Levi to Be Attorney General of the United States.* 94th Cong., 1st sess.

————. Committee on the Judiciary. *Nomination of Janet Reno to Be Attorney General of the United States.* 103rd Cong., 1st sess.

————. Committee on the Judiciary. *Nomination of Zoë E. Baird to Be Attorney General of the United States.* 103rd Cong., 1st sess.

————. Committee on the Judiciary. *The President's Nomination of Edwin Meese III to Be Attorney General of the United States.* 98th Cong., 2nd sess.

————. *Congressional Record.* Vol. 99, part 3 (10 April 1953): 2905–2906.

Uslaner, Eric. *The Decline of Comity in Congress.* Ann Arbor: University of Michigan Press, 1993.

"View from the Top of the Carter Campaign," *National Journal,* 17 July 1976, pp. 993–1002.

Vobejda, Barbara. "Hill Republicans Map Attack on Shalala." *Washington Post,* 20 December 1992, p. A13.

————. "Shalala: A Lifetime Spent in the Center of Storms." *Washington Post,* 14 January 1993, p. A13.

Von Damm, Helene. *At Reagan's Side.* New York: Doubleday, 1989.

Walcott, Charles E., and Karen M. Hult. *Governing the White House, From Hoover Through LBJ.* Lawrence: University Press of Kansas, 1995.

Wald, Patricia McGowan. Papers. Alumnae Office, Connecticut College.

"Walker Long Aide to Roosevelt Aims." *New York Times,* 1 September 1940, p. 2.

"Wall Street Populism." *New York Times,* 13 June 1972, p. 42.

Ware, Susan. *Beyond Suffrage: Women in the New Deal.* Cambridge, Mass.: Harvard University Press, 1981.

————. *Holding Their Own: American Women in the 1930s.* Boston: Twayne Publishers, 1982.

————. *Partner and I: Molly Dewson, Feminism, and New Deal Politics.* New Haven: Yale University Press, 1987.

Warshaw, Shirley Anne. *Powersharing: White House–Cabinet Relations in the Modern Presidency.* Albany: State University of New York Press, 1996.

Weinraub, Bernard. "Bush Will Retain Webster at C.I.A., Fills 4 More Posts." *New York Times,* 7 December 1988, p. 1.

————. "First Choice for Top Cabinet Post." *New York Times,* 10 November 1988, p. 1.

————. "President Designates Regan White House Chief of Staff, Switching Him with Baker." *New York Times,* 9 January 1985, p. 1.

————. "Shift at Treasury." *New York Times,* 9 January 1985, p. 1.

————. "Tower Considered for Defense Post in New Bush Move." *New York Times,* 22 November 1988, p. 1.

Weisberg, Herbert F. "Cabinet Transfers and Department Prestige: Someone Old, Someone New, Someone Borrowed. . . ." *American Politics Quarterly* 15, no. 2 (April 1987): 238–253.

Weisman, Steven R. "Black and a Woman Are Among 5 Named to Reagan Cabinet." *New York Times,* 23 December 1980, pp. 1, A12.

————. "Carter to Name Judge to Direct Education Dept." *New York Times,* 30 October 1979, p. C4.

————. "President Chooses Mrs. Dole to Head Transport Agency." *New York Times,* 6 January 1983, p. 1.

————. "Reagan Completes Cabinet and Keeps Mansfield as Envoy." *New York Times,* 8 January 1981, p. 1.

————. "Reagan Designates Eight to Fill Posts at Cabinet Level." *New York Times,* 12 December 1980, p. 1.

————. "Reagan Names Haig to State Dept. Post; Battle Is Expected." *New York Times,* 17 December 1980, p. 1.

Weko, Thomas J. *The Politicizing Presidency: The White House Personnel Office, 1948–1994.* Lawrence: University of Kansas Press, 1995.

White, Louise G., with Robert P. Clark. *Political Analysis.* 2nd ed. Pacific Grove: Brooks/Cole, 1990.

White House Central Files. Gerald R. Ford Presidential Library, Ann Arbor, Mich.

Whitney, Craig R. "Nominees Raise Both Hope and Worry Abroad." *New York Times,* 7 December 1996, p. 7.

"Who Runs Health and Welfare?" *New York Times,* 13 January 1982, p. 22.

Wieck, Paul R. "Cabinet Counterparts: Bentsen and Shalala." *Christian Science Monitor,* 23 December 1992, p. 19.

Williams, Dennis. "A Question of Loyalty." *Newsweek,* 30 July 1979, p. 30.

Williams, Juan. "President Names Ex-Rep. Heckler as Head of HHS." *Washington Post,* 13 January 1983, pp. 1, 8.

Williams, Melissa. *Voice, Trust, and Memory: Marginalized Groups and the Failings of Liberal Representation.* Princeton: Princeton University Press, 1998.

Williams, Winston. "Charles William Duncan, Jr." *New York Times,* 21 July 1979, p. 9.

Wilson, James Q. *Bureaucracy: What Government Agencies Do and Why They Do It.* New York: Basic Books, 1989.

Wines, Michael. "Friends Helped Labor Nominee Move Up, Then Almost Brought Her Down." *New York Times,* 12 March 1997, p. A16.

————. "President Speaks Out on Nominee for Labor." *New York Times,* 21 February 1997, p. A24.

"Without Being Spokeswoman for Liberation Causes, Several Firsts for Women Turned in by Dr. Kreps." *Durham Sun,* 20 December 1976. Further citation information unavailable. Source: Biographical File of Juanita M. Kreps, Duke University Archives, Durham, N.C.

Witt, Linda, Karen M. Paget, and Glenna Matthews. *Running as a Woman: Gender and Power in American Politics.* New York: Free Press, 1993.

"Woman Directs Labor." *New York Times,* 25 February 1933, p. 14.

"Women's Unit Hails Betty Ford." *New York Times,* 7 May 1975, p. 33.

"Woodin Advocate of Sound Money." *New York Times*, 22 February 1933, p. 1.

Wooten, James T. "Andrus Chosen for Interior Secretary." *New York Times*, 19 December 1976, p. 1.

———. "Bell Is Named Attorney General; Mrs. Kreps Gets Commerce Post." *New York Times*, 21 December 1976, p. 24.

———. "Carter Considering Splitting C.I.A. Post Between 2 Persons." *New York Times*, 19 December 1976, p. 1.

———. "Carter Names Friend as Attorney General and Selects Woman." *New York Times*, 21 December 1976, p. 1.

———. "Carter Names Three to Posts in Cabinet; One a Black Woman." *New York Times*, 22 December 1976, p. 1.

———. "Defense Secretary Today." *New York Times*, 21 December 1976, p. 1.

———. "Secretary of H.E.W., Director of C.I.A. and Chief Assistant for Energy Matters Designated." *New York Times*, 24 December 1976, p. 1.

———. "Transportation Choice." *New York Times*, 15 January 1975, p. 14.

———. "Washington Congressman Will Head Transportation Department." *New York Times*, 15 December 1976, p. 1.

Yamada, Mitsuye. "Invisibility Is an Unnatural Disaster: Reflections of an Asian American Woman." In *This Bridge Called My Back: Writings by Radical Women of Color*, ed. Cherrie Moraga and Gloria Anzaldua. New York: Kitchen Table, Women of Color Press, 1983.

Yang, John E., and Steven Mufson. "Businesswoman Named to Cabinet." *Washington Post*, 27 December 1991, p. 1.

Zuckman, Jill. "Martin: No Bush Clone." *Congressional Quarterly Weekly Report*, 2 February 1991, p. 298.

Index

Aberbach, Joel D., 45
Abraham, Spencer: 89(nn60,61),
180(table)
African Americans: Clinton nominees,
71–72; demographic profiles, 95,
132(n13); descriptive
representation, 8–9, 219; education
at black institutions, 118, 137(n45);
education of secretaries-designate,
118; endorsement of Griffin Bell,
207(n2); gains under George W.
Bush, 73; and Harris nomination,
67–68, 174(n52); proportional
representation, 33(n26); race as
issue during confirmation hearings,
194–197
Age, as profile variable: of Ford and
Reagan designates, 132(n12); of
secretaries-designate, 95(table)
Agenda, policy. *See* Policy agenda,
president's
Agriculture Department: "diversity"
nominees, 33(nn26,28);
Eisenhower's nomination of an
opposition leader, 80(n15); Espy
nomination, 2; Veneman
nomination, 73; women secretaries-
designate as outsiders, 61
Albright, Madeleine Korbel, 60(table),
82(n27), 114(table); Clinton's
nomination of, 71–72; and

confirmation committee, 203–204;
educational background, 118; family
of origin, 114(table), 115,
136(nn38,39); as gender insider,
125; as insider liaison at
confirmation hearing, 192–193; as
liaison, 18–19; marriage and, 117,
136(n42); media coverage of
nomination, 173(n35); opening
statements in confirmation hearings,
186; precabinet diplomacy,
212(n41); primary career, 109,
123(table), 137(n47); relevancy of
nomination, 62; strength and power
of nomination, 55
American Association of University
Women, 85 (n38)
American Federation of
Labor–Congress of Industrial
Organizations (AFL–CIO), 190
Ashcroft, John, 89(nn60,61),
180(table), 207(n2)
Asian Americans: descriptive
representation, 8, 219; gains under
George W. Bush, 73; stereotyping in
biographical articles, 159–160
Aspin, Les, 81(n20)
Attorneys General. *See* Justice
Department
Authority. *See* Power and authority

About the Book

Are female officeholders most acceptable when they most resemble men? Why has a woman never led the Departments of the Treasury, Defense, Veterans Affairs? Reflecting on these and similar questions, MaryAnne Borrelli explores women's selection for—and exclusion from—U.S. cabinet positions.

Borrelli considers how the rhetoric employed in the selection and confirmation of secretaries-designate establishes gendered expectations for the performance of nominees once they are in office. Analyzing the career paths of secretaries appointed from the 1930s through the first year of the George W. Bush administration, she demonstrates how gender shapes political judgments—by presidents, senators, and the nominees themselves—to reflect consistently masculine ideas about who should rule and how power should be exercised in the United States.

MaryAnne Borrelli is associate professor of government at Connecticut College. She has written several book chapters; her journal articles have been published in *Political Research Quarterly, Presidential Studies Quarterly,* and *Women and Politics.* She is the coeditor, with Janet M. Martin, of *The Other Elites: Women, Politics, and Power in the Executive Branch* (Lynne Rienner Publishers).